EVOLUTION
OR CHAOS

*Dynamics of Latin American
Government and Politics*

EVOLUTION
OR CHAOS

Dynamics of Latin American
Government and Politics

KARL M. SCHMITT
and DAVID D. BURKS

With an Introduction by
RONALD M. SCHNEIDER

FREDERICK A. PRAEGER, *Publisher*
New York • London

FREDERICK A. PRAEGER, PUBLISHER
64 UNIVERSITY PLACE, NEW YORK 3, N.Y., U.S.A.
49 GREAT ORMOND STREET, LONDON W.C. 1, ENGLAND

Published in the United States of America in 1963 by
Frederick A. Praeger, Inc., Publisher

Manufactured in the United States of America

Preface

This work was first conceived in the closing months of the Eisenhower Administration, at a time when the U.S. Government was taking its first cautious and hesitant steps toward new approaches and programs for Latin America. For several years, our economic and military assistance programs had been subjected to severe criticisms. Although some constructive measures had been adopted, such as the establishment of the Inter-American Development Bank, and some new attitudes could be detected, including growing friendliness to the non-Communist left and growing criticism of dictators, no new over-all policy seemed to be in the making.

Late in the summer of 1960, several Latin Americanists, all former analysts of the State Department's Office of Research and Analysis for the American Republics, discussed the possibilities of a new approach to relations between Latin America and the United States. Another discussion took place at the American Historical Association Convention in New York, in December, 1960. Out of these talks grew the idea of a book that would survey conditions in Latin America—not only the political, social, and economic institutions of the area, but also the ideas, prejudices, and psychology of the leaders and the people.

We believed that the deterioration in relations between the United States and Latin America, culminating in the stoning of Vice-President Richard Nixon in Caracas, in May, 1958, stemmed not only from our neglect of the area since World War II, but also from some basic misunderstandings among our policy-makers as to what Latin Americans thought, felt, and needed. We further believed that the beginning of the re-evaluation of U.S. policies toward Latin America that was in evidence by 1960 should be carried through to a complete rethinking of our goals in Latin America, as well as to a better understanding of the views of Latin

Americans concerning their own goals. It seemed obvious that what was needed was a better comprehension both of what we wanted and of what they wanted.

Not all wants, of course, can be satisfied. It is apparent that the United States can no longer work its will in Latin America as it pleases. The countries of the area are too well developed and too sophisticated for marines, customs directors, or admirals to run their political and economic institutions. Even the more backward countries are protected by the firm and solid support of the larger countries against this kind of intervention, which the United States stopped nearly three decades ago. Neither, of course, can all the wants of Latin America be satisfied. U.S. intervention, in the broad sense of the term, still takes place, though not so crudely and openly as before. It occurs constantly all over the hemisphere, in some form or another, because of the disparity in wealth and power between the United States and Latin America.

Intervention may take the form of nonaction (for example, *not* shipping arms) as well as action (*shipping* arms). Similarly, economic assistance may be either granted or withheld. The Bolivian regime is not viable without U.S. aid. Whether we send it or do not send it, whether we provide massive amounts or a mere trickle, vitally influences the course of Bolivian national life in nearly all respects. Therefore, although the desire of Latin Americans for an end to intervention in the narrow sense of the word has largely been satisfied, the subtler but even deeper forms of influence are felt throughout the area. The only way to escape this kind of U.S. intervention is to follow the Cuban example of accepting interventionist practices from someone else. Rather than reject this type of influence, however, Latin America has insisted upon not less but more economic aid. Although the United States is not wealthy enough to meet these demands fully, she is certainly in a position to do far more than what she did between 1945 and 1960.

For fifteen years, the U.S. Government resisted the idea of a Marshall Plan for Latin America, and the countries of the area were advised to seek private capital for economic development. U.S. capitalism was held up to them as a model of what could be accomplished through this kind of economic system. U.S. policymakers either did not know or did not care that "capitalism" carried strongly negative overtones to many Latin American political leaders and intellectuals. They also did not know, or closed their eyes to the fact, that social discontent was outstripping economic growth. Investments were more urgently needed in social welfare than in economic-development projects. But the former were expensive and brought little immediate return on the investment, while the latter could be measured in terms of miles of highway or power production. External aid was often necessary to prevent violent social disturbances and political revolt, but the U.S. Government insisted that its economic assistance be used in development projects, many of them large-scale and of little direct benefit to the discontented masses. It took the Nixon trip in 1958 and the implantation of Castro's regime in Cuba to awaken the United States fully to the needs of the area—their needs and ours.

Originally, then, this book was designed to influence the new Democratic Administration of President Kennedy not merely to continue but to broaden the recently adopted policies of his predecessor. Happily, however, Mr. Kennedy has moved more rapidly in policy-making than we have in writing this volume. This does not mean that we agree with everything that he has done. We regret the events of April, 1961, and have strong reservations concerning the Punta del Este Conference of January, 1962. We do wholeheartedly support, however, his expanded aid program for Latin America, particularly its social aspects, and his insistence that it be predicated upon agrarian, tax, and other internal reforms undertaken by the recipient countries. We recognize that both the aid and the reforms involve risks. They may even be the catalysts of violent and uncontrollable social revolutions in some of the countries. But we also believe that there is no real alternative to this policy; because without aid and reform—both on a large scale —violent social upheaval is a foregone conclusion for almost every country of the area.

Since Mr. Kennedy has beaten us to the punch, as it were, one might well ask what the justification is for our work. It is simply this: The Alliance for Progress, as the President has felicitously named his program, is expensive. The whole of the proposed aid, some $20 billion spread over a decade, will not come from the U.S. Treasury, but a substantial sacrifice must be made by the citizens of the United States to meet their share. Already, there is loud criticism of the program, especially since most of the larger countries of Latin America have balked at strong measures against Castro and appear to be lagging in self-help. Convinced that an informed public is the best guarantee of continued support for this vital program, we hope that the present volume casts some light not only on the difficulties and problems of Latin America, but also on the difficulties and problems facing our government in attempting to negotiate with and assist the area.

Our approach in this work has been topical. We begin by surveying broadly some basic ideas and attitudes of the Latin Americans toward their internal conditions and international relations. We then proceed to a discussion of social conditions and institutions, and to an outline of the economic factors impinging most directly on politics. The heart of our work is a more detailed investigation of interest groups, political parties, and the interaction of these political forces. Most of the discussion is on an across-the-board basis; however, in several places, we have included a series of brief studies of individual countries. Not all countries are covered in this manner, but the largest and most important are treated in each section, along with enough of the others to give the full range of significant variations.

In the preparation of this study, the authors are deeply indebted to their former colleagues in government service for long but pleasant hours of discussion, criticism, and advice. Our gratitude is extended first of all to Dr. Ronald Schneider, without whose counseling, encouragement, and goading the volume would never have been completed, and to whom we owe much of the substance of Chapters 4–7. Our thanks go also to Mr. Robert Dean, of the Foreign Service, who furnished much of the original inspiration for the work, carefully read the manuscript, and offered numerous suggestions for both content and style. Many others read all or part of the manuscript and offered valuable commentaries. These include Mrs. Elizabeth Hyman, Mrs. Mary Manzoli, Miss Lois Carlisle, Dr. Joseph Barager, Dr. Rollie E. Poppino, Mr. Henry Quintero, Mr. William Simonson, Mrs. Anita D. Schneider, Miss Elizabeth von Thurn, and Miss Rosita Rieck Bennett.

The authors also wish to express their regrets that two of their early associates, Dr. Robert Potash, of the University of Massachusetts, and Dr. Robert Gilmore, of Ohio University, were forced to abandon plans to participate in the project because of other commitments. Their role in the early conferences and their advice as to organization and general content were invaluable, and our work unquestionably suffers from their absence. As a result of their withdrawal, Dr. Schmitt took up the task of completing the manuscript, while Dr. Burks carried out his original commitment to write the social and economic chapters.

We wish also to recognize the contribution of our secretaries: Mrs. Margaret D. Anderson, Mrs. Joan Parker, Mrs. Sara Givens, and Mrs. Marilyn Allday—all of whom devoted long and tedious hours to typing and proofreading the many drafts of the manuscript.

Finally, we wish to beg forgiveness of our wives and families, whom we frequently abandoned during the past two years in pursuit of the facts, figures, and ideas that went into this book. We appreciate their unflagging support of our efforts and their good-humored resignation to playing second fiddle to a manuscript.

The authors assume sole and full responsibility for fact and interpretation contained herein.

K. M. S.
D. D. B.

August 1, 1963

CONTENTS

EVOLUTION
OR CHAOS

Introduction

by RONALD M. SCHNEIDER

The convulsions racking Latin America today far surpass in scope and depth the revolutions and turmoil of the nineteenth century. Cuba, once a faithful follower of the United States, has joined the Soviet orbit and is now striving to draw other members of the Inter-American System into that obedience. The countries of the Caribbean area, particularly those with unstable regimes, are most immediately threatened. Despite the failure of revolutionary forces launched from Cuba in 1959 and 1960, and the continuing protection offered by U.S. military and naval forces, the Caribbean political situation remains unsettled. Fidel Castro of Cuba has not renounced his intention of spreading political revolt and social reform throughout the hemisphere; he has only changed his methods. In place of armed might, he has been utilizing propaganda and agitation measures within the countries he hopes to subvert. Cuban diplomats have often spearheaded these operations, but now that a majority of countries have broken relations with Cuba, Castro has had to rely more heavily on nationalists and Communists determined upon emulating the Cuban experiment. Thus far, these movements have everywhere been contained in the Caribbean, and in most countries, notably Mexico, Castro's influence has declined as his regime has become more oppressive, his economy dangerously weakened, and his social revolution more slavishly modeled on the Soviet experiment. The threat of violence, however, hangs heavily over the area.

In the remainder of Latin America, Castro has his devotees in every country, but the personal bonds seem less close than in the Caribbean. University students have invoked his name in Peru and Chile, peasant leaders in Brazil, and labor leaders in Bolivia. In these countries, however, Castro is the symbol of the kind of reform that they expect to achieve in their own countries, not the

3

immediate source of support and assistance that he is to Caribbean revolutionaries. The Argentine extremists are still more distant, for they look for leadership to their deposed dictator, Juan Domingo Perón, who imposed a partial reform on Argentine society in the decade of his rule (1945–55). Adding to the ferment, the Communists in every country sustain and encourage the radical nationalists, hoping to capitalize on the growing discontent in all Latin America to swing the hemisphere from dependence upon the United States to subservience to the Soviet Union. It was in the light of this crisis that President Kennedy early in 1961 called for an Alliance for Progress between his country and all the Latin American states to ward off the threatening revolutions. In a bold plan for social rehabilitation and economic growth, he pledged aid from various sources totaling $20 billion over a ten-year period, in return for massive internal investments and reforms within Latin America. The program was officially launched with the signing of the Charter at Punta del Este, Uruguay, in August, 1961. With this document, the Latin American leaders finally had their own Marshall Plan, for which they had for so long pleaded in vain.

To many U.S. citizens, the events in Latin America of the past decade have been a "puzzlement" indeed. What has become of our "Good Neighbors" of the 1930's and our allies of World War II? Has not the United States been assisting Latin America generously with military and economic aid for the past fifteen to twenty years? Have we not been paying good prices for its products such as sugar, coffee, and metals? Has not Latin America been more prosperous since World War II than ever before in its history? And if all this is true, then why have so many Latin Americans become so anti-United States? Why are so many so radical, so discontented, so prone to violence?

The twenty countries of Latin America are undergoing rapid political change, reflecting a process of social upheaval and reorganization that has been under way for some years and an irrepressible demand for rapid economic development. Recent trends indicate that there is a real possibility that in many countries existing institutions and economic resources may prove inadequate for this task of political and social reorganization. In a number of the larger and more advanced countries, the institutional structures show greater evidence of changing to meet the new demands; in these countries, constitutional representative government may continue to evolve. The others are apt to turn to "democratic" dictatorship and may develop in the direction of mass-based semi-totalitarian systems. Thus, in terms of political organization, the problem in the next decade is to establish political and governmental systems that can accommodate social change and thereby contain its more explosive effects.

The United States and the other American republics have long enjoyed close relations resting upon a common Western heritage, a broad community of interests, and a multiplicity of ties between dominant Latin American groups and the United States. However, these relations have also been marked by suspicion and antagonisms arising in part from cultural differences, the striking economic disparities between the two regions, and the predominant power position of the United States in the Western Hemisphere. Moreover, changes in Latin American societies in recent years have raised new issues and have intensified certain traditional attitudes that may adversely affect relations with the United States. The Latin American countries, particularly those that have made substantial progress toward development into modern nation-states, are aware of the changes in the international power balance that have occurred since the end of World War II, and are beginning to demand that the United States stop taking their support for granted and begin treating them as equals. The example of Castro's Cuba as an extreme alternative lends weight to their demands. A major aim of Communist strategy in the area is to exploit existing antagonisms and to turn the forces of change against U.S. interests. This strategy is gaining support from expanded Soviet operations in the area.

The other American republics are members of Western society through cultural tradition, political institutions and alliances, and economic affiliation. Culturally, they remain faithful to their centuries-old Latin-Catholic tradition. Their strongest intergovernmental ties to Western society are with the United States, both on a bilateral basis and as members of the Organization of American States. Their economic ties to the Western countries appear in trade and investment patterns that reflect the area's long-standing position of raw-material supplier to the industrial countries. With social and economic shifts in the Latin American countries, these ties have been in the process of change, but without altering the broad interdependence of Latin American and other Western economies that has obtained since the discovery of the New World.

Latin American relations with the United States, although close, have been affected not only by differences in levels of economic development but also by striking cultural disparities. These include variations in language, religion, racial composition, and the origins of their European cultural patterns. There have also been marked social differences between the two areas arising from the continued predominance in Latin America of a traditional social order comprising a dependent mass under a narrow landholding, mining, and commercial upper class.

In recent years, internal changes taking place in Latin American societies have brought new pressures to bear on the dominant groups that have traditionally been friendly to the United States, and have tended to alter the composition of these dominant groups and, consequently, their attitudes toward the U.S. A broader segment of the Latin American population is demanding a share in the benefits of economic development and is insisting that the state assume a larger role in industrializing the economies. Currently, the governments are still most responsive to sectors friendly to the United States, but they are under increasing pressure from the forces of social and economic change, which impel them to assert greater independence of action.

In recent decades, Latin American society has experienced substantial changes in numbers, distribution, occupations, and expectations. Changes in traditional social patterns have taken place at an accelerating rate, particularly in the larger countries, with a direct and at times profound impact upon political and economic institutions. These changes have given rise to pressures for adjustment in those institutions that cannot easily be accommodated within the existing social structure.

The heterogeneity of Latin American societies is reflected in the diversity of values among classes, regions, and cultural groups. The once-consistent value systems of both upper and middle groups have been disrupted by the appearance of new ideological currents produced by urbanization and industrialization. The humanistic emphasis is losing ground to the desire for more of the material benefits of industrialization and for the more equitable distribution of such benefits. Popular expectations have outrun actual achievements, creating demands for benefits whose cost is beyond the capacity of the economies at their present stage of development. One long-standing ideological current that has, however, been strengthened by the course of social and economic change is the belief that the state is the best vehicle for implementing extensive welfare organs and developing the economy.

Although the area in general is in a state of flux, the rate of change varies greatly, with those countries that are still essentially agrarian the least subject to disruptive forces. With movement from rural to urban areas, disintegration of family ties, orientation of more and more people to the money economy and the growing dominance of the cash nexus, traditional social relations are already altered and weakened. Characterizing social change throughout the area is a determination to bring about more social welfare and more equality, and an overriding concern with security, reflecting the loss of stability under the old system despite measurable economic gains. The family, the patron-worker relation, the religious ties of the village, the land relationships are now weakening, and are less and less a source of stability in a time of changing values and aspirations.

A strong force for social change has been sustained population growth, of such magnitude that it constitutes a "population explosion." Improvements in health and sanitation have resulted in a marked increase in the rate of population growth, which has been higher than that of any other major world area since 1920. In this period, the total population of Latin America has more than doubled; it now stands at more than 215 million and is expected to increase by at least another 50 per cent in the next fifteen years.

As striking as is the over-all population growth of Latin America, the rate of urbanization has been even more spectacular. Latin America is one of the most heavily urbanized areas in the world, and, in fact, is surpassed only by the United States and Western Europe in percentage of urban population. A generation ago, there were not more than two cities with 1 million inhabitants in the entire area, while today there are ten, nine of which are national capitals. Hundreds of thousands of persons, attracted by city lights and hope for employment in industrial establishments, service industries, or burgeoning government projects, have moved into the urban centers from rural areas and small towns in the interior.

Urbanization and the drive to industrialize have brought about shifts in the size and composition of social classes in many of the other American republics. A propertied group with urban-based economic interests has effectively challenged the hegemony of the traditional agrarian ruling groups. In the more highly developed countries, this group has won a large share of political power, as evidenced by the favored treatment granted it by governments. Two other groups have become important elements in the social fabric of the larger Latin American countries. These are: (1) the wage-earning urban labor force, and (2) a dependent, salaried middle class, including some professionals, and ranging down to low-paid white-collar employees of commerce, industry, and government.

The urban worker group is numerically the most rapidly increasing new force in much of Latin America. In large part, this element is composed of recent migrants to the cities, barely literate, and otherwise poorly prepared for urban existence. It has active, if ill-defined, aspirations for social status and economic improvement that have not been realized. While urban labor generally has benefited from the social-welfare services available in the larger cities, its level of living has remained static in most countries, and may even have declined in some, since 1950.

The dependent middle class is literate, articulate, likely to take an active part in politics, and willing to endorse proposals for radical solutions to pressing economic problems. Entering this sector brings marked material improvement. Nevertheless, in the past decade in a number of countries, the economic level of the middle group has been eroded by inflation, with the result that tensions in the group as a whole have increased.

Although all twenty Latin American countries have adopted a republican form of government, few approach the ideal of a stable, mature, representative democracy. All are, to varying extents, becoming modern nation-states, but accident, history, and resources combine in differing ways to give widely disparate results. Diversity in this respect has reached such a point that it is difficult to make valid and meaningful generalizations concerning the politics of the area as a whole. Mexico, Brazil, Argentina, Chile, Colombia, Venezuela, Uruguay, and Costa Rica (which together comprise four-fifths of the area and contain more than three-quarters of its population) manifest in varying degrees most of the essential characteristics associated with the concept of a modern nation. Peru, Ecuador, Bolivia, Guatemala, and El Salvador are at intermediary stages, and their evolution as modern nations is held back by both economic deficiencies and the presence of a large unassimilated Indian population.

Political life in much of the Latin American area is still highly personalistic, and there is often little meaningful relationship between party systems and the social order. Nevertheless, broadly based and relatively impersonal political institutions have developed in a number of the more advanced nations. Mexico is the outstanding example of the operation of the dominant one-party system without crudely repressive tactics. Opposition parties do exist, participation in them is not a crime, and they do serve to organize dissident opinion. However, they do not have the strength to win an election at the national level, and hence do not offer the voter a real alternative. The governing party is not monolithic; basic decisions are worked out within it by leaders of the middle class, labor, military, and new industrial interests of which the party is composed. Colombia has a relatively stable two-party system; its leaders are seeking to overcome the political strife that led to the Rojas Pinilla dictatorship (1953–58) by institutionalization of an agreement to alternate the Presidency and share other offices on a party basis. Chile offers the area's best example of a stable multiparty system, with each party closely corresponding to a particular segment of society. Venezuela, Uruguay, and Costa Rica have also made considerable progress toward the development of impersonal political institutions. This is, however, a slow process, and in many countries traditional political institutions have proved inadequate—incapable of accommodating the increasing demands for rapid and extensive changes in the economic, social, and political fabric of the nation. In these countries, large segments of the population are becoming alienated from the existing political system as their demands for a voice in national policy-making are not heeded by the entrenched elites.

In the postwar period, there has been a kaleidoscopic procession of scheduled and unscheduled changes in government in Latin America, most of which have involved recognition of an underlying current of general dissatisfaction and demand for rapid, if not revolutionary, socio-economic transition. During the war years and immediately thereafter, regimes appealing for popular support and with avowed social-reform policies replaced a number of dictatorships and authoritarian governments closely identified with the traditional landed aristocracy. Later, roughly between 1948 and 1955, more moderate or conservative administrations, frequently imposed by the military, came to power in response to growing disillusionment with attempts at quick, radical solutions to basic social and economic problems. In general, under these governments, labor pressures were controlled or suppressed but not satisfied. After 1955, the military-based regimes came under strong pressure and were generally replaced by representative civilian administrations.

As elsewhere in the Western world, political parties in Latin America are the most immediate channel for pressures exerted upon the governments. A few Latin American parties may still be regarded as frank spokesmen of the traditional elite, but for the most part political leadership has passed to representatives of the urban upper and middle groups who are acutely aware of the significance of the urban vote and who tailor their appeals to the grievances and aspirations of the urban more than the rural electorate. Parties based upon an urban-worker following have sprung up in nearly all the more highly industrialized countries. Even parties that have been identified in the past as representatives of the propertied groups are deliberately wooing the city worker with promises of increased socio-economic benefits. At the same time, the demand for representative and democratic government, a continuing force in Latin American politics, has strengthened with urbanization of the societies and with expansion of articulate groups that have a stake in political freedom.

Since 1955, with a return to wider representative government in Latin America, the prodemocratic groups have waxed strong, and now appear more influential than at any time in the past. Important parties supported by these groups are more moderate than in the 1930's or the immediate postwar period, notably Acción Democrática of Venezuela and the Apristas of Peru. Small but growing parties supported by lay Catholics have also joined the ranks of prodemocratic reform groups in the area. The groups that have most strongly sought democratic government are "anti-imperialist" and at times inclined toward anti-U.S. nationalism. Their ties of sympathy with the United States, to the extent that they exist, are based on admiration for the U.S. tradition of democratic government and sympathy for reform movements in the United States. Their attitudes toward the U.S. Government and toward the State Department are still significantly affected by the belief that "big business" governs the course of U.S. policy.

The attitudes that affect relations with the United States are of varying intensities in different sectors of Latin American societies, and motivations and interests differ widely at each social level. The wealthy or well-to-do sectors, least provincial in outlook, undoubtedly have the strongest sense of belonging with the dominant groups in Western society. Their nationalism is based largely on expedience. They are more aware of world problems than other classes in the society, and have a more direct self-interest in maintaining ties with the Western industrial nations because their position is based on property. At the same time, preoccupied with internal problems caused by social change threatening the domestic *status quo,* they tend to regard foreign policy chiefly as an instrument to gain economic objectives, and in turn to achieve greater stability and control over their own societies.

The attitudes of the dependent salaried classes, including the intellectuals, are less influenced by a sense of common bonds with the industrial countries of the West. Unlike more affluent parts of society, these middle groups do not have direct economic ties with the United States or other Western countries. Members of these groups view Western society in the light of an education and experience that is essentially bounded by the traditional culture of their own country. To the extent that they are vitally interested in the offerings of the Western industrial world, their interest reflects future goals, including opportunity for the individual to rise in an expanding economy and to achieve maximum self-expression. This group looks to its own national government to provide these goods, and regards the United States with approval to the extent that it helps governments toward political and economic progress. Among members of this class may be found the greatest propensity to ascribe omnipotence to the United States, and to blame this country for the consequences of their own weaknesses and failures.

Among the workers there is a general ignorance of the United States and little sense of common cause with this country or, indeed, with Western society. U.S. motives, if they are examined at all, are far too frequently seen in the light of an anticapitalist indoctrination that breeds mistrust of U.S. policy. Latin American workers form their impressions of Western culture in a haphazard way, through such diverse channels as the Catholic Church, Marxist indoctrination, Hollywood movies, and advertising displaying material possessions beyond their reach. Personal insecurity and a sense of remoteness contribute to reduce their interest in external affairs. On the other hand, Communist propagandists find this lack of interest or understanding a barrier to mobilizing Communist-influenced labor groups in direct support of Soviet foreign policy.

Latin American attitudes on issues in relations with the United States are fairly uniform throughout the area, but expression is of widely varying intensity. Under liberal governments, there is freer expression of antiforeign, anticapitalist attitudes, and of grievances against authority in general. In periods of authoritarian rule, anti-U.S. expression may be discouraged over a long period, and the reaction toward liberty is apt to be disorderly and at times explosive. Also important is the extent of economic friction in U.S. relations with countries of the area, which tends to be greatest where there is most dependence on the United States combined with serious problems of adjustment to changing social and economic conditions.

The attitudes now common throughout Latin America, however differently or sporadically they find expression, may also be affected by a country's prospects for adjusting to new social and economic patterns. The larger countries—Argentina, Brazil, Mexico—are drawing away from their smaller neighbors at an accelerating rate. In these larger republics, along with qualitative social and economic changes, significant differences are appearing in official, business, and popular attitudes. The ruling groups generally include a larger number of men who represent a break with attitudes of the past, and nationalist feeling may have a less fearful and more confident note. With greater assets than other countries of the area, Argentina, Brazil, and Mexico are now in process of building economies that can respond better than traditional economies to modern social pressures, and that promise to differ radically from the dependent and static economies of most other Latin American countries.

In other countries of the area, the traditional patterns and attitudes are less changed despite extensive social and economic shifts. Relatively small in population—none except Colombia and Peru exceeds 10 million—these countries cannot look to industrialization greatly to abate their economic problems. In the small and middle-size countries, U.S. enterprise in developing raw materials has been a major factor in economic development. This is true in most of the Central American countries, Venezuela, Peru, Chile, Panama, and Cuba. It is in these countries that resentment against foreign companies may be most deep-seated and persistent, and most open to political exploitation.

The social and political patterns and trends sketched above are found throughout the area, but there are wide variations in stages of development, capabilities, and practical problems. Many economies are painfully weak, and existing government organization is generally inadequate for the vast task of social reorganization. The pressures for far-reaching change appear in the long run to be irresistible; if they cannot be satisfied through existing institutions, these will be swept aside by revolutions designed to overturn the existing order and place political power in the hands of new groups. Thus, the major division will be between countries capable of developing along an indigenous course by adapting their institutions to change and accommodating the interests of emerging groups, and those whose resources and institutions will prove inadequate for this task.

The Alliance for Progress was designed to secure the former alternative by encouraging present leaders in Latin America to undertake needed reforms on the promise of large-scale outside assistance guaranteed by the United States. August 17, 1962, marked the first anniversary of the signing of the Charter of Punta del Este. By that time a widespread feeling had developed, both in the United States and in Latin America, that the Alliance was off to a disappointingly slow start and had failed to pick up the momentum expected after a year of operation. In sharp contrast to the exuberance displayed among U.S. political leaders when the program was launched, the first birthday of the Alliance was noted with much sobriety. Teodoro Moscoso, Alliance coordinator in the United States, remarked dryly: "We observe it; we do not celebrate it." Behind this sober attitude lie the realities of the Alliance.

Latin Americans have complained of, and U.S. critics have bemoaned, the lagging pace of U.S. disbursement of funds committed for Alliance programs. The fact remains, however, that the rate of disbursement is about on par with that of the international lending agencies, and that the most serious obstacles to the implementation of the Alliance lie in the political and cultural limitations within Latin America itself. Long-range planning, for example, has proved to be enormously difficult. Only three countries—Colombia, Chile, and Bolivia—all of which were wrestling with the problem prior to the Alliance, had devised acceptable plans by the end of 1962. In most countries, there were critical shortages of trained personnel, a scarcity of basic statistical and cadastral information, and woeful lack of government planning agencies capable of formulating plans for effective use of large-scale aid. Nine countries, including the three largest—Argentina, Brazil, and Mexico—had to establish new planning agencies within their governments to cope with the problem. Because of the planning difficulties, sights were being lowered during the second year of the Alliance from ten-year plans to two- to four-year plans in addition to immediate and short-range social objectives. Moreover, powerful political groups in almost every country were opposing the fulfillment of Latin America's responsibility for social reform as its contribution to the Alliance. Tax and land reforms were moving slowly, if at all; national legislatures frequently packed with upper-class Congressmen and Senators, whatever their party affiliation, were reluctant to undermine the economic and social predominance of their class. Reform bills were bottled up in committee or bogged down in endless debate, or stymied by lack of congressional quorums. Such procrastination placed the United States in the difficult position of having to decide whether to refuse aid until the social reforms were forthcoming or to disburse it on the promise of future performance. Either decision posed a dangerous risk. Withholding aid could well precipitate immediate violence, but aid without reforms could only delay the day of reckoning. Unfortunately, the very fear of violence and Castroism has been limiting private investment, both local and foreign. Continued failure in this sector could also prove disastrous for the Alliance since Latin American entrepreneurs are expected to raise two-thirds of the $80 billion that Latin America is to invest, and U.S. capitalists about one-third of the $20 billion promised by this country. And this enormous effort is expected to achieve the modest result of raising per capita income 2.5 per cent annually over the ten-year period.

Even with its own "Marshall Plan" then, Latin America has obviously no guarantee of escaping further Castro-type revolts. Institutional weaknesses, timidity of leadership, widespread failure of social consciousness, and long-ingrained traditions of violence indeed militate against peaceful democratic change. On the other hand, the situation appears far from hopeless in many of the countries that have begun the painful process of modernization. The most powerful immediate factors currently prodding the Latin American ruling classes to reform their societies are the twin threats of internal revolution and foreign intervention. Just as the Russian Bear impelled the first moves toward unification of Western Europe despite the counterweight of history and tradition, so the Cuban Fox, with the Bear behind him, is hurrying the pace of reform in Latin America. The outcome of the struggle is yet to be decided. Indeed, at the midpoint of 1963, it appeared that many, if not most, of the Latin American countries had one foot on the road to peaceful transformation and the other on the path to revolutionary chaos. Some were standing still, while others were moving unevenly down both roads, the strain increasing with each step.

R. M. S.

Columbia University

1. The Latin Viewpoint

There is no "voice of Latin America," nor, for that matter, is there a voice of Cuba, of Mexico, of Argentina, or of any other country. There are many voices—some strident, some barely audible; some critical of, some complacent about, the *status quo,* whether in domestic or foreign affairs. There has always been discordancy in Latin America, but perhaps more so today than at any time since it gained independence.

BASIC CONSIDERATIONS

At the time independence was won, and throughout most of the nineteenth century, few Latin American leaders seriously considered upsetting the traditional social and economic patterns inherited from the colonial period. Most thought in terms of political organization and orientation: relations with the mother country, the problems of Church and state, federalism and centralism, executive authority and legislative power, landed and urban interests, democracy and autocracy. The conflicts that arose concerning these issues were settled by various means in the several countries, ranging from long and protracted civil wars to peaceful evolutionary adjustments. In most countries, however, little real progress was made toward political democracy or distributive justice in social and economic affairs. Land was more greatly concentrated by the end of the nineteenth century than at the beginning, as confiscated Church properties and Indian lands were acquired by the old rural and new urban elite groups. Urban intellectual, professional, and commercial interests struggled for, and in some instances gained, a share of power; but urban labor, not to mention rural labor, barely maintained its living levels, and in many areas they actually retrogressed.

15

ATTITUDES TOWARD CHANGE

These historical political conflicts have continued in part to the present. However, lower-class drives for material and cultural benefits developed with the introduction of modern industry and technology, large-scale rural migration to the cities, and the spread of socialistic and reformist ideas from abroad. Populist leaders, sprung from a new generation of nationalistic and reform-minded intellectuals, have challenged not only the naked power but also the very value system of the governing elite. Beyond deploring the misery and wretchedness of the poor and oppressed, these critics have asked by what right do the elite monopolize national power and wealth, by whose dictum are the workers consigned to a position of subservience, and by what infallible authority have the Indian and Negro races been declared inferior.

Cries of change have not been heard simultaneously in all parts of Latin America. Nor have they been heard in the same tone or for the same purposes. They have varied, depending on the magnitude of the problem, the awareness of the possibility for change, the ability of reform leaders, and the position of the elite. For the most part, change came slowly from the late nineteenth to the early twentieth centuries, but as mid-century approached, the demands for reform grew ever more insistent. After World War II, it became clear that the lower classes were no longer to be denied. Now it is not a question of whether or not the elite can maintain the structure (they cannot); it is rather a question of when, how rapidly, how deeply, and by whom reform will be imposed on the political, economic, and social structures of Latin America.

Despite the deep-seated social conflicts that are current in Latin America today, the opposing forces are not irreconcilably divided on all issues. Nationalism in its many guises, the drive for industrialization and self-sufficiency, programs for improved health and education, the creation of greater national wealth and commerce, and government intervention in the economy—all cut across class lines. These form the basis for a peaceful settlement of disputed issues in those countries in which the economic potential is favorable, and where compromise on social questions has not been made impossible by mutual intransigence and hatreds built up over many years. In other countries, however, the situation appears almost hopeless, and seemingly, only a series of miracles can stave off violence and radicalism. In no country will the transition be made easily and smoothly.

Industrialization requires a large working force, part of which must be technically trained and educated, and all of which can be organized for the attainment of improved social and economic conditions. The very nature of such an interest group leads inevitably to far-reaching changes, or demands for such changes, in the whole structure of the community. Limited demands for economic betterment lead inevitably to demands for political power. Both those demands drastically threaten the position of the ruling groups. Not only will the elite find themselves forced to share power with the lower and middle classes, but in time they will find their very mode of existence subject to change. Domestic service will slowly become more costly, until only a very few families will be able to maintain large houses and sizable staffs of nursemaids, gardeners, and caretakers. Labor-saving devices will increase in popularity, new industries will thereby be stimulated, and more workers will be required.

From the point of view of the economy and the general welfare, these changes may well be lauded by all, but the social changes they entail will be lamented by many. Families of means will be forced eventually to perform tasks that in Latin America have historically been considered demeaning. A large number of upper-class families in Latin America, although encouraging the growth of the economy, seem unaware of the related social and political changes that are sure to follow. Instead of planning carefully over a long period to ease the transition, most families seem to have set their sights on preserving the social *status quo*. Some, still affected by the traditional Hispanic disgust with the corruption and inefficiency of the state, espouse a broad *laissez-faire,* "rugged-individualist" economic doctrine. Still others ignore the problems, blithely assuming that their lives will not change and that somehow "it will all work out." A few families remark: "After us, the deluge."

This is not to imply that the reformist-nationalist position is without contradictions. Too often, the reformers combine opposition to foreign capital with demands for immediate division of wealth, and state planning for expensive welfare and investment programs. Such a position is as unrealistic as that of the elite, for it ignores the question of where the funds are to be found to build the economy. In their quest for more equitable distribution of the nation's wealth, these reformers ignore the fundamental problems involved in exploiting the nation's resources and the construction of the plant and facilities necessary for industrialization. Such projects are enormously expensive and normally beyond the capabilities of underdeveloped countries. Not only must profits be plowed back into expansion of the existing plant, but more often than not, outside assistance must be sought. Until agreements and adjustments in these respective positions can be worked out, the prospect of internal strife and radical solutions remains a strong possibility in many areas of Latin America. Currently, there is little evidence that sufficient thought is being devoted to reasonable solutions to the problem. The voices of moderation are too frequently drowned out in the urgent cries for radical social revolution on the one hand, and ignored with an ominous silence on the other.

NATIONALISM

In the nineteenth century and well into the twentieth, most Latin American leaders, though locally ambitious, were patient if not complacent about their impotent role in international affairs. Differences arose among Latin Americans, however, over the question of with whom they should ally themselves. In the 1820's, some liberals opted for the United States, then still a small power and one not yet seen as a threat to any Latin American country. In common with their own government, the government of the United States was a republic, then a rather rare political form; it was also an opponent of colonialism, imperialism, and monarchy, and was isolationist with respect to European wranglings. More conservative Latin Americans, however, felt greater kinship with Great Britain's constitutional monarchy, and a few reactionaries, questioning the wisdom of their break with Spain and Portugal, attempted to restore cultural and economic, if not political, ties with the mother country. In philosophy, learning, and the arts, almost all upper-class Latin Americans looked to France for leadership.

As U.S. politico-military predominance grew in the Caribbean, Central America, and Mexico, the early feelings of friendship and common political purpose of Latin Americans—even the liberals—began to fade and give way to an almost universal fear and hostility. Still not questioning their minor position in world affairs, even the larger countries acknowledged their inadequacy to meet the U.S. threat. As a matter of self-defense, they turned eagerly to Europe for foreign assistance in stabilizing their political institutions and building their economies. Argentina, Chile, and Brazil sought British aid at various times; the Dominican Republic turned temporarily to Spain; and Mexico, admiring yet fearing U.S. technological and administrative advances, sought by the late nineteenth century to counterbalance U.S. influence and investments with others from various European sources. Nationalism was present in every country throughout the nineteenth century, but it was not so virulent in form as to cause outside assistance to be rejected or placed under stringent limitations and controls. Actually, the very freedom permitted to foreign investors has been a vital factor in creating the xenophobia of twentieth-century Latin America. Beginning with Uruguay at the turn of the century, and Mexico a decade later, virtually every Latin American country, large and small, has undertaken to gain control of major foreign enterprises within its boundaries, and to oppose all attempts of foreign governments to protect the property of its nationals. Many foreign-owned businesses have been nationalized; the remainder have been made subject to local law, with no appeal for diplomatic protection.

The above discussion implies unanimity of opinion. This is far from the fact. The nationalization of foreign holdings was accompanied in most cases by bitter internal political feuds and, in the case of Mexico, by a bloody civil war succeeded by twenty years of political conflict. Many Latin Americans had a stake in foreign investments and the traditional organization of the economy. These protested the changes vociferously, but the march of events was against them. The dominant voice in the twentieth century has been that of the reformers and nationalists, and they may be found in all social and economic classes. No "patriotic" Mexican, Chilean, Peruvian, or any other Latin American may oppose the march of "national progress," and the nationalization of foreign-owned property has frequently been the first step on the road.

National progress itself implies several specific goals: a high degree of economic independence and self-sufficiency, strong and stable political institutions, and a larger role in hemisphere and world politics. These have had almost universal appeal, and specific policies advocated to achieve these ends are difficult to combat. One set of proposals may successfully be opposed only by another set—designed to achieve the same ends, but allegedly more efficiently, more realistically, more harmoniously. In some areas, land reform, for example—though it may be basic to any long-term political and economic growth—is successfully opposed by appeals to short-term national interests. However, out-and-out opponents of all change have been either virtually silenced or relegated to a fringe area. In recent years, only a Trujillo could openly and with impunity publicly take the position that his country was closely bound to the United States. But his was a voice of the past. Latin American leaders today must talk in terms of independence or, at most, cooperation with the great powers. A semineutralist position in the Cold War is popular in Mexico, and a call for renewal of diplomatic and economic relations with the Soviet bloc—as a mark of independence from the United States—will gain a Latin American politician wide popular support. Warnings against such moves are, at best, muted. No responsible leaders outside Cuba, however, advocate subservience to the Soviet bloc—a position that is recognized as only another form of dependence.

Latin American nationalists, in contemplating the world in which they live and the position of their countries among the family of nations, make two basic assumptions, one political and one economic, that are not entirely in accord with reality. As a result of these assumptions, they are thoroughly dissatisfied with their present condition and tend to place much of the blame for these circumstances on others. This, in turn, creates international tensions between the Latin American countries and the outside world, particularly the United States. Thus a search begins for solutions that are in large part unattainable, and therefore unrealistic.

The first of these basic assumptions is that the world community of nations is composed of equal, sovereign, and independent countries that have absolute control over their own destinies with regard to foreign and domestic policies. From this assumption, the nationalists quickly move to the position that no country should intervene in any way in the affairs of another. In 1957, Luis Quintanilla, then Mexican Ambassador to the Organization of American States (OAS), said: "Latin Americans reject not only outright intervention, but any sort of interference in their domestic or external affairs." Latin Americans, he continued, "insist on remaining the exclusive masters of their national destiny. Their form of government and their government's ideology are their concern, and theirs alone." From this concept of international relations, developed of course from their experiences since independence, has stemmed the Latin Americans' vehement opposition to any situation resembling extraterritoriality, to the use of force even when sanctioned by accepted international law (as for the protection of one's nationals and property), and to the use of diplomatic recognition or nonrecognition as an instrument by one state to pressure another into policies objectionable to the latter. They also object strongly to conditions attached to grants and loans from foreign sources, but at the same time, they view denial of assistance as another form of interference.

The second basic assumption, this one economic, is that each country, to assure its political independence and economic progress, should become almost entirely self-sufficient in agricultural and industrial production. To achieve this end, steel mills have been constructed, feverish searches for oil have been undertaken, and laws have been passed limiting the exportation of nonrenewable natural resources. In so far as possible, each country wants to free itself from dependence on the unstable world prices of the raw materials that it produces, as well as on the high cost of manufactured goods that it must import. A recent limited compromise on this position was the establishment, early in 1960, of a common market among seven* of the larger states. What practical measures will result remains to be seen, especially in view of the paucity of articles the members have to exchange, and the desire of each to attain self-sufficiency.

Neither the assumption concerning political independence nor that concerning economic independence is entirely erroneous, but neither is entirely accurate. The point need not be labored that the world is not composed of absolutely equal, sovereign, and independent states—it never has been. Rather, all nations are dependent, but some nations are more dependent than others. Unquestionably, the political leaders of Latin America recognize this truism of international politics. They cannot publicly admit it, however, because of the high degree of emotionalism involved in the concept of sovereignty. And they must frequently act as though they do not recognize it. Therefore, Latin American leaders, whatever the degree of their nationalism, are confronted with an embarrassing dilemma. This is the negative type of nationalism that shouts its condemnation of imperialists and colonialists in the same breath in which it demands internal reform and development, which cannot be accomplished without the aid of those same imperialists.

As a further complication in their relations with the United States, these nationalists combine their political and economic

---

* By the spring of 1963 the number had been increased to nine. They were: Argentina, Brazil, Chile, Colombia, Ecuador, Mexico, Paraguay, Peru, and Uruguay. Economic integration is also going forward in Central America.

principles to take a view of their position in world affairs that frequently places their northern neighbor in an impossible situation. With their strenuous objections to intervention, interpreted in the broadest possible terms, they have at one time or another condemned almost every type of U.S. action in the hemisphere. At the same time, however, with their tendency to blame the United States for most of their ills—from dictators to one-crop economies—they also demand that the United States take positive action to remedy their problems. Never was the dilemma so well pointed up as at the Santiago Conference of American Foreign Ministers in 1959. Venezuela and Cuba, both with new revolutionary governments, preached the doctrine that intervention was not intervention when carried out collectively to overthrow a dictator. Not one other Latin American country was willing to adopt this policy to overthrow Trujillo, of the Dominican Republic, despite the fact that he epitomized the term "dictator" in the Americas. The doctrine was not even mentioned at the San José Conference in 1960, and it was further made clear that diplomatic relations were broken with Trujillo at that time not because he was a dictator, but because he had intervened in the internal affairs of Venezuela, going so far as to order an attempt on the life of President Rómulo Betancourt.

Despite this reluctance to assume joint responsibility for the overthrow of dictators, these Latin American critics imply time after time that the United States should "do something"; but they simultaneously cry intervention when we act in some other capacity, even to strengthen or assist a Latin American country in a manner that does not meet their complete specifications. Intervention is not intervention *only* when the United States does what the nationalists want, when they want it, and in exactly the manner in which they want it—in other words, assistance with absolutely no strings attached. Apart from the question of waste or misuse of funds within the recipient country, such a program would not be politically possible to adopt in the United States or in any other country, democratic or authoritarian.

No amount of rational argument, presentation of statistical data, or recounting of political or historical facts will effect any significant change in this nationalist Latin American viewpoint. Neither will any amount of U.S. soul-searching, gnashing of teeth, or high expenditures bring about a solution to the tensions and frustrations between the United States and Latin America. They will continue to exist indefinitely, and all that can reasonably be expected is some amelioration of relations while the United States works, as far as possible, in overcoming Latin America's most pressing internal political, social, and economic problems. The "how" of whatever the United States does is at least as important as the "what"—perhaps more important. The lessening of Latin American dependence on the United States may well prove disadvantageous to our economic interests in the short run but, in all likelihood, advantageous to our political interests over the long haul, particularly if the future should hold out only the prospect of more and better *Castrista* Cubas in the hemisphere.

ATTITUDES ON CONTEMPORARY ISSUES

The primary desires of major Latin American political and social groups are for the most part theoretically attainable, but not always in the manner and at the pace that reformers demand. Some of their goals are not attainable in the foreseeable future, and some not without further changes in the ingrained habits and traditions with which they are reluctant to part. Progress toward these goals will be slow and painful, whether revolutionary or more moderate means are utilized, as the examples of a half-dozen or more countries have clearly demonstrated. There are no short cuts.

CURRENT POLITICAL TRENDS

Many of the major political conflicts of the nineteenth century have been muted, if not completely quieted. Regionalist struggles have not disappeared, but for many years they have not been the source of serious disturbances. The old theoretical quarrels of federalism versus centralism have been laid to rest through practical compromises. Church-state relations have not been definitively settled (nor can they ever be), but adjustments are constantly being made with few disturbances to the political structures of the various countries. The urban-rural conflicts of interest among the elite have been compromised almost everywhere, and commitments to republican representative political institutions are well-nigh universal. Where they have not been fully achieved, they remain among important sectors of the populace as ultimate though indefinite goals, even in such dictatorships of the left and right as Cuba and Paraguay.

The growing complexity of Latin American society has increased and complicated normal political tensions. New groups are striving for power, with the elite reluctant to surrender their monopoly.

Everywhere, however, the pressures are being firmly applied, and in a number of the more advanced countries, changes are already well under way. Mexico, Bolivia, and Cuba have experienced the most thoroughgoing revolutions, with consequent social and political changes. Argentina, Brazil, Chile, and several others have attempted the road to evolutionary change through less violent means. In so far as improvements have not kept pace with demands (as legislation has not been enforced, and election promises have been disregarded), large sectors of the lower classes have become cynical about democratic political institutions. Their own experiences have taught them that the high-sounding phrases of equality of opportunity, liberty for the individual, and fraternity among men have applied in practice only to the ruling elite. When they see further that authoritarians such as Juan Perón, Getúlio Vargas, and Jacobo Arbenz implemented what the elite only talked about, and that Fidel Castro is fulfilling promises to the lower economic groups faster than Betancourt, they are gravely tempted to abandon the course of political evolution and moderation for revolution and radicalism. Such sentiments are, of course, encouraged by the Communists throughout Latin America. The Latin American masses have not yet actively thrown their weight behind authoritarianism, but the ease by which they were led to do so by an ostensibly democratic leader in Cuba should give pause to the most optimistic observer.

Social and economic changes have brought about not only new interest groups clamoring for power, but also new forms of political organization. In the more advanced countries, well-organized labor unions, bureaucrats, and professional groups, as well as the older employer associations and business associations, exert pressure on the government to fulfill their demands. With these complexities, the nature of political parties has changed from the simple liberal, conservative, or personalist orientation to a multiplicity of forms representing widely divergent political and economic philosophies. Party loyalties are scarcely anywhere so firm as they are in the United States, but hard cores have been built not only by the Communists, but by democratic socialistic reformers, Christian democrats, and propertied interests. Personalist agglomerations tend to proliferate at election time but quickly evaporate with defeat. Parties with broad-based programs appear to be the trend of the future.

Despite the ferment and the change that have already swept through Latin America in the twentieth century, several deep-rooted political attitudes persist that are at variance with the new trends. Latin Americans have for centuries been attracted by the powerful personality, the "father figure." They still are, despite a move toward the institutionalization of political instruments. A Betancourt or an Haya de la Torre is more than the leader or symbol of his party—he is the personification of his organization to a degree that a Dwight Eisenhower could never become in the eyes of U.S. citizens. Even in Mexico, where the political process has developed much further, the President, during his term in office, is the father of his people, the symbol of the state, and the leader of the nation—to a degree that John Kennedy or Franklin Roosevelt could never attain.

Secondly, the Latin American remains far more highly individualistic in his politics than the average U.S. citizen. Compromise comes hard. Personal pride, often masked as rigid adherence to principle, is so deeply ingrained as to seem inborn. Political fragmentation is a constant threat to interest groups and parties. The Latin American is learning fast, but the course is difficult, and the final examination has yet to be passed.

Thirdly, the Latin American—despite his respect for authority, his reverence for the strong personality, and his inclination to "let the government do it"—has long had an abiding cynicism concerning government and politicians. And with good reason. The bureaucracy has been notoriously inefficient, with little sense of public service, and addicted by circumstance to the "pay-off." Elected officials and higher appointees have made personal fortunes through their offices, and positions of public trust have been regarded as roads to personal enrichment rather than as opportunities to serve the nation. Efforts have been made in recent years to change these conditions, but the obstacles are well-nigh insuperable. Necessary improvements would entail higher technical competence, a reduction in force, higher wages, and above all, a retraining in basic public morals not only of politicians and government workers, but of the whole population. Habits of thought and action cannot be revolutionized overnight.

ATTITUDE IN THE COLD WAR

The dominant groups in Latin America identify culturally with the West, as they always have, but because of the growing internal pressures accompanying economic growth and social changes, they have steered their governments away from binding political or military commitments with members of the Atlantic Community. Many of the rising middle and lower classes do not experience even this sense of cultural attachment to the West, and many are but vaguely aware of any relationship. As a result, they are more easily persuaded to establish contacts of various types with the Soviet bloc in the hope of ameliorating their social and economic distress. To this end, they are encouraged by the local Communists and extreme nationalists, who are bitterly opposed to the United States. U.S. opposition to such ties, on the grounds that the Latin countries are not sufficiently strong or mature to withstand Soviet and Chinese blandishments, have only goaded the nationalists to more strident demands that their countries conduct normal relations with "all countries of the world," and break their dependence on the United States.

The most extreme response to this appeal has been that of Castro's Cuba, which not only has restored diplomatic relations with the Soviet Union, but has exchanged ambassadors with Red China, all the Asian satellites, and all the East European satellites. The Castro regime has also bound the Cuban economy almost entirely to the Soviet bloc. Castro and his leading associates have explained their seizure of U.S. business enterprises on the island and their vitriolic verbal attacks on the U.S. Government as measures necessary to free the island from Yankee imperialism. Referring to alleged U.S. plans to overthrow the Cuban revolutionary regime, Ernesto Guevara, Castro's second-in-command, declared in Moscow in December, 1960: "The people of Cuba trust in the strength of progressive humanity, in the strength of the socialist camp led by the U.S.S.R. I am confident that this strength will not allow Americans to plunge into a dangerous adventure against the independence of Cuba." The posture of the Cuban revolution is well summed up in the popular slogan "Cuba, yes! Yankees, no!" No one who has remained loyal to the Castro regime has yet raised the question, at least openly, of whether Cuba has not exchanged one master for another.

Next to Castro, President Jânio Quadros, of Brazil, prior to his resignation in August, 1961, had developed the strongest independent or neutralist position with regard to the Cold War. Seemingly anti-Communist by conviction, Quadros adopted an enigmatic attitude toward the United States and the Soviet bloc during his campaign for the presidency and during his first few weeks in office. Although he referred to the historic ties of friendship between the United States and Brazil, he gave evidence that he was reconsidering Brazil's relations with the Soviet camp. Rumors circulated from Quadros' circle that the new government was contemplating renewing diplomatic relations with the Soviet Union and concluding a trade agreement with Red China. Within a month of taking office, Quadros clarified his foreign policy position of "independence." His Minister of Foreign Affairs spoke of a "sovereign" foreign policy and hinted that Brazil would establish diplomatic relations not only with the U.S.S.R. but also with the People's Republic of China. Quadros himself replied to a greeting from Khrushchev with a statement that closer relations between Brazil and the U.S.S.R. would contribute to international peace and prosperity. He balanced the remark the following day, in answer to a greeting from Kennedy, by saying that he hoped to strengthen the spirit of co-operation between his country and the United States. His subsequent actions, however, did not support the latter statement. He was cool to U.S. envoys, including Adolf Berle, and ordered his U.N. delegation to support debate on the seating of Red China. He also spoke of eventually withdrawing recognition of Nationalist China. Nonetheless, Quadros gave every indication that he intended to continue past policies of seeking aid from the United States in credits and food supplies.

An early explanation for Quadros' "independent" foreign policy was that it was designed to placate the Communists and the extreme left in the hope of lessening their opposition to the austerity program with which he planned to end Brazil's catastrophic inflation and stabilize the economy. His enemies on the left did not respond to his first friendly gestures to the bloc, but Quadros continued and even expanded them. His resignation did not change the basic realities of Brazilian political life, and his successor, João ("Jango") Goulart, has continued to pursue a nationalist, semi-neutralist, and independent foreign policy to gain and maintain popular support. In November, 1961, the Goulart Government re-established diplomatic relations with the Soviet Union.

Except for a few of the more conservative and rightist regimes, such as those of Nicaragua and Paraguay, the remainder of the Latin American governments are wary of taking a position that the nationalists could interpret as being subservient to the United States. Only with reluctance did the majority of the Latin American countries sign the Caracas Anti-Communist Declaration of 1954, and then only after it had been clarified that joint hemispheric action would be taken only against foreign Communist aggression in the hemisphere—not against local Communist governments. Even with this proviso, Mexico refused to sign, and has maintained this position to the present, for fear that the declaration may be used as justification for intervention. Mexico has also refused to sign a military pact with the United States, or to tie herself in any way to the Western alliance. However, in the face of the Cuban missile crisis of the fall of 1962, the Mexican Government revised its long-standing position on self-determination of nations to declare openly that a Marxist-Leninist regime was incompatible with the principles of the Organization of American States. Many of the others have let their desire for armaments override their inclination to adopt an independent attitude on military aid.

Most of the Latin American governments are also under pressure to increase their trade and diplomatic relations with the Communist bloc. Several Latin American countries have exchanged ambassadors and consuls with bloc countries, have made some gestures toward increasing trade relations, and have declared in favor of debating Red China's entry into the U.N. Except for Cuba, trading activities with the bloc during the past five years have not been spectacular. Only Argentina, Brazil, and Uruguay have channeled more than 5 per cent of their total trade into exchanges with the Communist nations. Soviet and Chinese offers elsewhere have progressed little beyond the talking stage, but no government can afford to turn them down without some gesture of consideration. Bolivia, for example, dependent on U.S. aid ($20 million annually since 1952) to keep its government solvent, apparently did not believe that it could safely reject outright a Soviet offer of credit to build a tin smelter in the country, and a Bolivian delegation was sent to the Soviet Union to discuss the project. Nationalists envision the processing of Bolivia's major mineral resource within the country, although the plan is probably not economically feasible. But the nationalists cannot be ignored, here or anywhere else in Latin America.

THE CUBAN REVOLUTION

No event since World War II has so shaken the Inter-American System, and each Latin American country individually, as has the Cuban revolution. In the two years of armed conflict waged by Fidel Castro against President Fulgencio Batista, Latin Americans in overwhelming numbers, at least a majority of U.S. citizens, and much of the press in both areas favored the young idealist against the aging dictator. Mexicans and Bolivians quickly identified the Cuban revolution with their own earlier struggles, while the Democratic Action (Acción Democrática, or AD) Party in Venezuela, the reformist APRA (Alianza Popular Revolucionaria Americana) in Peru, and nationalists, reformers, and liberals everywhere saw reflections of their own victories or aspirations. The people of the United States were not so emotionally involved but, with their natural sympathy for the underdog, cheered on Fidel and his small band of determined fighters. As the officially recognized ruler of the island, an anti-Communist, and a close collaborator with U.S. Government and business interests, Batista had numerous supporters in the United States. Although Latin Americans hailed Castro's final victory with unreserved enthusiasm, the United States responded more cautiously, and government and people alike, though willing to grant immediate recognition to the new regime, reserved final judgment until they could ascertain the orientation of Castro and his cohorts.

The gap between United States and Latin American views on Cuba soon began to widen. U.S. offers of economic assistance and political support for the revolution were unceremoniously rejected, and the new government began a campaign of nationalization of U.S. interests and vilification of the U.S. Government that grew to such proportions that eventually all vital political and economic ties between the two countries were broken. As recompense for the losses impending and resulting, Castro sought the support of the Sino-Soviet bloc, which was quickly forthcoming. The Latin American response was at first one of some satisfaction at the discomfiture of the United States, and of criticism at the latter's increasingly hostile attitude toward Cuba. This attitude has been modified but has not disappeared. Concurrently, considerable alarm began to grow among all Latin Americans, except among the Communists and their allies, at the degree of dependence upon the Communist bloc that Castro not only permitted but encouraged, and at his repeated threats to carry his revolution throughout the area. By the spring of 1963, fourteen Latin American countries had broken relations with Cuba—the Dominican Republic, Nicaragua, Haiti, Paraguay, Guatemala, Peru, Ecuador, Panama, Colombia, Venezuela, Costa Rica, Honduras, El Salvador, and Argentina. At least half of these have been directly threatened with revolt by *Fidelistas* and/or Communists. Some are rightist regimes, but in Peru, the reformist Víctor Raúl Haya de la Torre, leader of APRA, publicly supported his government's condemnation of

Castro. Moreover, the democratic regimes of Costa Rica, Venezuela, and Colombia supported the resolution of the Punta del Este Foreign Ministers' Conference in January, 1962, to exclude Cuba from participation in the Inter-American System. All nineteen supported the U.S. quarantine of Cuba imposed to force the withdrawal of Soviet missiles and other offensive weapons from the island.

Despite the fact that many Latin Americans have begun to mute their earlier enthusiastic acclaim for the Cuban revolution, the gap between their views and those of the U.S. Government has not been closed, only narrowed. Some politically active Latins, predominantly students and intellectuals—but including, too, some lower economic groups—have continued to support Castro. Their governments believe that they must still proceed with caution, but during the closing months of 1962, the strength of the pro-Castro groups appreciably waned. None of the major Latin American countries, Mexico or Brazil in particular, is ready to countenance intervention singly or jointly. Only with reluctance and with verbal reservations did they sign the San José Declaration of August, 1960, in which the OAS condemned intervention or the threat of intervention from "an *extracontinental* power in the affairs of the American republics," and declared that the acceptance of such intervention by any American state jeopardizes American solidarity and security.

Latin American and U.S. differences were clearly pointed up by the variant interpretations given the declaration. Christian A. Herter, then U.S. Secretary of State, believed that it constituted a "clear indictment" of Cuba. Cuba agreed, but Manuel Tello, Secretary of Foreign Affairs of Mexico, stressed its general character and insisted it did not constitute a condemnation of Cuba. Most of his Latin American colleagues concurred. A more critical view of Cuba has been apparent throughout Latin America since San José, particularly since the missile crisis of October-November, 1962, but the sentiment against intervention goes deep. Unquestionably, the United States will continue to encounter significant resistance to any attempt to invoke the mutual-security provisions of the Rio Treaty against Cuba in the foreseeable future. Most Latin American governments are disenchanted, but not all of their citizens; most governments are alarmed at the Soviet threat and the threat of spreading revolution, but they cannot bring themselves to intervene; most governments sympathize with the U.S. position and are ready to take advantage of the new sugar quotas, but many are not overly unhappy about the U.S. embarrassment, and cannot appear to be unduly sympathetic on specific issues. They would like the Castro threat removed, but they will do little to assist its overthrow.

ECONOMIC DEVELOPMENT, INTERNATIONAL TRADE, AND FOREIGN ASSISTANCE

Intimately linked with the political questions involved in Latin America's position in the East-West conflict are the area's problems of trade channels and sources for economic development. Nationalist feelings run high in discussions and consideration of both these subjects.

In the forefront of Latin American drives and ambitions stands the desire, amounting at times to near frenzy, to achieve national economic self-sufficiency. Chafing at the restrictions that a one- or two-crop economy imposes upon them, as well as at their dependence on foreign markets and foreign imports, most countries hope to achieve economic independence through the establishment of new manufacturing plants and the development of auxiliary enterprises such as transportation and communications systems. Lacking sufficient domestic private capital to finance these undertakings, and wary of the entry of foreign private capital into vital economic areas, many governments in Latin America have been rapidly expanding the promotion, control, and management of their national economies. Mixed enterprises, with stock divided between government and private investors, have come to be a favorite form of business organization in large-scale undertakings such as steel production. In nonrenewable natural resources such as oil, and in certain natural monopolies such as railroads and public utilities, government ownership or general control is preferred. Government promotion through credit extension, tax relief, or outright grants is favored by businessmen for private economic development, and by the lower classes for health and welfare programs.

Unfortunately, in most Latin American countries, development programs have led to deficit spending, unbalanced economies, galloping inflation, and resultant political instability. Only Mexico, Bolivia, and Cuba have made any radical attempts to increase and diversify agricultural production and to improve the standard of living of the agrarian masses. Their results have been far from spectacular. After more than ten years, Bolivian economic problems appear as far as ever from solution; Cuba cannot yet be judged; and Mexico has failed to raise the level of living of her vast peasantry to approximate that of her urban workers. Mexico has, however, achieved balanced economic growth, increased production in basic food stuffs, and a controlled inflation, with the result that social unrest has been minimal and political stability unthreatened for twenty years. Elsewhere in Latin America, the farm problem has hardly been touched. Not only has land remained overly concentrated, but efficient production methods, improved strains of plants and livestock, wide-scale irrigation, and diversification of products have been neglected. Credit, too, for agricultural experimentation and expansion has been lacking. Not every country has neglected every aspect of agricultural improvement, but no country except Mexico has pushed on a broad front to maintain a balance in national economic growth between agriculture and industry.

The fact that the great majority of the Latin American countries sell their principal products primarily to the United States, and purchase their needed supplies there, has led to bitter criticism of the United States for what the Latin Americans regard as an inequitable system: high and stable prices for their manufactured imports, and low and fluctuating prices for their raw-materials exports.

To remedy this unfavorable condition, the nationalists, aided by the Communists, have demanded a further diversification of their markets to include the Communist-bloc countries, but these new markets have not taken up much of the slack. Many businessmen and politicians have urged the establishment of international price supports for commodities such as coffee, cocoa, and copper, and market quotas guaranteed by the United States, such as those in effect since 1934 for sugar. Until the Punta del Este Conference of 1961, the United States had refused to become a party to any such agreement or treaty for price supports, but for the preceding two years had sent observers to international conferences seeking to establish quotas for coffee marketing. The United States has insisted further that production be cut, and government subsidies be ended on items of which surpluses have resulted. Political pressures from the powerful coffee barons within the Latin American countries concerned have made this advice difficult, if not impossible, to follow.

A third group, one that might be labeled idealists, has proposed a common market, or perhaps a series of common markets, within

Latin America to improve its trade position with respect to the rest of the world. Thus far, two have come into being, one a modest attempt by five* Central American countries to reduce tariffs over a period of years, and a more ambitious one of eight South American countries and Mexico. The success of these ventures is open to doubt inasmuch as most of the members of these respective organizations are basically competitors in the sale of raw materials and, among the nine, of manufactured goods, as well. For example, all the larger countries are trying to increase their production of petroleum, steel products, and textiles. In view of the economic nationalism within each country, it appears uncertain that realistic agreements can be reached by which their economies will complement, rather than compete with, each other.

The Latin Americans are also demanding assistance from foreign governments in the form of loans and grants for economic development and social advancement. Prior to World War II, these matters were of much less concern to Latin America, and counted for little in its international relations. Franklin D. Roosevelt, it is true, sponsored the creation of the Inter-American Economic and Financial Commission, which recommended an Inter-American Fund. Out of this suggestion grew the 1939 convention for the organization of a bank, but only a few countries ever ratified the instrument, and the coming of World War II destroyed the plan. After the war, Latin America had to be content with existing organizations, such as the World Bank, the International Monetary Fund, and the Export-Import Bank. The United States, meanwhile, turned its major attention from hemisphere problems to European and Asian difficulties.

Beginning in 1948, with the vast Marshall Plan aid program for Europe, Latin America felt increasingly neglected by its onetime good neighbor and began to clamor for U.S. attention to hemisphere problems, reminding the United States of the area's aid to the free world during the war. Latin Americans were particularly incensed when General Marshall, then Secretary of State, informed them at the Ninth Inter-American Conference, at Bogotá, that they were excluded from the U.S. plan for European recovery; Marshall Plan aid was to be granted only to rebuild war-shattered economies. The Latins were advised to seek private capital for their development, as the United States had done in the nineteenth century. The United States maintained this position for ten years, in the face of

* Membership is open to Panama should she wish to join.

ever-growing Latin criticism and discontent, and specific demands for an inter-American lending agency.

At the Tenth Inter-American Conference, at Caracas, in 1954, Secretary of State John Foster Dulles extracted from reluctant Latin American delegations an anti-Communist declaration (obviously aimed at Guatemala) but refused to listen to their economic problems at that time. Consenting to an economic conference later in the year (the first of its kind), the United States rejected even a proposal for a study on the feasibility of an inter-American bank. Continued Latin American pressure and the growing deterioration in U.S.–Latin American relations led to a more flexible attitude by 1957 and, finally, to consent by the United States, in 1958, to the establishment of such an institution. Unfortunately, the growing success of Castro in Cuba, and the hostile reception accorded Vice-President Nixon in his hemisphere tour, made it appear that only violence and mob action could persuade the United States that its Latin American policy needed re-examination. It was a question of perhaps too little, and certainly too late.

Since 1958, when the first concrete steps were taken toward the establishment of the Inter-American Development Bank (IDB), Latin American leaders have raised an additional problem for the United States. The aim of the IDB is to assist the Latin countries in developing their economies: to provide jobs, increase productivity, and, ultimately, raise the standard of living. But in many areas, immediate social improvements are necessary, involving investments that will bring no immediate monetary return. Schools, houses, hospitals, medical care, and agrarian reform are needed now in order to satisfy political pressures and, to some extent, to pave the way for further economic development. These require capital investments beyond the scope of the Latin American countries, unless they receive foreign assistance. Initial U.S. resistance to this kind of aid evaporated in the face of the Cuban revolution, and in 1960, President Eisenhower recommended $500 million as a beginning. Unfortunately, Castro was able to take a good deal of credit for bringing this about, and his fellow Latin Americans, though unfriendly, felt that they had to give the devil his due.

The question remains: Why has Latin America pushed so hard for an Inter-American Development Bank, that is, for this particular kind of credit institution? The question may best be answered by examining first the other forms of possible assistance to economic development and the causes for their rejection or lack of preference. The earliest postwar proposals by the United States—

that Latin America invite private capital for development—were largely unacceptable to many segments of the people. Under the broad cloak of nationalism, diverse and, at times, conflicting economic and political groups united to restrain and narrowly limit foreign private capital. Entrenched local industrialists viewed the introduction of foreign (particularly U.S.) businesses, with their more modern techniques and equipment, as a threat—at best to their monopoly of the domestic market, at worst to their very existence. Nonbusiness nationalists opposed their entry on the grounds that the extraction of nonrenewable resources resulted in a net loss to the Latin American country; that millions of dollars of profits were taken out of the country instead of being retained and reinvested; and that foreign capital perpetuated a colonial economy for their country since it was attracted primarily to the extractive industries and to money crops that did not contribute to needed diversification. In other words, the Latins have complained that foreign private capital, motivated by its quest for profits, did not respond to considerations of national interest in the host country.

An acceptable alternative to private investment was, and still is to a large extent, government-to-government loans, such as those made by the Export-Import Bank and the Development Loan Fund of the United States. Only the extremists have opposed such aid outright, on the grounds that it tends to make the recipient amenable to pressures from the lender, again the United States, to join in political and military alliances or agreements. Nationalists of moderate views have not been unresponsive to this argument, if only for its propaganda effect. More practically, the borrower, especially in Latin America, has seen himself restricted in the uses to which such funds could be put. For example, it was U.S. policy until early 1961 to deny government loans for oil-development projects undertaken by Latin American government oil corporations, such as Pemex in Mexico or Petrobrás in Brazil. The lack of logic in the U.S. position has been particularly annoying to the Latin Americans, and they have felt themselves subjects of discrimination and pressure to force their oil development into the hands of large foreign oil companies. Therefore, even though the Latin Americans have no strong objections to government loans, they have come to prefer a third alternative—loans from international lending agencies.

For several years after World War II, the Latin American nations seemed fairly well content with their abilities to borrow either from the World Bank, for development, or from the International Monetary Fund (IMF), for balance-of-payments difficulties. Beginning in 1954, however, they began to exert considerable pressure on the United States for a hemisphere agency. The real reasons for this are not entirely clear, especially in view of the fact that loans from the World Bank, the Export-Import Bank, and IMF rose substantially throughout the mid-1950's. The Latin American problem is perhaps threefold: social, economic, and psychological. First, these institutions, including the Export-Import Bank, have been reluctant to lend funds for social overhead—welfare projects on a long-term basis, for example, education and housing. Secondly, the international organizations are themselves responsive to world financial opinion and are therefore in a strong, independent position to insist that needed economic and financial reform be undertaken by the prospective borrower. A bank controlled by Latin Americans can, on the other hand, more easily be persuaded to bail out a Latin America country in financial difficulties. Psychologically, Latin America, feeling slighted by the announcement of the Marshall Plan, in 1948, hoped its special status would again be recognized by U.S. foreign-policy makers—specifically, by the creation of a hemisphere bank, over which Latin Americans would have considerable direction. Felipe Herrera, a Chilean, was chosen first President of the bank, and although he and his associates have announced that it is a financial—not a political—institution, they cannot close their eyes to its political origin, or to its future political role in a seething continent. How well it operates is yet to be seen.

THE MILITARY PROBLEM

One of the obvious signs of great-power status, and therefore of independence and sovereignty, is military strength. Prior to World War II, when most of Latin America was little concerned with making its mark on world politics (but vitally interested in obtaining from the United States a promise of self-denial as embodied in the Buenos Aires declaration on nonintervention in 1936), Latin American leaders, including the military, seemed little inclined to insist on heavy and expensive equipment. With the approach of World War II and the adoption of the policy of hemisphere solidarity and cooperation, Latin America was given at least a token role in defense plans, and some armaments to fulfill it. Modest grants during the war whetted appetites for more. Following the war, the United States devised various measures to continue some further military assistance and finally, by the Mutual Security Act of 1951, made larger supplies available to Latin America on a regular basis. The United States attempted to standardize armaments, secured a virtual monopoly in military missions, and outfitted some forces with heavy equipment such as tanks, artillery, aircraft, and warships. The Latin Americans responded with alacrity. The more they were given the more they wanted—until by the mid-1950's, their supplier became aware that a veritable arms race was on. When the United States refused to supply further warships and planes, the Latin Americans sought and obtained them in Europe. With unmistakable evidence before them of deep-seated popular discontent in Latin America, some members of the United States Government began to question the U.S. joint hemisphere-defense policy, and to urge Latin American governments to spend less on arms and more on economic development and social welfare.

The Latin American response to this suggestion has not been nearly so favorable as might have been expected, judging from nationalistic and liberal cries for economic development and reform. It is true that Eduardo Santos and Alberto Lleras Camargo, of Colombia, and Pedro Beltrán, of Peru, have condemned U.S. arms aid, and that President Jorge Alessandri, of Chile, has called for a conference on limitation of armaments. But they are not typical. Alessandri's conference has not materialized, and it is questionable whether or not the subject will be on the agenda of the next Inter-American Conference. Although it can be argued that reluctance to cut armaments stems from the objections of the military—admittedly strong in most countries—it is also apparent there is little popular support for arms reduction. In fact, the opposite can be demonstrated, both with the popularity of Perón's military bombast among the working classes, especially in his early years of glory, and with the broad popular support, at present, of the Castro military machine in Cuba—the mightiest native armed display ever seen in Latin America. In fact, the show of Soviet and bloc arms, and the threatened use of them against any possible U.S. intervention, are taken in themselves as indications of independence from U.S. control.

Of the major countries of Latin America, only the Mexican political leaders have sufficient control over their military and sufficient security in their international relations to feel that they do not need the gaudy display of modern weapons to convince

their people and themselves that they have international importance. Mexican displays of independence have taken quite the
opposite tack. Mexico has consistently rejected offers of U.S. mili-
tary-grant aid under the terms of a bilateral treaty. Reluctantly,
she has from time to time purchased necessary equipment for
minimal efficiency of her armed forces, and publicly acknowledges
that they are for internal order and assistance in crises. Mexico
makes no pretense of any ability to participate in hemisphere defense against outside aggressors. She has virtually no air force or
navy, only a small quantity of artillery, and an army of at most
50,000 men, of whom only a few thousand are armed with modern
small arms. But among the large states Mexico is unique. In virtually every other country, intense national pride is taken in the
country's armed might; criticism of the military comes chiefly from
those they oppose in internal struggles for power. Moreover, with
the military now tending to surrender political administration to
civilians and to support moderate reform and economic development, arms-limitation programs will probably continue to have little
appeal—particularly in view of rising nationalism among all sectors of the population and the availability of arms from either the
United States and Western Europe or the Soviet bloc.

The arms build-up in Cuba, Castro's success against the invasion
of April, 1961, and his threat to carry revolution throughout the
continent may well be expected to strengthen demands for increased military preparedness—not necessarily ships and tanks,
but rather training, counterinsurgency tactics, and the arms and
supplies necessary to maintain internal security in the face of
Castro techniques. These new types of assistance imply a new
military relationship between the United States and Latin America.
The result may well be the scrapping of Latin America's role of
participation in hemisphere defense from outside attack, and the
adoption of a more realistic role of counterinsurgency and guerrilla-
type warfare to contain the more real danger of subversion and
attack from within.

INTERNATIONAL AMBITIONS

The international ambitions of the various Latin American powers have been confined largely to the Latin American area itself
and, more specifically, to the immediate neighborhood of glory-
seeking and imperialistic rulers who have appeared from time to
time. For the most part, too, such aggressive drives as have mani-

fested themselves have resulted from the ambitions of strong leaders rather than from popular sentiments, but once nationalism has been aroused among the masses, it is difficult to dampen. Today, however, the prospects for serious, large-scale war within the hemisphere are remote. Repeated commitments to the peaceful settlement of disputes by all countries, the unifying force of the threat of extracontinental aggression, and the assorted machinery for hemispheric peace help prevent disputes from breaking out into protracted fighting. On the other hand, remote too are the possibilities of greater Latin American political unity in view of rising nationalism in the area.

Bolívar's dream of a united Spanish America collapsed in the face of an early nationalism associated, in the minds of the newly independent Creoles, with provincial and local jealousies and ambitions. Even Bolívar's creation of Gran Colombia fragmented before the Liberator's death. Moreover, Central America split into five countries and Argentina was taxed to the utmost to keep a semblance of unity within the interior provinces; Uruguay and Paraguay did succeed in breaking away. Only Portuguese America was able, for a variety of reasons, to retain its colonial unity, but it did not wholly escape secessionist movements. Efforts to achieve some degree of political, military, or economic cooperation have succeeded only under pressure and in collaboration with the United States.

Not only has Latin America failed to achieve a high degree of unity, but the area has been agitated repeatedly by threats of war and, on a few occasions, by open fighting over boundary disputes dating from the colonial period. The War of the Pacific, of the 1880's—involving Chile, Peru, and Bolivia—and the Chaco War, of the 1930's—between Bolivia and Paraguay—have left lasting bitterness among the disputants. The still-raging Peruvian-Ecuadorean boundary dispute, which has resulted thus far in effective Peruvian control over the disputed area, has not been definitively settled, since Ecuador repudiated the 1942 agreement on the grounds that it was forced upon her by Peru, the United States, and other Latin American countries as a measure of wartime solidarity. Brazil, on the other hand, has aroused no deep-seated hostility, despite the fact that boundary settlements with almost all her neighbors have resulted in her favor. The explanation lies probably in the fact that the areas under dispute lay in the inaccessible and seemingly worthless upper reaches of the Amazon and its tributaries.

Other sources of discord are more recent, and of different origin. The disputes between the late dictator of the Dominican Republic, Rafael Trujillo, and his neighbors in the Caribbean were largely personal and ideological and sometimes a combination of both. His early quarrel with Batista, of Cuba, was personal, and his repeated threats against Haiti resulted in part from his desire to dominate the whole island of Española, and in part from his racial hostilities. His quarrels with the liberal José Figueres, of Costa Rica, and his feud with Betancourt, of Venezuela—which extended to assassination attempts—had their roots in personal antagonism as well as in ideological differences. Personal and ideological elements counted heavily in the repeated quarrels between Costa Rica, during Figueres' Administration, and Nicaragua under Anastasio Somoza. Following the election of Mario Echandi in Costa Rica, in 1958, and the succession in Nicaragua of the less dictatorial Luis Somoza, son of the old dictator, hostilities between the two countries declined and some cooperation has been achieved in preventing revolutionaries from using the territory of either to launch attacks on the other. This sort of cooperation would have been unthinkable a few years back.

There is a third type of rivalry and ambition that has been marked by little or no open hostility, and certainly no threat of war. Mexico, for example, long regarded herself as the leader of Middle America, if not of all of Latin America. Luis Quintanilla, then Mexico's Ambassador to the OAS, presented his country's aspirations, if not her actual position, when he stated a few years ago: "Mexico, today a good neighbor of the United States, and the only Latin American country sharing its borders, is viewed by Latin Americans as a faithful and reliable sentry of the extensive Latin American world." At the other end of the hemisphere stands Argentina, which has long desired to lead a Latin American bloc, either within the Inter-American System or outside it. This goal was not new with Perón, but he expanded the program to lengths far beyond those of his conservative predecessors. By means of trade pacts, military understandings, threats, and an inter-American labor organization, he hoped to extend his influence throughout Latin America, particularly southern South America. Uruguay, Paraguay, Chile, and Bolivia were his immediate targets. His success was minimal, although he did take a highly independent position within the OAS by refusing to ratify most inter-American agreements, treaties, and conventions.

There has also been a long-standing rivalry between Argentina and Brazil for prestige and economic leadership in Latin America. The most recent evidence of this continuing competition was the acquisition in the late 1950's by first one, and then the other, of an aircraft carrier. Neither country seriously believed that such military expenditures were necessary for protection against the other, or that they contributed substantially to hemisphere defense. Brazil further attempted to raise her prestige among her neighbors in 1958–60 by promoting Operation Pan America. Another device to secure greater U.S. economic aid for the area, the plan called for a collective attack on underdevelopment as the most effective means of combating Communism. Brazil has, in addition, insisted that her voice be heard in international councils on peace and disarmament. She sent troops under U.N. auspices to the Gaza Strip and the Congo. Argentina, still in the throes of economic and political crises following the overthrow of Perón, has not been able to meet this challenge, and has probably slipped in prestige relative to her larger neighbor.

Long dominated and overshadowed by the United States in the Western Hemisphere, the Latin American countries welcomed the establishment of both the League of Nations and the United Nations as possible counterweights to the northern "colossus." Ten countries joined the League as charter members, seven others shortly after its formation. The remaining three joined somewhat later, but several countries eventually withdrew. The Latin American nations tried to obtain a League definition of the Monroe Doctrine that would limit U.S. activities in the Caribbean, but they were quickly disabused of this notion. Under Article XXI of the League Covenant, the Monroe Doctrine was recognized as a regional arrangement, and the organization refused to define the doctrine for fear of offending the United States. (In joining the League, several Latin American states specifically refused to recognize Article XXI.)

All the Latin American states are charter members of the United Nations. On the whole, they have cooperated with the United States and the Western alliance against the Soviet bloc. Their position on colonial questions has been moderate, their primary divergence being their hard push for economic-assistance programs for underdeveloped areas. Guatemala under Jacobo Arbenz (1951–54) proved uncooperative, as has Cuba under Castro, since 1959; but these have been exceptional in that they adopted not neutralist but pro-Soviet positions. Arbenz was overthrown by force, and Castro is now under considerable pressure, although it appears insufficient

to topple him in the near future. With greater confidence in the
Inter-American System, with limitations on U.S. interventionist
policies, and with greater influence in the comparatively new OAS
(founded in 1948) than in the U.N., the Latin American states,
with the exceptions noted above, have been unwilling to transfer
hemispheric disputes to the world organization and have preferred
to handle American problems within the inter-American community—a striking contrast to the early interwar years.

CONCLUSIONS

Latin views, then, are diverse—varying not only from country
to country but within each country. Latin Americans are deeply
divided among themselves in their attitudes toward solutions for
their internal political, social, and economic problems and the role
they should play in international relations. Depending upon their
personal and national interests, their ideological orientation, and
their cultural levels, they either adhere to the *status quo,* countenance slow but cautious change, or demand radical solutions.
Some wish to strengthen their ties to the United States, some wish
to loosen them, and some call for close relations with the Soviet
bloc. U.S. policy-makers, faced with these variant and often powerful voices, are called upon daily to make vital decisions affecting
the interest of the United States and its southern neighbors. In
recent years, these policy-makers have been subjected to ever-
rising crescendos of criticism, both at home and in Latin America,
as U.S. relations with the area have steadily deteriorated.

What are the policy-makers to do amid the babel of advice?
Support dictators or conspire with reformers? Intervene on behalf
of constitutionality, freedom, justice, and economic and social well-
being, or adopt a policy of strict nonintervention in internal political affairs? Pour U.S. Government money into the area, or advise
our neighbors to seek private investment for economic development? Grant them arms to participate in hemisphere defense, or
withhold military equipment and training on the grounds that none
of them can really contribute anything significant to joint defense,
and that the arms are too frequently used to uphold an inequitable
status quo? Set up marketing quotas and price supports for the
area's raw materials, or let the world market set the prices? Push
hard for a hemisphere-wide anti-Communist pact, or let each
country handle its Communist threats as it sees best? Adopt policies
and exert pressures to bind the Latin American countries more

closely to the United States, or loosen the bonds and permit them (with our blessings) to experiment freely with economic, political, and cultural relations with other, including Soviet bloc, countries?

Before any of us can attempt to assess U.S. policy in the post-World War II era, we must investigate at greater length not only what the Latins are thinking, but also the realities and problems of the area. This we propose to do first by examining prevailing social and economic conditions, and then by studying the complex political scene, with emphasis upon interest groups and political parties—the vehicles through which viewpoints are transformed into policies.

2. The Social Setting

The Pattern of Society

The social organization of Latin America is strikingly diverse and complex, varying from country to country and from region to region within a single country. Although all twenty countries have a common Latin-European origin and, with the exception of Brazil and Haiti, a common colonial history, they have developed distinctive national characteristics and problems since independence. In addition, most of the twenty republics suffer from marked and divisive regionalisms, and several, with large Indian populations, from the lack of a pervasive nationwide culture. There are also striking differences in the rates of social change from one country to another, and even within the same country. Because of the multiform nature of the area, scholars in Latin America and in the United States have debated over the years whether the name "Latin America" has enough foundation in fact to justify its use. Some have suggested "Indo-America," others "Hispanic America," but none, in writing the history of the nineteenth and twentieth centuries, has been able to do much more than examine each of the countries as separate entities. Generalizations about Latin American society, therefore, often tend to be artificial and superficial. Yet, it is apparent that there is sufficient cultural unity in the area to distinguish it from the United States and to support a few carefully formulated generalizations.

For the societies of most of the countries, we have so little reliable information (of the kind sociologists and anthropologists have prodigiously assembled on the United States) that it is easier to generalize about the whole than to analyze the individual countries. Precisely because we in the United States wish to understand Latin America as an area with a way of life different from our own, it becomes necessary to study it as a unit. This tendency is reinforced by the efforts of Latin Americans to establish loose political, and now economic, regional groupings that constitute recognition of shared problems and assets.

Latin America possesses social systems that in many essentials are characteristic of underdeveloped countries everywhere. Behind this similarity is a more than casual relationship. In Latin America, as in Africa and Asia, the social structure has been a major factor retarding economic development, and the economy has in return supported antiquated and inflexible social habits. As the U.S. delegation stated at the first Punta del Este Conference, in 1961, Latin America, as an underdeveloped area, has many developmental needs that can best be satisfied by planning on an area-wide basis.

SOME GENERAL PROBLEMS

Latin American society today is marked by profound social and ideological cleavages, as well as by very rapid change. Long-established institutions and customs are in a state of flux almost everywhere, and social unrest is actually or potentially a powerful force for far-reaching economic and social upheavals. Such periods of rapid change are not new to Latin Americans, but in contrast to previous periods of unrest, the present crisis seems destined to produce a more fundamental reorganization of basic social institutions. Today's rapid change arises from the interrelated processes of urbanization and industrialization, as well as from new concepts of social reform, Marxist and non-Marxist, which have had a far-reaching impact upon the leaders of the region. For the first time, broad and important segments of society are profoundly conscious of the differentials in urban–rural, upper-class–lower-class, and Latin American–North American levels of living. The unwillingness to tolerate these age-old social and economic inequities has been aptly called the "revolution of rising expectations." The change in attitudes—preceding, as it does, substantial and rapid economic growth—has produced demands that cannot be immediately satisfied, and thus threatens the existing social, economic, and political structures.

No one can foretell whether the institutions of Latin America will meet the challenge of imminent mass demands. If they do not, severe and lasting social disorganization may result, or the appeal of Castroism-Communism may prove overwhelming. The inherent instability of Latin American society has been laid bare for all to see by popular reactions to the Marxist-Leninist regime in Cuba. The Castro government failed when it sought to export its revolution in 1959 by sponsoring invasions of Panama, Nicaragua, Haiti, and the Dominican Republic. When the Cubans shifted to indirect subversion through propaganda, best exemplified by the operations of *Prensa Latina*, their official news agency, they were able to stimulate enough unrest to give pause to those political leaders who wished to adopt an anti-Castro position. Although Castro has now identified his regime as Communist as well as pro-Russian, destroying its earlier enchantment for most middle-class radicals, the attraction of *Fidelismo* still runs deep for a vociferous minority including elements of the lower class. Free elections and other paraphernalia of political democracy are of little moment to many, compared to the high standard of living Castro has promised his people, and the destruction of the aristocracy and upper-middle class that he has already accomplished. The missile crisis of October, 1962, did besmirch the Castro image, but the effects were limited and transitory, scarcely affecting the hard-core Castroites.

Cuba, Mexico, and Bolivia have each experienced a sweeping social revolution. In all three countries, a basic rearrangement and reorganization of society and the economy has taken place. Guatemala experienced an abortive social revolution which, although it was cut short in 1954, did effect some changes in social institutions. In all these countries except Mexico, societal forms are unstable and in a state of flux, with the ultimate forms yet to appear. All of these social cataclysms began as political revolutions to remove dictators who were wedded to the *status quo*. Once the dissolution of the existing political system produced anarchy, long-repressed demands for economic and social reform came to the fore.

The issue in the countries as yet untouched by social revolution is the adequacy of the existing institutions. If the traditional institutions of family and Church are not viable enough to adjust rapidly to new ways of doing and thinking, they will be drastically changed. An example of what can happen is the acute problems of Bolivia, where the government keeps its head above water through the medium of U.S. aid and the leadership of men like Hernán Siles Zuazo, who, when he was President, resorted to the hunger strike to dramatize to the people the necessity of his policies. The frequent small-scale battles between various groups in Bolivian rural areas is ample evidence of the disintegration of traditions and habits which help maintain order. Colombia, on the other hand, is a country which has not experienced a sweeping social revolution. Yet serious social disorganization has been apparent for about fifteen years in Colombia, as a consequence of changes moving the country in the direction of a developed, modern economy. The weakening of those beliefs and interpersonal relationships tying society together has produced long periods of endemic and destructive guerrilla warfare. The country's political leaders have largely failed, until very recently, to come to grips with this state of near-anarchy, and it may be that the social malaise has progressed so far that a gradualist solution is no solution at all.

CLASS STRUCTURE

Most Latin American societies are sharply stratified, some having class structures so rigid that they approach caste systems. In some countries, such as Peru or Guatemala, numerous indigenous groups constitute a distinctive society living apart from the dominant Western-oriented groups. The late nineteenth and early twentieth centuries brought the emergence of professionals, intellectuals, small entrepreneurs, and white-collar workers—a heterogeneous body of essentially urban people sometimes referred to as the middle class or the middle sector.

Upper Class. Although, in each country of the area, the upper class plays a distinctive national role governed by its make-up, size, and power, in every country the upper class has more political and economic power than does its counterpart in the United States. In Peru, Ecuador, Colombia, Nicaragua, Honduras, and Panama, the upper class forms a power elite; until very recently, this was also the case in the Dominican Republic and El Salvador. However, in Costa Rica, Uruguay, Venezuela, Argentina, Brazil, and Chile, it constitutes a more loosely organized grouping rather than a caste. In Bolivia, Cuba, and Mexico, the old upper class was annihilated by the forces of revolution, but in Mexico and Cuba, a new upper class has risen from the revolution itself. Where the elitist nature of the upper class is predominant, the middle class is weakest, and the gap between upper and lower social levels most extreme according to economic and social criteria.

In the nineteenth century, high social status was derived primarily from the ownership of a large estate. Although other criteria for upper-class membership have grown in importance, the *hacendado,* or owner of a large estate, is still automatically a member of the upper class. The wars of independence, as well as early political conflicts, affected the position of the landed aristocracy only slightly. In the late nineteenth and early twentieth centuries, however, mercantile and industrial wealth began to contribute important new elements to the upper class. These *nouveaux riches* were not readily accepted by the landowning families, who continued to place great stress upon possession of an old and established family name. Many of these newly rich purchased land. Combined with the passage of time and some intermarriage with old families, this landownership completed the process of making the new aristocrats acceptable to the old.

In their outlook toward life, the elites have always regarded themselves as an integral part of the Western world, and their financial resources have permitted them to travel, study abroad, and in other ways maintain contact with Europe and the United States. They have not, however, developed a strong social conscience. Although the wealth is available, foundations of the kind established in the United States by the Carnegies, the Rockefellers, and the Fords are highly unusual, and are certainly not regarded as particularly honorific. Rather, the Latin American elite engage in charitable activities of a personal nature and on a much smaller financial scale, often in a manner emphasizing the dependent position of the recipient. Many charitable activities are channeled to distantly related, but less fortunate, members of the family and to servants whose misfortunes are considered a family responsibility. The elites have not proved, in the majority of cases, amenable to reformist currents, particularly to demands that they peaceably relinquish some of their political power, wealth, and social position. Therefore, in the eyes of the reformers, they have forfeited any moral claim to political power and the loyalty of their fellow citizens.

Middle Class. The middle class in Latin America is more disparate in size, status, and cohesion than either the elite or the poor. Some Latin Americanists maintain that members of middle-income groups are so disunited and heterogeneous as to constitute not one but a range of classes. Countries like Paraguay, Honduras, El Salvador, Nicaragua, Haiti, Peru, and Ecuador possess virtually no middle-class grouping; others, such as Argentina, Costa Rica, and Uruguay, have clearly definable groups between the upper and lower classes. The remaining countries range somewhere between these poles, but nowhere in Latin America are the middle sectors comparable to the United States middle class in the possession of shared ideals and unifying relationships. In general, the various elements comprising the middle sectors do not have a vital understanding either of the concept of "middle class" or of their interests as a class. Divided among themselves, the middle groups in Latin America have not, as a class, exercised political power commensurate with their wealth and education to the extent achieved by their counterparts in more developed nations.

Many middle-class members consciously ape the upper class. Rather than consume conspicuously in intraclass competition, they consume beyond their means in order to emulate their economic betters by the purchase of land, luxury houses, and private education for their children. Unquestionably this type of mimesis reflects a widespread feeling, usually not explicit, that "middleness" is untenable as a permanent position: One must either attain upper-class status or risk falling into the lower class.

The middle class has been the most nationalistic of the classes. Its members have most consistently sought national economic, cultural, and political independence, and have attempted most persistently to produce a broad national philosophy acceptable to all groups. This national consciousness may be attributed mainly to the fact that most intellectuals belong to the middle class. Consequently, this class may offer the greatest hope for resourceful leadership in Latin America. The record of the Cuban middle class in this regard was less than happy, however, for it failed to use its power to combine economic development with economic and social reform. Although this failure resulted partly from close ties with U.S. economic interests, the Cuban middle-class leaders were on the whole incapable of providing imaginative policies and honest government. They talked much about using the sugar industry as a means for capital accumulation to develop light industry and agriculture, and for lessening dependence upon a single export crop, but they accomplished little or nothing in this direction. Middle-class individuals expended their income to achieve an extremely comfortable life, or to accumulate capital in the United States instead of risking investment in Cuba. Or if they invested in Cuba, they placed their money in sugar, real estate, and other less useful enterprises. Although Cuba had a radical constitution dating from 1940, and a wide range of social legislation on the statute books, effective programs were few and far between, permitting a marked social distance to appear between the urban middle and the rural lower classes. It was, indeed, to the rural disinherited that Castro made his strongest appeal, and from whom he has received his most devoted support.

The dependent middle class (those employed by others) is composed mainly of white-collar workers in business and government. Historically, the bureaucratic segment of the middle class was one of the first to appear, and as government agencies have continued to expand and proliferate, this segment has continued to grow. At present, an estimated 5 to 14 per cent of the labor forces of the various Latin American countries is employed by government agencies; in Castro's Cuba, the percentage is much higher. Civil servants are usually better educated than the average citizen, but they have not reached the level of technical competence and professionalism of the civil service of Western Europe and the United States. Many are still trained narrowly in the law, despite a growing trend toward a broader education. Unions of white-collar government workers are common throughout the area. The white-collar worker holds strategic positions in most countries because of the critical shortage of trained personnel.

The enlargement of this status-conscious and politically important group is directly dependent upon the further development of government services. Its members are committed to the philosophy of a socialistic or welfare state, partly because they have a direct financial interest in expanding government functions, and partly because they consider the government the only truly national instrument of progress. So much large and important private enterprise has been foreign owned, especially in the smaller countries, that government workers have indelibly associated "exploitation" with private initiative. The greatest potential for the expansion of the bureaucrats originates in the widespread and persistent demands for rapid economic development and for redistribution of income—policies that have assigned, and will continue to assign, to government an ever-larger role in national life. Nevertheless, civil servants more often favor gradual rather than revolutionary change, and are not averse to blocking policies contrary to what they consider their own legitimate interests. In most countries, prevalent corruption and poor morale, arising from low pay and uncertain tenure, tend to create an unfavorable image of government employees in the eyes of the general public, thus somewhat limiting their influence.

The other element in the dependent middle class consists of the clerical and professional employees of business enterprise. As U.S. corporations operating in Latin America have long since learned, their Latin American employees have an outlook on many aspects of life that is different from that found in the United States. Generally more status conscious and "face" conscious, they jealously guard their position as people who do not demean themselves by physical labor.

The independent middle class consists of self-employed professionals, businessmen, and small farmers. Only the professionals enjoy social and economic security and find the road to the upper-middle or upper class relatively easy. A foreign education and/or financial success open the door to the upper class almost everywhere. The small businessman has always been dependent upon government or the favors of elite families for survival, and the medium-sized farmer has found competition with the large estate a losing proposition without government-provided credit and technical assistance. The independent middle class is further fragmented by the existence of small-town and larger-city segments and by regional differences.

In Argentina, the independent middle class has been growing rapidly in numbers and power, but only in Costa Rica, Uruguay, and Cuba before Castro has it attained sufficient size and strength as a group to hold in its hands the balance of political power.

In summary, although the middle class is well established in a few countries, in most it has as yet attained relatively little cohesiveness, class awareness, or status. In some countries, it lacks leadership, since many of its ablest members are often absorbed by the upper class; in others, it is divided by the great differences between urban and rural elements, regional groups, and lower and upper sectors. Currently, inflation is almost everywhere threatening its economic security. It has been limited in forming effective political organizations and influencing the course of national policy. Politically speaking, in fact, the day of the middle class may have passed before it ever arrived—unless, as is taking place in Castro's Cuba, a largely new middle class is created by social revolution.

Lower Class. In the nineteenth century, the lower class, like the elite, was clearly defined. This large social class consisted almost entirely of landless peons and owners of very small farms (*minifundia*), often too small to support a family. Except in Costa Rica and Colombia, an extensive group of yeoman farmers has never developed in Latin America. In the twentieth century, demands for agrarian reform have stressed the creation of a sizable small-holder group, but only in Bolivia, Venezuela, and Mexico has this come to pass. In Mexico, Cuba, and Guatemala, land reform has also produced collective ownership under various names; and in Cuba, it has produced state control and operation.

The lot of the rural proletariat of landless peasants and poorer tenants is usually worse than that of the less numerous small farmers. The landless work on *latifundia*. However, on the Central American banana farms, working conditions approximate those in urban industry; and the workers are less interested in land reform than in their labor unions, which are their chosen vehicles for achieving higher wages and better working conditions. Where capital-intensive agricultural methods are not in use, the peasant league is the more common organizational form through which agrarian reform and social-welfare benefits are sought from the state. Peasant leagues are open to Communist infiltration because the landless peasant has the greatest potential for violent and socially disruptive action. In Mexico five decades ago, landless peasants led by Zapata demanded land reform; in Argentina, they temporarily supported Perón when he promised to break up the great cattle and wheat estates; and now in Brazil, some are backing Francisco Julião and other leaders. Peasant societies currently face very grave problems, chief among them the need for capital investment in agriculture, better rural living conditions, and agrarian reform.

The industrial worker is a large component of the lower class in Mexico, Brazil, Chile, Argentina, and Cuba; that is, in the countries with large-scale industrial and mining enterprises. In the more isolated and underdeveloped countries, such as Paraguay and Honduras, the worker constitutes a barely measurable quantity. Only where his number is legion has he succeeded in establishing strong unions based on the principle of lower-class solidarity. Because they are urban dwellers, he and his family do not find educational opportunities so foreshortened as do their rural brethren. Cities have more and better schools, and governments have been prone to respond favorably to urban workers' demands. Thus, the future within the existing system often holds more hope for them than for the peasants, although their everyday living conditions may be more affected by the vagaries of the business cycle. Other urban lower-class groups, from domestic servants to semiskilled laborers, are largely nonunion and are usually worse off than their rural counterparts. They have lost the stable kinship ties of rural areas and the assurance of subsistence that was fairly dependable no matter how inadequate. They are recent arrivals, facing the complexities of urban existence for which they are ill-prepared. They are an ever-present element in street mobs, attracted by demogogic leaders of all political hues. Frequently, urban labor has seen its level of living either remain static or decline, although social-welfare services may have in small part offset this trend.

Lower-class hatred for the middle and upper classes has always existed, but it is now more overt, direct, and violent than in the past. For the lower class, the Communist is only repeating a truism when he expounds the inevitability of class antagonism. Paradoxically, however, there lingers among the lower classes of Latin America a demeaning attitude of subservience toward upper- and middle-class people, who in return are expected to grant certain favors. This is sometimes referred to as the *"patrón"* tradition. The lower class is not loyal or even neutral when it looks "upward at its social betters," and for this reason, it can be led by demagogues and dictators. Because of its illiteracy and lack of sophistication, the lower class is more attracted than are other classes to the charismatic leader, or the absolute dictator. There is no doubt that Castro's position during his first year in power was based mainly upon his crude appeals to class hatred and his ability to pose as a divinely inspired leader who could bring heaven on earth. But the Somozas and Trujillos have also been successful in mobilizing lower-class backing.

Indians. The Indian is defined primarily according to cultural rather than racial criteria and lives apart from Western society. In Latin America, an individual is not classed as an Indian primarily because of his physical appearance, but rather because he lives in an Indian cultural style or in an Indian community. The use of the term "Indian" here is perhaps misleading to the average reader, since most Indian cultures in Latin America have drawn not only from pre-Hispanic Indian cultures but also from Western European traditions. In the blend, the proportion of each varies in each major aspect of life and from one Indian group to another. In southern Mexico, for example, Christian beliefs are predominant in religion, with the pagan gods superstitiously respected as evil spirits. In Peru, Christian and pagan faiths have fused to create a new religion possessing its own integrity. Even in those cases in which the Indian has absorbed many Western traits he has usually retained enough of his own culture to be clearly distinguishable as non-Western in essential aspects of daily living. Sometimes, an individual or individual groups cease being Indian by accepting the cultural ways of the Westernized people. For example, the Indian in Guatemala, by discarding his native language, using only Spanish, and wearing shoes, can disassociate himself from the Indian community and become a Ladino.

According to 1950 estimates, the Indian constituted about half of the population of Guatemala, Bolivia, and Peru; about a third of the population of Ecuador; 15 per cent, or less, of the population of El Salvador and Mexico; and a tiny percentage in the other countries of Latin America. Where the Indian exists as a majority or a large minority, he is a passively disruptive element, militating against the emergence of the cultural nation. Even after education, transportation and communications, and other modernizing forces begin to make inroads in Indian-populated sections, assimilation progresses very slowly, requiring more than one generation. When Indians move into the labor force in cities, integration advances more rapidly but less smoothly. Where the integration is orderly and proceeds under the control of ruling groups, Indian and transitional elements generally come to accept the prevailing value system of the social class into which they have moved. But almost without exception, the process of change is a very difficult one, partly because non-Indians have never been able to agree on the best way to proceed. They have not even been able to agree on the desirability of proceeding, and the governments have not had the financial resources for ambitious programs. Even if large-scale programs to promote assimilation were undertaken, completion of the process would be very slow.

The Indian, on the other hand, more often than not tries to protect the integrity of his way of life. Too often, he has learned that change does not bring improvement. Living at a subsistence level in small, often socially unstructured groups, the Indian has a caloric intake about two-thirds of that recommended by health experts, and a diet badly deficient in proteins and vitamins. Health services are nonexistent; educational facilities are practically unknown; and in general, living levels are barely adequate for existence. Only Mexico and Bolivia have consciously adopted sensible, though modest, programs to ease the transition of Indians to Western civilization. Those who are making the transition are, in a very real sense, marginal people, living as they do on the boundary of two mutually exclusive cultures, disturbed and unhappy because they do not know which value system should govern their personal behavior. They frequently become city slum dwellers of the most hopeless kind.

Social Mobility. Class lines are sufficiently rigid throughout the area to foreclose for the vast majority of lower-class people the prospect of moving into the middle class in the near future. The barriers against social mobility have given a ring of validity to the Marxist-Leninist concept of class war and have restored the vigor of the Latin American concept of the corporate state. According to the latter, the government should recognize the permanence of social stratification, incorporating representatives of class-based economic organizations in the governmental framework. Although in the United States we seldom think of the lower class as a threat to political stability, upper- and middle-class Latin Americans view it only in these terms because it is an ever-present threat to their privileged position. For this reason, although we regard labor unions as one of many competing interest groups, Latin Americans tend to regard them as a weapon of the lower class.

Social mobility is on the increase in Latin America, but it has not attained the fluidity and ease found in the United States. In almost all countries, it is more difficult than it is in the United States for the individual to move up from one segment of a class to another, or from a lower to a higher class, on the basis of certain acquired characteristics. Because of the personalistic nature of the society and the strength of the family, the road to success is substantially easier if the individual has a protector, whether friend, godparent, or relative. An anonymous and neutral system for recognizing and rewarding talent by universities, businesses, and governments is well-nigh unknown in Latin America. Relatively open societies exist in Mexico, Brazil, Chile, Argentina, Costa Rica, and Uruguay; at the other extreme, it is virtually impossible to move upward in Peru, particularly into the upper class, with its castelike rigidity.

Slow and often negligible growth of educational facilities has been a major obstacle to the development of mobility; education gives able people a chance to move, particularly from the lower class to the middle class. A great premium is placed upon education in countries in which only a few are well educated, particularly because this has long been a distinguishing characteristic of the upper class. Primary education boosts a person's standing within the lower class, but usually secondary education is essential in order to move out of that class. The low rate of secondary-school attendance is indicated by the 1950 figures on the percentage of population completing four or five years of secondary education. In the Western Hemisphere, the United States ranked first with 25 per cent of the population in this category, but Latin American countries ranged from just under 6 per cent to less than 0.5 per cent. In higher education, the differential between the United States and Latin America is as great.

The army has been a pathway for socially mobile persons. For officers, the armies have provided training not only in military matters, but also in medicine, law, and engineering; for enlisted men they have offered an increasing variety of technical and semi-technical skills. Political revolution has brought quick promotion to especially able officers who have entered the government. Some, like Fulgencio Batista in Cuba, have been accepted socially by the middle and even upper classes, but only after many years. To a much smaller degree, the Church has served to assist the upward movement of individuals; for example, in the 1930's, Archbishop Sanabria of Costa Rica came from the lowest social level. Labor unions have also served to move their leaders up the social scale, but the difficulties in gaining acceptance faced by labor leaders of proletarian origin are typified by the experiences of the chief union officials in Mexico. These men move in the upper political levels, but socially they are generally unacceptable in the "best" circles of society and even in the professional segments of the middle class.

BASIC INSTITUTIONS

The predominant institutions of Latin America are the Catholic Church, the family, and the state; but only the last named has been strengthening its position in society. The preponderance of these institutions is not checked by the self-generating and self-sustaining social organizations corresponding to the club and community activities in the United States. Such organizations are fewer in number, less effectively organized, and often short-lived. Nor does the corporate form of business organization exist in large enough numbers to have as great an impact on society as it does in the U.S. In contrast to the people of the United States, who are frequently guilty of overvaluing conformity, Latins lean more to individualistic behavior. Latin Americans are as a whole less group-minded and more self-reliant than their neighbors to the north. Civic and social organizations do exist, but they are almost exclusively concentrated in the larger cities. They also show less initiative and rely much more upon the state for support. As a result, the individual is faced with fewer competing loyalties or alternative choices in terms of joining and, therefore, relies much more upon the family, and sometimes the Church, to satisfy needs of this kind. This thesis can obviously be overstressed. Nonetheless, the visitor to Latin America is struck by the all-encompassing nature of the family in comparison with the deficient and imperfect role of other types of social organizations.

The Family. Despite its shrinking size and functions, the Latin American family remains, today, a relatively stable institution. Frequently it includes within its confines a larger number and variety of persons than does the family in the United States. Often more than two generations, including cousins several stages removed and, in the case of upper-class families, servants, live under one roof or in adjacent houses. Only now is the simple, or nuclear, family of husband, wife, and children replacing the older form, and this change is occurring chiefly among the urban middle class. The upper-class family—buttressed by wealth, family name, and hoary tradition—has resisted the new tendencies tenaciously; but it, too, is being affected by the new ways. Among the rural and urban lower classes, the extended family continues to thrive, because the combined earning power of extra hands offers an advantage over the nuclear family. Even in city slums, large family groups often occupy apartments in the same building. Because all members work—some at home in marginal handicrafts, a few as beggars, and others in modern factories—survival at a minimal level is possible.

The reach of the family is extended by *compadrazgo,* or co-parenthood. By this universal Catholic relationship, those who become godparents of a child are expected to assume some responsibility for his religious and moral welfare. In Latin America, however, *compadrazgo* has been traditionally broader in scope, including concern for the physical welfare of the child, and even for the well-being of the child's family. Families prefer to find god-parents in a higher social class, for, if the godparent fulfills his obligations, he will benefit both family and child. Like the family itself, co-parenthood has been debilitated by a variety of pressures, so that in urban society in Chile, Mexico, Brazil, and Argentina, it has frequently become an empty relationship. But among the peasants it is taken seriously, and candidates for godparents are carefully screened.

The extended family is patrilineal, with authoritarian powers in the hands of the dominant male. Women continue to be subordinate and submissive, with marriage the most acceptable career. In some areas, however, the status of women is being significantly modified by economic, social, and legal means. Improvements in the legal status of women include, in many countries, the right to vote, obtain a divorce, and own property. Middle-class women are entering active economic life in larger numbers, and lower-class women have long worked outside the home, mainly as servants. But the bias of law and social custom in favor of male dominance endures in the face of the battle for women's rights.

Latin American patterns of sexual behavior are often judged by Americans according to popular misconceptions of actual practice in both types of societies. In Latin America, consensual or common-law marriage is very common among the lower classes, although campaigns by Church and state for mass marriage ceremonies have slightly reduced the percentages in some countries. Consensual marriage seems to be a function of economic conditions and literacy as well as tradition. Latin American males of the upper and also of the middle levels (if they can afford it) do often have mistresses or even establish a second family with a woman of lower social standing. The legal status of illegitimate offspring varies greatly from country to country. In Brazil, little distinction is made, in practice, between legitimate and illegitimate children, but in Peru, the members of the second family suffer from serious discrimination. In Central American countries, they are legally recognized but often have difficulty protecting their rights. Except in Brazil and among the lower class elsewhere, they suffer from social stigma and often become bitter and disgruntled. (It is worth noting here that Fidel Castro was the illegitimate son of a wealthy planter and that he was sent to school in Havana because he was ostracized in Santiago at the first school he attended.)

The Latin family is a very effective mutual-aid society. Its members help each other find employment and work together in a multitude of ways. The family has traditionally assumed considerable responsibility for the ill, the unemployed, and even the insane. Friendships outside the family's existing circle of friends are entered into only cautiously and are relied upon only when *confianza* (a kind of trust or intimacy) has been established. Out of the family's cooperative attitude originates the nepotism seen everywhere in business and government, for a person with a position of influence is expected to advance the interests of his family. The strength of familial ties interferes with the development of impersonal institutions in political and economic life and serves as a source of political corruption and irresponsibility. In Latin American eyes, one of the most striking early acts of Fidel Castro was his disloyalty to his family, as evidenced by the confiscation of his half brother's hacienda and his open disagreement with his mother over his failure to protect family financial interests.

With regard to the future, the state is slowly absorbing family functions through public education, social insurance, and a plenitude of other services. Yet the family remains a source of national strength, even while in transition, for it has given continuity and equilibrium to a society otherwise very much shaken by change.

The Catholic Church. The power of the Roman Catholic Church in Latin America is frequently overestimated by North Americans. A distinction must here be drawn between the Church as a self-conscious force in society and politics, and the Catholic religion as an integral part of the daily lives of the people. Catholicism does supply ceremony and rhythm to daily life, particularly for women, because community life in smaller towns and the countryside is organized around fiestas and other religious activities. The Church does not, however, derive full political benefit from this basic cultural influence, except in Colombia and perhaps Argentina. Some have attributed the limited influence of the Church to the supposedly conservative political views of its leaders. Although this is a factor, it is to some degree balanced by the liberal, and even radical, social and economic views of some of the parish clergy and members of the regular orders (such as the Franciscans), as well as a few of the bishops.

The character of the Church in each country has also reflected rather faithfully the mores of society, tending to make it a captive of local prejudices and restricting its ability to shape and change society and to impose norms of behavior. In a more diffuse sense, the burgeoning secularization of society contributes to the Church's lessened influence; the state has absorbed many educational and charitable functions. Furthermore, the growing popularity of a materialistic philosophy is inconsistent with the asceticism of the Christian religion. As a result, for many years, there has been an insufficient number of candidates for the priesthood, although this is not true of every area. In southern Brazil, the Church attracts enough recruits, but in the country as a whole, 40 per cent of the priests are foreign. In Cuba, Bolivia, and Central America, the Church is also forced to rely upon Europe and the United States for additional clergy. Because society continues to demand higher moral and religious standards from women, the recruitment of nuns is almost nowhere a problem. The financial position of the Church has altered somewhat, for the prolonged battle with the classical liberals in the nineteenth century stripped the Church of most of its wealth almost everywhere. However, where separation of Church and state is an accepted fact, voluntary contributions are sufficient to supply its basic needs.

Between World War I and World War II, the Church reassessed its defensive and negative position and undertook once again to become an authoritative social force. Some incentive was supplied by the Vatican with Christian social doctrines (the papal ency-clicals *Rerum Novarum* and *Quadragesimo Ano*), and by the growth of Catholic political parties in Europe. After World War II, Church leaders moved to establish a Latin American equivalent of the U.S. National Catholic Welfare Conference, and to examine realistically the Church's weaknesses as an institution. At an inter-national meeting in the early 1950's, Catholic lay and clerical leaders agreed that one of the primary weaknesses of the clergy in Latin America was the fact that it has long regarded itself as a part of the state apparatus, performing spiritual functions as a civil servant performs secular functions. Therefore, many of the clergy have had no sense of real service to the people, or, in Catholic terminology, no sense of an apostolate. These moves resulted from Vatican prodding, as well as from a growing awareness of social unrest. To overcome these limitations, the Church has stepped up its effort to organize labor under its auspices, and has sought, by giving such unions spiritual guidance, to lead them away from Marxist concepts. Lay organizations have been given renewed emphasis, and the parochial-school system, new to Latin America in its presently organized form, is slowly being established.

In recent years, the Church in Mexico and Guatemala, and in Cuba since the establishment of the Castro government, has an-nounced that it accepts social revolutions as consistent with—in-deed, directly relevant to—Christianity. The clergy are engaged in a great number of socially ameliorative activities, running the gamut from agrarian reform, rural development, and the improve-ment of working conditions, to the betterment of mental health, hygiene, and the living conditions of lower-class families. This is in addition to their concern with the traditional moral precepts of the Church. The influence of the Vatican has been directed to improved discipline of the clergy and a reorientation of the clergy away from narrowly defined pastoral duties and toward social action. The 1961 social encyclical *Mater et Magistra* reiterated the principle of the earlier documents and expounded the Vatican's views on more current problems; in regard to underdeveloped areas, it noted the responsibility of the great powers and of the local elites to hasten economic and social reform.

It can be argued that the Church is more vital, and therefore has more ascendant influence, in a modernized, Westernized society like Mexico than in the tradition-bound society of Peru. In the former, it stands on its own feet with little or no government support and, in fact, opposes the government on some issues. In the latter, the Church is the captive of the elite, who have opposed introduction of Catholic missionaries from the United States; and if the elite falls from power, the Church is likely to suffer severely.

In conclusion, it should be stressed that with the Church, as with all else in Latin America, there is little uniformity between one area and another. The Church generally retains some political influence in all countries, and very great influence in Argentina and Colombia; but it is now only one among several interest groups competing for the favors of the government. It is generally on the defensive, because religious goals are no longer national goals, nor are they the personal goals of most present-day political and intellectual leaders.

TYPES OF SOCIETIES

For a valid discussion of the importance of societal factors in the political life of Latin America, it is necessary to examine briefly the manifold variations of the basic pattern analyzed above. This we have done by classifying the countries of the area into three groups, according to social trends, and then examining examples of each type. These are, first, the countries (Mexico, Bolivia, and Cuba) that have experienced radical social revolution; second, the wide range of countries (Argentina, Brazil, Chile, Venezuela, Guatemala, Costa Rica, and Colombia) in which substantial social change is under way, but at a measurably slower rate; and third, the countries (Peru and Nicaragua) whose social systems are among the most traditional and least affected by social change.

REVOLUTIONARY SOCIETIES

In Mexico, Bolivia, and Cuba, social revolution has fundamentally altered the class structure, in addition to redistributing
wealth and political power. The experience of these countries
accords with the definition of social revolution as a rearrangement
of part or all of the existing social structure and a basic alteration
in institutions.

Mexico. The Mexican revolution has had a profound effect upon
Mexican society. The revolution began in 1910 primarily as a
political movement against the dictatorial Díaz government. Once
the power structure of the old regime had been broken, demands
for economic and social reform emerged in the resulting near
anarchy. In order to consolidate their power, political-military
leaders responded to these demands, often despite their own conservative leanings, with radical socio-economic policies. Many
of these demands were placed in the 1917 Constitution, which
is in the economic and social fields still one of the most radical
constitutional charters in Latin America. Mexico was in 1910, as
it still is now, an agricultural country in terms of use of the labor
force, and the most important reforms were those implemented
in the rural areas.

Beginning in 1913 and continuing to this day, land has been
confiscated and distributed in an attempt to redistribute wealth.
Drawing upon Indian and Spanish traditions, the semicommunal
farm, or *ejido,* was created as the preferred, but not exclusive,
method of giving land to the peasants. In 1910, about 1 per cent
of the population owned 97 per cent of the land; the remainder
was owned by villages (1 per cent) and small farmers (2 per cent).
Today, although *latifundia,* or great estates, are not unknown in
Mexico, only about a quarter of the arable land is in farms of
500 acres or more. The agrarian reform has not made the *campesinos* (farmers) members of the middle class, but it has raised
well over half of all farm families to the status of landowners. The
rural lower class as a whole has been elevated sufficiently so that
the social and economic distance between it and the rural lower-
middle class is much smaller than ever before in Mexican history.
The *campesino,* on the average, is living better than before 1910.
Furthermore, he has greater educational opportunity, though this
is still not adequate by any modern standards. The economic and
social foundations for a politically active peasantry have been

created, and the growing political awareness of the peasants has been reflected in the political system. The land reform has begun the long and slow process of converting the peasantry into a free citizenry, capable of producing its own leaders and protecting its own interests. Although progress has been disappointing in this area, there are signs that agrarian reform has contributed to the growth of a pluralistic society, to social mobility, and to a lessening of class antagonisms.

Large agricultural-development programs have been associated with agrarian reform, especially in recent years, and these are largely responsible for the increased productivity that in normal years permits Mexico to feed itself. Money has been invested in irrigation, machinery, fertilizer, improved seeds, insecticides, and community development. If the Mexicans had invested the same amount of capital in the hacienda system, instead of assisting the lower class, it would have forced the insecure tenants or day laborers off the land. Fortunately for Mexico, its hacienda was not a modern commercial farm, for it was labor-intensive rather than capital-intensive; and the breakup of the hacienda did not destroy an efficient agricultural system depending upon an export market. In any case, once the revolution had begun, its leaders could not afford to reinforce their enemies, the *hacendados*. Consequently, the association of land redistribution and economic development was inevitable. A basic problem now is what to do with those still remaining landless, especially the children of families who received land, for now these children swell the surplus labor force in rural areas.

In urban areas, the revolution had an equally drastic impact upon society. In essence, the old ruling elite—intellectuals, government officials, professionals, wealthy businessmen, and landholders, who usually resided in the cities—lost some of their wealth, power, and, consequently, social position. The land reform destroyed the *hacendado* segment of the upper class, forcing many of its members into other types of economic endeavor and into the middle class.

Not enough is known to make it possible to say exactly where all these people moved in the class structure. Some, with assets other than family name and landed wealth, moved horizontally into the new upper-class groups. Thus, the well-educated, particularly the professionals, lost wealth and political power but not class status. Others were definitely forced into the middle class, their children becoming white-collar workers (even their daughters sought employment). The core of the elite—the people around Díaz—drifted back to Mexico after the revolution and formed an enclave within the new upper class. They were socially isolated, although still important enough to be featured in the society pages of the big dailies of Mexico City. Their children, however, tended to drift downward into the middle class.

The small, divided, and weak middle class suffered severely during the first eleven years of the revolution—a period of physical violence—mainly because of property losses. By the 1920's, when Calles and Obregón came to power, the revolutionary leadership had become essentially middle class, and by the 1940's, when Ávila Camacho became President, the revolution turned more conservative, in response to the demands of the middle class and the new upper class. The middle class had by then been augmented by important new elements who owed their wealth, education, and political positions to the revolution. The creation of the modern bureaucracy, and its steady growth, gave lower-class individuals upward mobility; so did the top positions in the new labor organizations, peasant unions, and new industry created in the wake of the revolution.

The "popular class," as Mexicans are wont to label the lower class, has been diminished in relative size by the revolution. Its heterogenous elements include growing numbers of urban workers, landless agricultural workers, and most of the new small holders and members of *ejidos*. It is also divided into Indian, Western, and transitional groups. The transitional, or marginal, elements are a large but diminishing group within the lower class and within the total population. Their way of life is part Western and part Indian, in a wide variety of combinations and proportions.*

Economic progress in Mexico has raised the living standard of most Mexicans but has also accentuated the social and economic extremes. Social mobility is increasing, however, and is open to more people than in most of Latin America. Educational expansion is lagging behind needs, but the López Mateos government has a forced-draft program under way to put all elementary-age children in school. If even partially carried to completion, this program will increase opportunities for upward social mobility, but it may also promote unrest if employment opportunities are not commensurate with the improved educational levels reached by the lower class.

* For a study of the adjustment difficulties of the transitional groups, see Oscar Lewis, *Five Families: Mexican Case Studies in the Culture of Poverty* (New York: Basic Books, 1959).

The revolution has changed the life of lower-class Mexicans more in the economic than in the social sphere, but even in the latter, it has increased the size of the middle class.

Bolivia. The 1952 political revolution led to a profound social revolution that has not yet run its course; it has not yet reached the stage of institutionalization. Under the predominantly middle-class leadership of the Movimiento Nacionalista Revolucionario (MNR), the revolutionary government has only tenuous command of several major sectors. Worker and peasant militia units have assumed primary responsibility for maintenance of law and order, although the government has a regular army of 10,000 men. Because of political necessity and social desirability, the regime also pursues economically unsound national policies. An ineffective and corrupt bureaucracy plagues the leaders of the revolution as they attempt to stabilize the political situation and implement their policies.

The principal social impact of the revolution has been the restructuring of the class system, principally by the destruction of the upper class. The seizure of *latifundia* and the confiscation of the tin mines destroyed the economic foundation of the elite. They were eliminated as a political factor by being forced into exile and by destruction of the regular army, upon which they had depended. The existing middle class was partially destroyed, and its remaining segments are represented in the Falange Socialista Boliviana. New elements have been slowly added to the middle class, as a result of the 1952 revolution, by the building of a loyal bureaucracy not associated with the Falange.

The redistribution of wealth in mining and railroading took the form of government ownership and operation. In agriculture, it consisted of the breaking up of the large estates into small peasant holdings. Education has been actively promoted, but only at the basic level of reducing illiteracy, rather than as a means of raising lower classes to middle-class status. Although these steps have encouraged upward social mobility, it is too early to evaluate their practical impact. The educational problem is readily understood when it is noted that from the 1920's to the early 1950's, only one or two new schools were built in all Bolivia, and that since 1952, the government has of necessity poured available funds into economic development.

The revolutionary government, as in Mexico, has tried to integrate the Indian into Western culture and make him a participating member of the political system. The obstacles in the way of eliminating this internal proletariat are almost overwhelming. Many of the Indians speak only an Indian language. With an actual literacy rate of perhaps 15 per cent, they are far from ready to assume the responsibilities of free citizens (although all Indians over twenty years of age received the vote in 1952). Most suffer from poor health and dietary deficiencies, which have held life expectancy to about forty years. That the Indian has been reached by the revolution is evidenced by growing unrest in Indian communities. To date, however, only the more Westernized Indians of the Cochabamba Valley have fully shared revolutionary aspirations.

Cuba. The Cuban revolution led by Fidel Castro and the Communist Party of Cuba is still in the stage of rapid, drastic, and ideologically motivated social changes. It is far too early to assess the long-term meaning of all that has happened in Cuba because the full impact of the social changes has not been felt. If the regime should fall from power tomorrow, many of the new organizations and institutions would be, at most, only partially modified, and others would remain untouched by any regime that might follow Castro's.

Measured by social and economic criteria based on U.S. and West European experience, Cuba before Castro was one of the most advanced countries of Latin America. A high literacy rate, the fourth highest per capita income in Latin America, and a solid basic structure for economic development were among its assets. But not all parts of society received a fair share of national income; rural–urban and upper-class–lower-class differences were especially extreme. In modern Havana, the relatively large middle and upper classes were able to maintain a high standard of living. By contrast, the poorest families—the *guajiros,* or peasants, of the Sierra Maestra—were mostly squatters who practiced slash-and-burn agriculture, i.e., first clearing the land, and then cultivating it until its fertility is lost. Organized labor was strung out somewhere between these extremes. Castro came to power with the Sierra Maestra peasants supplying the bulk of his army and the middle class furnishing military leadership, as well as financial and political support. Organized labor stayed apart from the struggle because it believed it had nothing to gain from the overthrow of Batista.

Once in power, Castro proceeded to throw the existing social structure into disarray. The upper and middle classes were eliminated by seizure of their wealth and political persecution, which drove them into exile. Castro had always made a special appeal to the petty bourgeoisie in his fight against Batista, and he seemed willing, at first, to permit them a tenuous role in the new Cuba. As he drifted closer to an open policy of Marxism-Leninism, he talked increasingly in terms of a peasant-worker alliance as the basis of his regime.

The Cuban revolution has stimulated and facilitated a high degree of social mobility. Loyalty to the Marxist-Leninist revolution is a major qualification for moving upward in Cuba's socialist state, which, significantly, is almost the only source of the wealth, education, and power necessary for achieving high social status. By 1962, the state owned more than 80 per cent of industry and more than 40 per cent of the arable land; but even more important, it tightly controls the remainder of both. A new upper class is being created out of individuals who have been filtered through the apparatus of the state, where they have been tested for devotion to Communist doctrine. Most top leaders were members of the Integrated Revolutionary Organizations, the first-stage Marxist-Leninist party soon to be replaced by a more elitist United Party of the Socialist Revolution (Partido Unido de la Revolución Socialista, or PURS). How this process operates can be seen in the sugar cooperatives, which the government has placed in the hands of inexperienced workers who were formerly manual laborers. These men have jumped overnight from lower to middle or even upper class.

As the Communist bureaucracy grows, a new type of Leninist civil servant is emerging to establish the new middle class, composed chiefly of people of peasant and worker origins. The new upper class appears to be formed of elements of the revolutionary leadership, drawn from both lower- and middle-class backgrounds, along with a sprinkling of survivors from the old upper class.

From the beginning, the peasants have been given some economic and social benefits, especially in health and education, and they stand to be the chief beneficiaries of Cuban economic plans for creation of light consumer industries and diversified farming. The rural-development program planned by Castro is intended to reduce rural-urban disparities, thus putting the peasant on the same economic and social level with the worker. Urban labor is now apparently so completely cowed that Castro believes it is politically possible to force them to accept a deterioration in living standards. This decline was produced first by inflation, wage reductions, and forced unpaid labor, which were later augmented by a general malaise of the economy. The housing, education, cultural, tourist, and sports programs of the revolution are devised to benefit all elements of the lower class. Thus the Castro regime seeks to narrow the social extremes significantly by raising peasants to the equivalent of pre-revolution lower-middle-class living standards. The success of these programs, however, remains in doubt.

GRADUALLY CHANGING SOCIETIES

The second of our three groups of countries consists of those that have experienced some important social changes, but not so abruptly as have Mexico, Bolivia, and Cuba. Four of these countries—Argentina, Brazil, Chile, and Venezuela—have made such great strides toward middle-class dominance that they have undergone a peaceful, gradual social revolution that has now been in progress for many years. Two others—Uruguay and Costa Rica—have gone even further along this evolutionary road. Guatemala entered the stage of violent upheaval in 1944, but in 1954 the revolution was cut short before its full impact could be felt. Since then, Guatemalan society has evolved at a much slower rate, and the coup of early 1963 will probably have little or no effect on this process.

Colombia. In many ways Colombia is similar to the other Latin American countries in social structure and economic development. Dominated in the nineteenth century by a landed oligarchy, plagued by a series of *caudillos,* or would-be *caudillos,* supported by the labor of an inarticulate peasantry, the country has taken its first steps into the modern world through the typical process of urbanization, industrialization, and the growth of a middle class. But Colombia has done this in its own way. Unlike Mexico or Bolivia, it has not undergone a violent revolution; nor like Uruguay, Costa Rica, and, more recently, Venezuela, undertaken far-reaching social reforms by evolutionary methods. On the other hand, neither has Colombia dragged its heels as badly as Peru or Ecuador. The Colombian elite are partly enlightened, relatively flexible, and conscious of the approaching crisis. The lower classes (there are but few unassimilated Indians), both urban and rural, and the growing middle class are raising their voices in protest against the existing inequities in Colombian life. Reform legislation has been introduced in Congress, and some has been passed; but the ruling classes appear to be paralyzed in taking decisive action, in translating words into deeds. The energies of Colombia's leading statesmen have been centered on the political arena in an attempt to restore peace after years of violence and bloodletting which resulted from the quarrels of the country's two major political parties.

Strong party allegiances, extending from the major cities to the agricultural villages, have prevented, thus far, ideological polarization or class conflicts. Although for over a decade (1948–58), Colombia suffered from conditions approaching civil war, the strife revolved about the struggle for power between the Liberals and the Conservatives at all levels—a struggle embittered by local and regional feuds and intensified further by outright banditry. Violence has not yet ceased, but the killings have declined from a peak of several thousand monthly to about two hundred, and are now caused almost entirely by outlaws. The parties have compromised their power struggle and differ only in degree on the questions of the rate and extent of social reform. Neither, however, has shown much enthusiasm for rapidly implementing thoroughgoing changes.

Colombian society has been changing slowly since World War I, and noticeably since World War II. The discovery of oil, and its exploitation through foreign capital, beginning in the 1920's; the shock of the economic Depression of the 1930's; and the shortage of manufactured goods during World War II—all have contributed toward the drive for industrialization, with its consequent weakening of the traditional rigidity of the country's class structure. Well into the twentieth century, the upper class had the characteristic of a caste, in that membership was restricted almost exclusively to those families who could trace their lineage back to colonial landholders. The middle class, small and unaware of itself as a group, consisted primarily of urban people who had managed by commerce, skill, education, or just plain luck to raise themselves above the level of poverty. The lower classes consisted of all the rest, the poor—Indians, Negroes, persons of mixed blood, and whites. It was extremely difficult to move from the lower to the middle class; it was virtually impossible to move to the upper class. On occasion, members of upper-class families could slip downward into the middle class, and disasters of various kinds could push middle-class families into the lower ranks.

In the past several decades, the rigidity of the structure has begun to give way to a more flexible system in those areas affected by economic development, particularly industrialization. In these more modernized parts of Colombia, such as Bogotá and Medellín, upper-class status—enjoyed by about 5 per cent of the population —now rests not only upon lineage, but also upon wealth and education. Industry, commerce, coffee planting, and ranching have all opened the doors to the upper class for those families, native or immigrant, who could amass wealth in these enterprises, which in turn made possible the education of their children. The middle class, comprising about 20 per cent of the population, has also expanded with the growth of urbanization and industrialization, as it has in many other parts of Latin America. The types of persons that comprise this sector of society are also similar: white-collar workers in government and private business, professionals, small tradesmen and service people, and about 300,000 small commercial farmers, chiefly coffee growers. Some of these are descendants of upper-class families whose original fortunes were dissipated or divided among numerous heirs. Many middle-income families, however, share upper-class values—in fact, to such an extent that the validity of the term "middle class" has been questioned. It appears, however, that a sufficient number of persons in this economic category recognize their status as above the proletariat, but below the elite, to permit us to use the term in a limited manner. The lower class, making up the remaining 75 per cent of the Colombian people, live in squalor, disease, and illiteracy. The majority of these, who live in rural areas, have little or no opportunity at present to rise above their station; the urban proletariat has some chance through education and the acquisition of skills.

Several programs have recently been undertaken to alleviate the most pressing needs suffered by the lower classes: land, education, and decent standards of living. Some pilot projects have been undertaken to improve conditions, and if the current efforts can be broadened to full-scale development, as anticipated, Colombia's social pressures will ease considerably. But the difficulties are imposing because of the base levels from which development must begin. Two-thirds of the farmers own only 10 per cent of the productive land, while 1 per cent owns more than half. Schools are available for only about half the school-age population. Although the over-all growth rate is only 2.8 per cent per year (the average figure for Latin America), the cities have experienced a rapid expansion that has taxed their facilities to the breaking point. Cali, the most extreme example, has been growing in recent years at the rate of 8 per cent annually. Medellín has rivaled this figure, and Bogotá has grown at about 4 per cent. Since the overthrow of the dictator Rojas Pinilla, in 1957, the percentage of the budget allotted to education has nearly doubled; some housing projects, public and private, have been constructed; and the agrarian-reform law has passed the legislature. The effects, thus far, have been minimal, but the Colombian elite do demonstrate at least an awareness of the problem. What is needed urgently is the will to act, and to act quickly.

Argentina. The Argentine middle class is numerically the largest in all Latin America (with the possible exception of Brazil, for which adequate figures are lacking), and relative to the total population it is exceeded only by Uruguay and Costa Rica. The growth of the middle class has taken place mainly since 1900, and has been accompanied by rapid urbanization. Today, it amounts to well over 40 per cent of the total population of nearly 22 million, as compared to less than 10 per cent for the upper class and about 50 per cent for the lower class. This conversion of Argentina into a middle-class-oriented society constitutes a type of gradual social revolution that is similar in some ways to the rise of middle-class dominance in the United States. The expansion of education, which has been a major force for social mobility, provides one of the better indexes of the growth of the Argentine middle class. From 1895 to 1948, the number of secondary students rose from 1.6 to 10.7 per 1,000 inhabitants. At the same time, students at this level have shifted from an interest in liberal arts to greater emphasis upon commercial, industrial, and professional training. Similarly, from 1917 to 1944, the number of university students per 1,000 inhabitants increased from 1.1 to 3.4.

Although the middle class has grown at an astounding rate, within this class the relative importance of the dependent sector has been favored by the growth of government, industry, and service enterprises, all of which require large numbers of salaried, white-collar workers rather than self-employed individuals. Immigration has also been a factor in middle-class growth, even though a majority of immigrants entering the middle class have gone into the independent sector of that class. In rural areas, the middle class has also grown, though not so rapidly. Census figures for housing conditions indicate that well over 30 per cent of rural dwellers are middle class. Even renters who operate fruit or wheat farms often have enough money to send their children to universities.

The Perón regime in Argentina did not revamp in a major way the social structure of Argentina, but rather accelerated existing trends. The most significant changes came in the cities, which now contain about 70 per cent of the population. During Perón's rule, a substantial accretion to the middle classes in the cities took place in the course of more rapid urbanization. The extremely liberal social benefits granted labor to ensure its political support, and the efforts at industrialization, attracted large numbers of rural dwellers to the cities. Members of the lower class moved into the lower-middle class by establishing a variety of service establishments to serve the swelling population. The broadening social benefits, the state-sponsored industrialization, and the creation of the repressive apparatus of a police state opened new middle-class positions by greatly expanding the bureaucracy. It is difficult to estimate with precision the growth of the middle class resulting from these changes, but it seems probable that it increased by about one-sixth during the Perón era. The upper-class elements of urban life experienced a downward change in political power, but not a similar drop in class status. The financial and commercial interests that supported the two major opposition parties lost most of their political power, although the economic foundations upon which that power rested remained intact. Many industrialists received greater economic protection and support, principally in the form of tariffs, but also from more direct government aid; they naturally supported the regime.

The relatively exposed position of the Argentine middle class is largely the result of Peronism's emphasis upon economic benefits for the *descamisados* (shirtless ones). Paradoxically, expansion of the middle class came at the same time that the influential position of that class was threatened by the rise of labor's economic standing. Today, highly skilled labor approximates the income levels of the lower-middle class, though inflation has weakened the economic status of many of its members. This income pattern is an important reason for the growth of middle-class unions, especially among white-collar government workers.

In rural regions, the chief social impact of Peronism was the exodus of large numbers of day laborers and tenants to the cities. Perón diminished total agricultural labor forces by 25 per cent. The resulting labor shortage gave the peasants a somewhat greater ability to defend their economic interests. Contrary to campaign promises in 1945–46, Perón distributed a negligible amount of land, seizing the haciendas of a few of his prominent political opponents, but more often permitting relatives—such as his brother-in-law, Juan Duarte—and various political allies to acquire the land for a nominal sum through the threat of expropriation. The wheat growers, primarily tenants on large estates, continued to be relatively well off, although angered by the high profits made by the government export agency, the Argentine Institute for the Promotion of Trade (Instituto Argentino de Promoción del Intercambio, or IAPI) in its early years. The large landowners, their political wings clipped but their economic power only temporarily limited, bided their time and re-emerged in politics after the fall of Perón, in 1955.

The most striking social change of the Perón era was in the status of women, a change that must be attributed to the personal bitterness of his wife, Eva Perón, as much as to the political needs of the dictator. Eva had experienced the exploitation that comes from being both female and lower class in Argentina. With her support, women began to abandon their semisecluded position to enter business, the professions, and public life. Although they did not engage in these activities in large numbers, the old tradition of female subservience was at least partially broken. Divorce was legalized (this law has since been repealed), and women received the vote in the late 1940's and won seats in the provincial and national legislatures as Peronista candidates in the 1951 elections. However, women were not granted control over their property, which remained in the hands of their husbands.

In summary, Perón did not consciously initiate a sweeping social revolution, and what little interference with existing social relations occurred was the result of political objectives, and had relatively limited impact. He accentuated the existing trend toward a middle-class society. Although it is too early to assess accurately the lasting effect of the appeal made to the lower classes, it seems clear that class antagonism grew and that lower-class people acquired a new sense of their rights and dignity.

Today, Argentina appears to be at the beginning of a new stage in its development. Either the bulk of the skilled workers will move into the middle class, with a consequent trend toward political conservatism, or, if economic development plans do not succeed, the lower sectors of the middle class will move economically into the proletariat. Argentina, in contrast to some of its neighbors, has few social problems that are insoluble given sufficient economic growth, and it has the advantage of a relatively low birth rate. Even without land reform, it has the social essentials for a stable, middle-class, reformist democracy. Argentina possesses not only one of the highest per capita income patterns, but also one of the most equitably distributed. However, from 1950 on, economic growth failed to keep pace with population growth, and there was consequent popular unrest as belts were, of necessity, tightened; in 1956, this development became even more pronounced.

Brazil. By far the largest country in Latin America in both area and population, Brazil has a correspondingly large degree of regionalism and diversity. Nearly all stages of social development and all types of social structure exist within Brazil's national territory, a fact that renders national averages nearly meaningless. The process of change began slowly at about the turn of the century, but was accelerated by the Vargas regime during the 1930's and by World War II. During the past decade and a half, the pace of change has accelerated even more. At least in the cities, social and economic changes have already touched society so deeply as to constitute a gradual, largely nonviolent social revolution. Brazil, as a society in transition, is experiencing all the stresses and strains of its Spanish American neighbors, but its problems are greatly magnified by the country's size and complexity.

Dangerous political pressures are building in Brazil; these, however, are not the result of continued rigid social stratification and upper-class, elitist domination, but rather of the gradual breakdown of a closed society and of the relationships that for many years supplied secure anchorage for the middle and lower classes. In twentieth-century Brazil, social change has modified the configuration of society in a multitude of ways and has created demands for a better life and a search for new leadership. Fortunately for the Brazilians, such demands have always been accommodated within existing flexible political structures.

Brazil is generally divided into six major regions, primarily on the basis of economic conditions as well as geographic factors. These regions are the North (the Amazon watershed), the Northeast (the eight states occupying the "bulge"), the East (Minas Gerais, Bahia, and Espírito Santo states), the West Central (Mato Grosso and Goiás states), the South Central (São Paulo, Guanabara, and Rio de Janeiro), and the South (the three states bordering Argentina and Uruguay). For our purposes, it is possible to confine this discussion to the four regions—the Northeast, the East, the South Central, and the South—where most Brazilians live. Of the estimated 1963 population of more than 76 million, approximately nine-tenths live in these four regions, which occupy a broad band of land along the coast. The rapid growth of Brazil's population as a whole since 1930 has been more than matched by the expansion of the urban population, which now comprises at least 40 per cent of the total. Although by far the greater part of the population growth has resulted from a high rate of natural increase, the growth is in some measure due to immigration. Italians, Portuguese, Spanish, Japanese, and Germans have supplied most of the estimated 4.5 million newcomers between 1875 and 1950.

Since World War II, there has been considerable internal migration, consisting principally of the movement of people from rural sections of one region to those of another, as well as from rural to urban environments. An important causal factor for this migration has been the rotational system of agriculture, which produces what Preston James, in his *Latin America* (1959), has called the "hollow frontier." Brazilian farmers, particularly on the frontier, use slash-and-burn agricultural methods, which destroys the fertility of the land. Then the farm family moves on into other undeveloped areas, leaving behind a lightly settled, largely uncultivated area, usable only for grazing or sporadic farming. A large share of the internal migration is also produced by the periodic and severe droughts in the Northeast, which have forced farmers into other areas in search of livelihood. Reverse migration occurs when economic conditions improve in the Northeast, encouraging people to return to their original homes. In recent years, the Brazilian interior (Mato Grosso, Goiás, Paraná) has received a significant influx of agricultural settlers, chiefly from the Northeast, but also from older, settled areas such as Minas Gerais and São Paulo, where available farm lands are generally scarce.

During the nineteenth century and much of the twentieth, the Brazilian upper class traditionally rested upon the foundation of the great estate. The upper class constituted an oligarchy based upon an extended family system. With the beginning of this century, the upper class in the South and South Central regions came to include many descendants of immigrants who had been successful in finance, industry, and commerce, along with the usual contingent of large landholders. Important remnants of the old upper class still exist today, particularly in the Northeast; but even in this region, the land has largely been taken over by anonymous corporations, in which they may or may not hold stock. There enterprises operate the large sugar plantations on the basis of efficient, modern mechanical methods. Consequently, today, the old plantation-based upper class is sharing its rung of the social ladder with groups composed of people with very different economic and social origins. Although it is still relatively difficult to break into the upper levels of society in Rio de Janeiro and São Paulo, this has been, and is being, accomplished by newly wealthy industrialists and businessmen, in ever larger numbers. By the 1930's, such un-Brazilian names as Matarazzo, Klabin, Lafer, Maluf, and Pignatari had joined, or were soon to join, high society. These *nouveaux riches* may be resented and resisted, but they are eventually incorporated in upper-class political and social life.

Below the upper class is a burgeoning middle class, both rural and urban. In Rio de Janeiro, São Paulo, Recife, Belo Horizonte, Pôrto Alegre, Salvador, Belém, Fortaleza, Curitiba, Campinas, and other cities and towns, the growth of industry, business, and government has opened vastly expanded opportunities for the white-collar worker. Like their counterparts in the Spanish American countries, these groups are highly motivated to obtain an education for their children because of its economic and social value. Their value system is diffuse and unconsolidated, since at the same time that they are stressing many of the traditional values of the old upper class, they are being forced by economic necessity to live according to another, more materialistic, value system. They are often on an economic treadmill, with a tendency to acquire more debts than they can handle, because of their desire to emulate upper-class living standards. The middle class exercises great political power, and though often politically and ideologically adrift, it supplies much of the leadership for the country and attracts substantial mass following in politics.

In the past, the Brazilian middle class has been strongest in the areas from Rio de Janeiro southward, and particularly in São Paulo, where large numbers of immigrants from Europe have settled. The chronic inflation of recent years may have slowed the growth rate of the urban middle class, but if so, it has done so only temporarily. The rural middle class is steadily growing as a result of the division of land among the large number of heirs in a wealthy family, who often sell or lease the relatively small farms they inherit. Another factor contributing to its growth has been the substantial increase in farm tenancy, resulting from the leasing of land by people moving to a new frontier. The small, independent farmer—migrating at will to new lands, which he develops and then rents or sells—has continued to be important. Although most tenants are lower class, some operate large enough plots and have sufficient income to be considered middle class.

A new type of rural lower class is appearing in ever-larger numbers all over Brazil. As the old family plantations,* most typical of the Northeast, have failed to compete successfully in the world market with export crops of sugar, coffee, cotton, and cacao, they have been converted into essentially commercial enterprises. This type of large farm employs a rural proletariat of semiskilled and unskilled workers, who are paid wages and receive perhaps some fringe benefits, but who are no longer in any sense a member of the family. The corporation regards them only as units of labor, and thus these workers must look to the politicians for leadership and protection. At the same time, the *patrão,* or master, has disappeared in many rural areas, leaving a psychological vacuum. The state has partially taken the place of the traditional bosses and plantation owners but is not yet fully effective in meeting the psychological needs of lower-class Brazilians. Such workers are good candidates for membership in Communist-led peasant organizations.

Perhaps the most rapidly growing sector of Brazilian society is the urban lower class. Industrialization and urbanization have swollen its ranks, while adding to its diversity as well. Only in such industrial centers as São Paulo does the classic proletariat exist in really significant numbers. Elsewhere, the bulk of the urban lower-income masses are "peasants living in the city." Like their rural cousins, they sorely miss the social institutions that gave them a sense of security and stability in their earlier existence in rural communities. They, too, are looking for a protector. Given improvement in their standard of living—even the *favelas* (slums) are an improvement over their previous way of life—they do not overtly manifest sharp resentment toward their more fortunate neighbors (although the slums of Rio de Janeiro are within easy sight of the luxury apartments along Copacabana Beach). Even though the demands of this first generation of migrants to the city have been relatively mild, their sons and daughters are acquiring new desires for material things and give evidence of losing their passivity when opportunity is not afforded them to move another rung up the socio-economic ladder.

Fortunately, social mobility in Brazil is probably as free as in any other country in Latin America. The major restrictions upon mobility are primarily economic and educational, with racial factors of only secondary importance. The depressed economic condition

---

* For a full description of these plantations, see Gilberto Freyre, *The Masters and the Slaves* (New York: Alfred A. Knopf, 1946; 2d ed., 1956).

of the lower class, however, has militated against large-scale move-ment into the middle class. Both urban and rural sectors of the Brazilian lower class spend about 75 per cent of their income for food, leaving nothing for personal savings. Despite the many re-forms of the Vargas period, even the urban-worker component of the lower class is little better off than many of the agricultural laborers and tenants in the South and South Central regions. How-ever, as urban dwellers, his children have access to free public education, which is not available to most of the rural population.

Although the educational system has provided important oppor-tunities for upward social mobility, it continues to be inadequate in a number of ways. Not only is there a serious shortage of school facilities, but the existing system is skewed in favor of middle- and upper-class students. Since the primary, as well as secondary, schools emphasize selecting and training for the universities, too little is done in the field of "fundamental" education. Upper-class children attend private institutions through the high-school level, then go on to a public university. The universities have normally received the lion's share of resources for public education. The neg-lect of lower-class education is shown, in part, by the failure of Brazil to reduce the literacy rate (highest among the lower class), which has remained constant in recent years at about 55 per cent of the adult population. The fact that the middle class is growing despite this serious restriction in one of the chief channels for social mobility is evidence that a relatively modest improvement in the educational situation could bring about even greater growth in their numbers.

With a considerable justification, Brazil claims to be the world's foremost racial democracy. Racial discrimination is specifically prohibited, both by the Constitution and by federal and state laws. Nevertheless, some social and economic discrimination against the Negro does exist, but it is frequently difficult to pinpoint because it is generally indirect and often subtle in form. Although mulattoes are found in large numbers in the middle and upper classes, the vast majority of Negroes belong to the rural and urban lower class. There is, however, a numerically small but wealthy middle-class Negro society in São Paulo and Rio. Nowhere does race constitute an impassable barrier to upward mobility, and friction between whites and nonwhites in comparable educational and economic brackets is minimal by comparison with the United States. When individuals of darker skin color have achieved economic and educational status, their position and prestige is very similar to that of their white peers.

Chile. In spite of appearances to the contrary, Chile is experiencing profound social change and, in some respects, has suffered greater institutional disorganization than almost any other country of the area. Population growth, government programs of social reform, and industrialization have all had an impact upon class structure. Since the late 1930's and early 1940's, the country's production balance has been shifting from agriculture to industry, particularly of the consumer and light varieties. The impact of these economic changes upon society has been uneven, with rural areas of central Chile the least touched, and Santiago the most affected.

Landowners still command the most prestige within the upper class, which today also includes wealthy industrialists and professionals. However, land is becoming increasingly esteemed for its economic value, rather than solely for the prestige accruing to the owner. Enough wealth to maintain an acceptable style of living, and admittance to the proper social activities are the basic standards for acceptance by the upper class. The majority of the aristocracy live in Santiago, where they maintain a distinctive way of life that includes membership in exclusive clubs, especially the Club de la Unión, visits to nearby summer resorts, and education of their children abroad. The upper class is growing in absolute numbers, although probably not as a percentage of the total population.

The Chilean middle class emerged as a social factor of importance in the nineteenth century, and as a political factor in the twentieth. It is composed of diverse groups. The independent middle class consists of small shop and factory owners, professionals, small- and medium-sized landowners, and owners of urban real estate. Some of these possess enough wealth to join the upper class, but for other reasons, they are unacceptable to the upper class, or do not wish to move up. Immigrants and their descendants are heavily represented in the independent middle class. Within the landowner segment, there is wide variation—from the farmers, whose level of living is often lower than that of renters, to those who approach the large landowner in wealth and importance.

The dependent middle class is composed of government employees and white-collar workers in commerce and industry. In 1956, government workers constituted about 7 per cent of the labor force—a rather large percentage, both because of the pen-

chant of governments controlled by the Radical Party for rewarding their followers with government positions, and because of the
expansion of government welfare services in the 1920's and 1930's.
Badly eroded by inflation, these social benefits have helped chiefly
the dependent middle class and the skilled workers. The dependent
middle class is growing faster than the independent, reflecting, as in
Argentina, the effects of industrialization and even greater educational opportunities. This part of the middle class relies heavily
upon government-provided hospital care, housing, credit, and pensions, and secondarily upon consumer cooperatives for these and
other needs. Having enjoyed a very stable economic position until
the late 1940's, the dependent middle class has since been concerned with defending its relative position within the middle class.
The galloping inflation has shaken the middle class as a whole,
arousing deep-seated fears for the safety of its position.

The lower class in Chile consists of three main elements: the
landless peasants, the industrial workers, and the groups of miscel-
laneous workers and small businessmen. The highest living standard
is enjoyed by the miners, skilled industrial workers, and transport
workers—who constitute a small percentage of the labor force and
are highly unionized. This group has been substantially aided by the
labor code of 1931. Other industrial workers have received some
legal protection, but little or no material improvement in their
living conditions. Indeed, the evidence indicates that many of these
workers have witnessed a deterioration in their economic position,
in both relative and absolute terms. Well over half of the industrial
workers live in slums or other inadequate housing and suffer from
an insufficient and unbalanced daily food intake.

The rural lower class consists, in large part, of *inquilinos* (tenant
farmers), whose extremely depressed economic and social status
has not changed importantly for many years. The deprived condition of the agricultural laborer is directly related to the practice of
labor-intensive farming, and to the system of land tenure that con-
centrates 56 per cent of the land in less than 2 per cent of the
fundos (estates). The tenant normally works 240 days a year for
the landowner in return for a small wage, a bit of food, a small
garden plot, and perhaps another piece of land to farm on shares.
Since the *patrón*-peasant relationship is still very strong, the peasants are generally under the political control of the landlord, i.e.,
voting as he directs, if they vote at all. No government-operated
social-welfare system, effective tenancy laws, or unions protect
these peasants living at a subsistence level. More than a third of

the peasants are illiterate, and because of the land-tenure system, they find it difficult to move to the city, where educational opportunity is more readily available. The by-products of this depressed social status are a high rate of illegitimate births, an often unstable family, and a life basically without hope of improvement. *Inquilinos* are concentrated in the central part of the country and near the larger cities. Paid agricultural workers live at approximately the same economic level, but are more numerous in the north-central region and in the far south. These two types of agricultural workers have been moving increasingly to urban areas, where they work in light industry or become petty entrepreneurs. The latter—street sellers, beggars, and small-time criminals—form the most depressed sector of Chilean society, receiving almost no protection or social benefits from the government, and only minimal help from private charity.

The landless peasants and the industrial workers—themselves only a part of the lower class—far outnumber the entire middle and upper classes combined. The lower class, as a whole, represents an estimated 70 per cent of Chile's population of roughly 8 million; the middle class, 25 per cent; and the upper class, only 5 per cent. Interpersonal relations between the rural and urban parts of the lower class are close and long-standing. These ties, combined with the efforts of socialists and Communist propagandists, have produced a strong class feeling that verges on hatred of the middle and upper classes. This feeling is not easily detected, since in personal relations with people of a superior class, it usually is consciously hidden by an attitude of humility.

Chile may be said to have a relatively open society only at the upper levels. Upward social mobility has prevailed mainly in the case of middle-class individuals seeking acceptance by the upper class; lower-class persons have been much less successful in their efforts to move into the lower-middle class. Elementary education has been expanded so slowly that since the 1930's, the over-all illiteracy rate has remained constant—at about 25 per cent. Expansion in education has been confined to secondary schools serving chiefly middle-class students who go on to universities for professional training (which in some cases permits them to join the upper class). Primary education has grown at a much slower rate, and the growth of population may even have brought a constricting of educational opportunities for the lower class.

The foremost social problem in Chile for the last two decades has been the impact of inflation, a major issue in elections since 1952.

The worker in Chile has been damaged by inflation and by the anti-inflationary steps taken by the Ibáñez government in the last three years of its tenure, from 1955 to 1958. A large part of the workers and indeed of the whole lower class had voted for Ibáñez in 1952, but were disappointed in him and voted for Alessandri in 1958, seeing in each of these two men a *patrón* able to solve their problems. Voting records indicate that the workers are politically independent only until such time as they find a reformist leader or party to follow. A large segment of middle-class individuals, having lost faith in the ability of the political parties to find practical solutions to economic problems, is also looking for new leadership. Inflation thus explains, in large part, why independents form the largest single voting group in Chile today.

Venezuela. Venezuelan society is plagued by chronic instability, arising from the country's rapid rate of political, economic, and social change. Urbanization and population increase are but surface evidences of this fact. Caracas, the capital, has grown to more than 1 million inhabitants from a pre-World War II population of about 200,000. Maracaibo, the second largest city, gained 100,000 people in three years during the late 1950's. The total population of Venezuela in 1920 was estimated at under 2.5 million; in 1961, at about 7.5 million. This growth has resulted mainly from natural causes, with the annual rate of increase running about 3.5 per cent since World War II. With urbanization and population growth have come social diversity and economic development, which have destroyed the old Venezuela of landed oligarchs, military *caudillos* (chiefs), and inarticulate *campesinos*. Mineral wealth, industrialization, new services, and, now, land reform have created an urban labor force, a money-oriented business community, a growing middle class, and thousands of small independent farmers.

The original impulse that eventually propelled Venezuela out of its colonial patterns of organization came from the discovery and exploitation of oil, in the second decade of the twentieth century. Favorable concessions and attitudes toward foreign investments on the part of government officials, and the very wealth of the fields themselves, attracted substantial quantities of foreign capital. This mushrooming industry has raised Venezuela, between 1918 and the present, from one of the poorest Latin American countries to the wealthiest, in terms of per capita income and gross national product.

The development of petroleum has affected all of Venezuela, but in varying degrees and ways. The Maracaibo lowlands, where the oil industry is heavily concentrated, has expanded from an unimportant provincial outpost of 15,000 people, in 1918, to become a modern urban center with a population of about 400,000. But the impact of the oil boom spread rapidly to other areas and sectors of the population. The old landowning class found itself forced at least to share, if not surrender, positions of political and social leadership to the newly rich businessmen and their associates— government officials, higher army officers, and foreign managerial personnel, all of whom were connected in some fashion to Venezuela's new-found wealth. The business community, organized in the Venezuelan Federation of Chambers and Associations of Commerce and Production, has continued to grow in numbers and power; wealth, along with education, now determines upper-class status.

The middle class has blossomed since about 1930, and particularly since 1945. It includes a wide range of occupations: military officers, politicians, small ranchers and merchants, professional people, and white-collar workers in private enterprise and government. Most of the nearly half a million immigrants (primarily people with skills) who have come to Venezuela since World War II also belong to the middle class. Middle-class elements played a key role in the overthrow of dictator Marcos Pérez Jiménez in 1958, and today, these people dominate national politics. The middle class, however, is not a cohesive, homogeneous grouping, and Venezuela's government should not be regarded as a middle-class government in the same sense as is the government of the United States. The middle class is divided within itself, but its members currently provide much of Venezuela's political leadership.

Although oil has diversified the social and economic structure of Venezuela, it has also served to widen the existing gap between the very rich and the very poor. Oil company employees enjoy good pay and generous fringe benefits, but they constitute only 2 per cent of the total labor force. Some other skilled employees also have satisfactory wages, but many of the unskilled and the remaining landless rural workers (agriculture still employs over one-third of the labor force) live a marginal existence. The Confederation of Venezuelan Workers, with 1.5 million members (both urban and rural), has ameliorated labor's lot to some extent since 1958; and the Betancourt government's land-reform program, combined with a steady influx of rural people to the cities, has eased the land problem considerably. On the other hand, this internal migration has added a new dimension to the urban problem. For many of these rural migrants, the attractions of the city have proved to be a chimera. Unemployed and unskilled workers have clustered into shantytowns called *ranchos,* particularly around Caracas, and as elsewhere in Latin America they are vulnerable to the blandishments of radical agitators and revolutionaries. The democratic, reform-minded government of Betancourt significantly faces violent and determined opposition from some of this lower-class proletariat, led by middle-class intellectual malcontents. The Betancourt government has attempted to meet the social and economic needs of this depressed part of the population through economic expansion and educational advancement. Unfortunately, it inherited the results of corruption and neglect from the Pérez Jiménez dictatorship that preceded it. Much of the oil revenue had been squandered, and illiteracy had grown from 49 per cent in 1950 to 58 per cent in 1958. Present plans call not only for rapid industrialization, but also for providing all children of primary-school age with sufficient schools and teachers by 1964—admittedly herculean tasks. The present administration is rapidly building new schools, however, and has already reduced illiteracy to 50 per cent.

Guatemala. Guatemala experienced the beginning of a social revolution during the years 1944–54, but the full impact had not been felt when Carlos Castillo Armas overturned the Communist-influenced Arbenz government, in 1954. Despite the manifold changes brought by revolution, the class structure remained substantially intact. Those Guatemalans whose culture is Western, the Ladinos, represent just over 45 per cent of the population, according to the 1950 census. Ladino society is generally conservative, based as it is upon the extended family, the Church, and Spanish traditions. The class structure in urban areas approaches a three-class system; only two classes are present in rural areas.

The events of 1944 and after reduced somewhat the social standing and political influence of the elite, but have influenced a few of them to invest in industry and commerce. Land continues, however, to be the primary economic basis for upper-class membership, and family name has lost only a little of its importance. The new ruling groups that came to power in the decade after 1944 quickly moved into the upper class, but in 1954, many of them were driven into exile, and the old aristocracy regained much of its social position and political power. This reversal was more complete in rural areas, where the revolution generally had less force than in the cities and towns.

A quasi-middle class first appeared in Guatemala City and some of the provincial cities in the late nineteenth century. Government workers, small businessmen, professionals, intellectuals, teachers, and all but the highest army officers belong to this category. Much of the motive power for social change after 1944 came from the middle class, which could count upon the sympathy of the army until the leaders of the revolution proposed organizing and arming a peasants' and workers' militia. The influence of Marxist ideology, and the controlling position of the Guatemalan Communists, depended upon the ideological inadequacies of the middle-class leadership, which intensely desired social change, but lacked a full-blown philosophy and technically qualified personnel to implement agrarian and other reforms. As it was, middle-class leaders accomplished almost nothing in their announced aim of helping the Indian, who still constitutes about one-half the country's estimated population of nearly 4 million. Without a doubt, economic changes since 1944 have increased the size of the middle class, but its members continue to lack class-consciousness and tend instead to seek admission to the upper class.

The rural lower class of Ladino society exists side by side with an Indian caste. The Ladino lower class in rural areas often shades imperceptibly into Indian, but in cities the cultural lines are clear. Most of the lower class is unskilled, except in Guatemala City, where a few small industries and the service trades require skilled workers. The land-reform program of the Arbenz regime, based on a law passed late in 1952, could have had a profound effect upon the organization of lower-class rural society but was reversed two years later. But the dissemination of the concept that agrarian reform would help them affected the attitudes of peasants in many sections of rural Guatemala. The 1952–54 program has been replaced by a colonization scheme, supported with U.S. funds, which avoids the issue of expropriation. Much of the new program has been carried on in the Department of Escuintla, the only area where the earlier land reform had progressed too far to be reversed.

The revolution did not significantly ease the process of upward or horizontal mobility. Education has been a means of social mobility, but one open to very few persons. During the fifty years or so before the 1944 revolution, less than a hundred public schools were constructed in all of Guatemala. The Arévalo and Arbenz governments speeded up school construction to a rate that has since been maintained or accelerated. The Castillo regime constructed sixty schools in three years, and the Ydígoras government (1958–63) launched a program seven times as large, based on substantial U.S. aid. The effect of the Peralta coup, early in 1963, on the education program remains to be seen.

Costa Rica. Costa Rica is often mentioned as the country with more schoolteachers than soldiers. Revolutions there are said to be infrequent, if not unknown. Although Costa Ricans have a justifiable pride in their way of life, it is not so different from that of neighboring countries in Central America as they like to think. Much of their sense of not being "Central American" arises from historical traditions of political apartness, rather than from social differences. (In the nineteenth century, Costa Ricans were able to avoid involvement in many of the Central American struggles over political confederation and other problems.) The society of Costa Rica varies from the Central American norm in terms more of degree than of kind.

Extremes of wealth and poverty are less marked in Costa Rica, and the class lines less rigid than elsewhere in Central America. The upper class, which includes some families dating from the colonial period, is small, and its wealth is based upon a variety of investments. Valuable coffee lands on the Meseta Central are the most common source of wealth, but the upper class has also invested heavily in urban real estate. The upper class has been relatively open to new recruits, including the *nouveaux riches* and their children. Some of the German immigrants of the last half of the nineteenth century, a few U.S. and English immigrants, and many of the political exiles from the rest of Central America have been accepted into the upper class over the years.

In this relatively open society, the middle class is large and includes not only the usual white-collar workers, but also owners of medium-sized *fincas* (coffee plantations). The latter have benefited from a successful government rural-credit system that lends money at reasonable interest rates, as well as from rural extension programs. The farmer, using the credit thus made available, is able to finance fertilizers, seed, and his other needs as a coffee producer. Middle-class political power is very great, as was demonstrated in the 1958 Presidential elections, which the National Liberation Party lost because it had antagonized the white-collar workers of the capital and other cities by radical economic proposals.

The urban lower class consists of domestics, manual laborers, and the very few industrial workers; its rural counterpart is composed of the landless and the owners of *minifundia*. The large estate also exists in Costa Rica, and controls its workers in the *patrón* tradition. On the largest coffee *fincas* and sugar plantations, workers tend to be politically docile and inactive. The labor laws of the government do not give these agricultural workers much protection. However, the large estate has considerably less effect upon economic and social life than elsewhere in Central America, because it is not the dominant form of land tenure. The majority of the employees of the United Fruit Company form a distinct element of the lower class; their wages are higher than average, and they receive extensive fringe benefits. The recent efforts of this company to convert to a contract system of banana production may well do serious economic harm to this laboring segment, which has a long history of pro-Communist leadership.

The large Negro population of the Gulf Coast, especially around Puerto Limón, maintains its cultural distinctiveness, speaking a West Indian English and supporting Anglican and Protestant churches. These people are descendants of British West Indian Negroes brought over to work on banana farms. Almost all of them are Costa Rican citizens, and live with their Spanish-speaking neighbors in an unsegregated social setting. Although in past years, attempts were made by provisions in contracts with the United Fruit Company to keep the Negroes from the Meseta Central, they have always moved freely, particularly to San José, where many find employment as servants and as members of the police force. The Negroes are predominantly lower-class, with a thin layer of middle-class individuals providing professional and other services to the Puerto Limón community.

The relative openness of Costa Rican society can be attributed to a variety of influences. The development of the small-farmer class in the colonial and early national period, and the general poverty of the country, prevented the emergence of a sizable landholding elite. The existence of large areas of land suitable for farming has permitted a slow expansion of land ownership. In recent years, the steady increase in the number of urban high schools has facilitated entry into the middle class, and the improvement in the University of Costa Rica has helped the growth in the number of professionals. Rural children attend school only through the second or third grade, and can expect six years of education, at most, unless they reside temporarily in a nearby town. But most lower-class children, in contrast to those in other countries of the area, do at least learn to read and write.

A major reason for the small degree of social unrest among lower-class Costa Ricans has been the early appearance of reformist governments dedicated to the improvement of lower-class living standards. Since 1940, when Rafael Calderón Guardia was elected President, every administration has offered the poor something in the way of economic and social readjustments. Significantly, such bitter opponents as Calderón Guardia and José Figueres followed the same general approach in domestic social policy—the former with the aid of the Communists, the latter in the face of their opposition. Thus, the Costa Rican Government has proved to be reasonably flexible in adjusting class conflicts and satisfying lower- and middle-class demands.

TRADITIONAL SOCIETIES

In the third group of countries whose societies we shall consider, social and economic change has progressed most gradually and its effects have been extremely limited. Of the two nations to be discussed here, Peru seems ripe for social revolution, while Nicaragua appears almost too depressed, economically and socially, for its people to rise in protest.

Peru. Present-day Peru possesses a social system that has changed less since independence than that of any other country in the area except Haiti and, perhaps, Paraguay. Relatively rigid social stratification has produced something approaching a closed society, with rule by a small aristocracy that resides in Lima. Regionalism has always been strong in Peru, and the process of national integration has always proceeded slowly. Western society is strongest in the coastal areas; Indian society predominates in the highlands.

Western society comprises about half of the country's total population of just over 11 million. Like most of the population located on the coastal plain, urban dwellers are almost entirely Western. In contrast, the population of the jungle areas east of the Andes is only 30 per cent Western in culture; for the highlands, the figure is closer to 20 per cent. Membership in Western society depends upon knowledge of spoken Spanish, adoption of Western clothing, abandonment of the use of the coca plant and observance of Western sanitary habits. If these practices are followed, it is possible for persons with Indian features to pass easily into the

Cholo, or Western, lower class. Those who serve in the army make this transition, and then often return to Indian culture at the end of their enlistment.

The Peruvian upper class includes less than 1 per cent of the total population. It functions as a power elite, dominating the government, the economic system, and the Church—with only the army maintaining some autonomy, because of its largely middle-class officer corps. The majority of the upper class resides in Lima, but a small number live in other cities and in the countryside. Land, considered a stable and honorable investment, is the economic base for this class, even though investments in other types of enterprise are not uncommon. Newer members of this class—those whose fortunes are based on guano and nitrate, European families who have been in Peru only a generation or two, and the younger generation of older families—have a somewhat more venturesome spirit in economic affairs. The extended family is a bulwark of the economic position of this class; the eldest sons normally manage the family interests, and the other sons assist, often by taking training in law and related fields. The upper class maintains a very high level of living, including ownership of airplanes and yachts and membership in exclusive private clubs.

The rigid conservatism of this upper class is the characteristic that sets it apart from the upper classes of neighboring countries. Closely allied with the Church hierarchy, which in Peru does not look with favor on the Christian-democratic political philosophy, and conscious of Spanish colonial tradition, the upper class displays almost monolithic opposition to social change. The aristocracy maintains its power with the support and assistance of members of other classes. Some of its most loyal supporters are the *validos,* or hangers-on, drawn from the middle class.

The façade of upper-class unity has shown some signs of cracking under the impact of diverse economic interests in Peru. Agricultural, mining, and industrial interests disagree over national economic policies, with the dominant landed group often opposing industrialization because of the changes it will bring. For the most part, however, such disputes are handled behind the scenes, with negotiations taking place at the social level. The upper class has been united against social reform, and its control of the press and its ability to manipulate elections has, in the past, effectively stifled political freedom. But marks of strain are beginning to appear in the structure.

The Peruvian middle class is neither well defined nor well developed. Small in numbers, weak in influence, it is almost without class feeling. It comprises about a third of the total urban population, but only about 15 per cent of the population of Lima, as opposed to well over 40 per cent of the population of other cities and towns. Although most of the usual elements of the middle class are present in Peru, the small tradesman is not generally considered to qualify for middle-class status. The bureaucracy is not large or well paid in Peru, and consequently contributes few members to this group. White-collar workers of all types are, however, the largest single element. Many of these people live under conditions that would be considered lower-class elsewhere in Latin America. The upper-middle class is comprised of owners of medium-sized farms, supervisory personnel of commercial farms, top army officers, university officials, professionals, and so on. The provincial middle-class leaders, rather than jousting with the elite, expend their energies in regional struggles. The rural middle class is least amorphous in areas where Indians constitute a clearly demarcated caste.

The lower class lives under abysmally backward and depressing conditions. Tuberculosis is endemic in the *callejones,* the slum areas of the cities. Although both general death rates and infant mortality rates have dropped, health and sanitary conditions are still primitive; only a few towns have potable water. Consequently, disease slows economic development significantly. The urban sector of the lower class, as a percentage of the total, is largest in Lima and Callao. The skilled craft workers and mechanics are literate, and competent in their trade. Unions, largely under Aprista leadership, are weak because the membership cannot afford strikes of more than a few days' duration. Because they do not seek to maintain a set standard of life, they are often better off than the lower-middle class, which must spend conspicuously. The largest component of the urban lower class is the menials who are migrants from Indian villages in the highlands. With an unstable family life and a high rate of illegitimacy, the group as a whole manifests a propensity to petty crime. Without protection and without political or economic power, they are potential targets for demagogues and the Communists. The rural lower class is composed of individuals who have basically abandoned Indian culture, but whose Western culture is mixed with many Indian traits. Those who are sharecroppers have become politically active and seek improved contractual terms from the large landowners.

Despite the rigid class lines and the generally static condition of

Peruvian life, social mobility is not unknown. Middle-class people pass into the aristocracy only rarely, but movement from the lower to the middle class is more readily achieved, by means of education, wealth, professional career, or government service. Education, particularly at the high-school level, is an absolute requirement for upward movement, but the limited facilities of the educational system make this difficult. Less than half of the school-age children (six to sixteen) are enrolled, and only 1 out of 100 of those entering first grade finishes high school. The 40 or so agricultural high schools, or institutes, and the more than 150 industrial high schools are inadequate for the country's needs; the universities, moreover, are retarded by insufficient funds.

A more important movement is horizontal—from Indian to Western society. Population pressure in the highlands (where per capita income is dropping), military service, and the need for labor on the commercial farms in coastal areas have all played a part in this movement. In the south of Peru, in the Arequipa-Puna-Cuzco triangle—an area suffering from severe drought—starvation has created political unrest approaching the point of revolution. Movement to the cities by newcomers who were unable to earn a living in their former places of residence has permitted the Communists to make dramatic gains in influence. These migrants, who are marginal because they are in the process of passing from Indian to Western culture, are restless and usually defenseless against exploitation and are therefore open to Communist appeal.

The draft system in Peru has furthered national integration. Although all men of a given age are legally obliged to register for the drawing of names, the illiterate Indians usually fail to do so; therefore, under the law, they are automatically required to serve. Trucks are sent around, and the delinquent Indians are gathered and enrolled. The net results are beneficial for the Indian, because he learns Spanish and has other opportunities for education. The large estate owners, however, often hesitate to hire Indians who have served in the army. For both lower- and middle-class Peruvians, the army has been a readily available means of upward mobility. Despite this process, the army as an institution has seldom opposed the interests of the elite.

The rapid population growth (between 2.5 and 3.0 per cent annually) and the declining per capita income are signs of serious troubles ahead for Peru. Social problems, from illiteracy to starvation, can be expected to get worse. Because the political system is undemocratic, and has allowed little or no opportunity for effective protest through legal means, serious social unrest may well lead to serious political disturbances.

Nicaragua. The social structure of Nicaragua is highly traditional, with a small upper class that dominates social and economic life, a middle class that is almost nonexistent, and a lower class that is fearful and subservient. The elite has always maintained a *patrón* attitude toward the lower-class masses, controlling and exploiting them. Recent efforts by elite leaders (who opposed the long-dominant Somoza family) to attract mass support have been hampered on the one hand by their fear of genuinely popular movements, and on the other hand by popular apathy. The Somozas more effectively exploited the ignorant lower class, as shown by the Frente Popular Somosista, a lower-class organization led by Nicolasa Sevilla, who was undisputed ruler of the Managua prostitutes. The Frente was often used over the years to further the Somoza dynasty's policies by brutally attacking upper-class oppositionists and publicly humiliating their wives and daughters. In 1958, the government encouraged the Frente to attack a radio station affiliated with the Conservative Party. The degree of class consciousness prevalent among the lower-class members of the Frente was not readily apparent, but opponents of the government have claimed that Nicaraguan Communists have worked closely with the Somozas in arousing lower-class feelings.

In addition to being underdeveloped, Nicaragua is undergoing prolonged, very grave deterioration of its social institutions. The Somoza family, while enriching itself substantially, has ruled in the economic interest of the 5 per cent of the population that owns more than 75 per cent of the country's wealth. The maldistribution of income is not redressed by any significant government tax or welfare measures; on the contrary, the concentration of wealth has been promoted by the Somozas' policies. The number of illiterates is growing steadily, as the inadequate school system fails to expand to meet the population growth. In 1950 only 1.4 per cent of the population had completed four or more years of secondary education. Without question, this figure is even lower in 1963. Social groups are confined to the upper class, with the exception of a few Church organizations, a small number of labor unions, and the National Guard. The dependent attitude of the lower-class individual is one reason that the Castro-backed invasions, early in 1959, aroused no widespread reaction. The lower-class Nicaraguan appears too downtrodden to rise in defense of his rights.

3. Economic Considerations

INTRODUCTION

Latin America is the most advanced of the so-called underdeveloped regions of the world. Among them, it alone has a basically Western-oriented cultural and political system. For more than three decades, the area has been altering its traditional plantation and mine economy, geared to the output of raw materials in exchange for imported capital, technology, and manufactured goods. Under stimulus of the Great Depression and World War II, the region as a whole began consciously to re-evaluate its position in the world economic system, and to examine its resources and potential. With only minor dissent, the conclusion was reached that greater economic self-sufficiency would offer a shield against the often adverse impact of a world market that was beyond its power to control. The construction of new industries, power plants, and communications systems was undertaken with enthusiasm; and, in the process, the region began to reweave the fabric of its own economic and social structure, as well as to set in motion a process of political reorganization. New interests groups were formed, new components of power entered the political arena, and new national ambitions began to influence government policy. To a considerable extent, these new power centers—urban industrialists, labor unions, commercial interests, and white-collar government employees—have almost everywhere forced some additional democratization of government. The broadening of the political base and the rise in the standard of living, at least in urban centers, have begun to erode the economic predominance of the old power groups of landed and exporting interests, and in turn have brought demands for further and faster political, social, and economic changes.

The dissimilarity in economic conditions from country to country, however, is so great that the impact of economic change on politics has been very uneven. Particularly in terms of industrialization, the economies of the larger countries have moved ahead of their smaller neighbors. Argentina is no longer simply a larger version of Paraguay, nor is Mexico an oversized Guatemala. The larger countries are also marked by greater awareness of their economic requirements, and by a greater willingness to shake their time-honored traditions. The Brazilians, especially, are proud of their vigorous racial mixtures, burgeoning population already in excess of 75 million, rich resources, and economic potential. With good reason, they consider their country an emerging world power. The Argentines, with a population well over 20 million, already possess the necessary base for steady economic growth. In fact, Argentina can hardly be classified as undeveloped or socially unprogressive, despite some poverty and illiteracy in the northern provinces. Its basic needs are to increase agricultural output and labor productivity, provide adequate housing, and improve the efficiency of its overstaffed bureaucracy. To a significant degree, this is true of Venezuela as well; the relative prosperity of its 7.5 million citizens rests upon the country's position as the world's leading exporter of petroleum. Although Venezuela's high national income is still very unevenly distributed, the social policies of the present reformist government are softening the impact of these striking disparities.

Mexico, with a population exceeding 35 million and a relatively low, but rapidly rising GNP, ranks among the most advanced in its progress toward economic development and in its attitude toward social welfare. Still motivated, in part at least, by the revolutionary mystique, the government attempts to respond within certain limits to mass pressures for increased social benefits. Colombia, fourth in population, with over 15 million inhabitants, ranks below Mexico and above Brazil in per capita GNP but is less industrialized than the latter. Still, it is making steady progress in this direction, and has taken steps to ensure that social development keeps pace with economic growth. Chile, whose nearly 8 million people enjoy an average income above that of the Colombians, trails her Argentine neighbor in both economic and social development. Economically as well as socially, Peru lags far behind her major neighbors—Chile, Colombia, and Brazil. The overwhelming majority of her 11 million inhabitants (one-half Indians) live closer to the level of their Ecuadorian or Bolivian neighbors than to that of the other large and medium-size countries.

Among the less populous nations, Uruguay and Costa Rica are favored with a high degree of racial and social homogeneity, in addition to a relatively developed if sluggish economy. With fewer extremes of wealth and poverty than the other small countries, they have evolved a substantial degree of social and economic justice. Despite one of the lowest GNP growth rates in Latin America (it still ranks high in per capita GNP), Uruguay is politically mature and socially stable. Its elaborate and generous system of social benefits tends to level out unequal incomes and goes far toward explaining the country's lack of social unrest. Costa Rica, like its less progressive neighbors in Central America, depends upon a few agricultural products for its dollar earnings; but like Uruguay, it has social-welfare benefits that have narrowed the gaps between rich and poor, with consequent social stability and popular faith in democratic government. The other small countries, except Panama (and here, it is the Canal that causes the difference), rank with Peru in the bottom ten so far as Latin American economic development is concerned. If we take per capita GNP as the yardstick, the Dominican Republic leads the way as the most fortunate of the unfortunate, followed in descending order by Guatemala, Nicaragua, El Salvador, Paraguay, Honduras, Peru, Bolivia, Ecuador, and Haiti.

THE URBAN-RURAL IMBALANCE

Discontent in Latin America stems, not only from underdevelopment and the skewed distribution of political power and wealth, but also from the social and economic reforms that have whetted popular appetites without fully satisfying them. One of the major economic problems of the area, which aggravates this condition, is the unevenness of economic growth. Not only does neglect of certain sectors of the economy increase the difficulty and eventual cost of restoring economic balance, but those elements of the population dependent upon the neglected sector, irritated and aroused by the progress in other areas, become easy targets for radical agitators and propagandists bent on stirring up political and social unrest. Nowhere is this problem more evident than in the neglect of agriculture, still the source of livelihood for 50 to 60 per cent of Latin America's population.

Industrialization has encouraged urbanization in Latin America, as it has in the more advanced countries of the West. Since World War II, some cities—Buenos Aires, Mexico City, São Paulo, and Rio de Janeiro—have mushroomed to rank among the largest in the world. The trend, however, has tended to exaggerate the old problem of domination by the national capital over the rest of the country. Always the focus of national life politically and culturally, capital cities have benefited disproportionately more than the rest of the country from investment in education, public works, and industry. Only Brazil, Colombia, and Ecuador have provincial centers that rival the capital, but elsewhere many provincial centers are nonetheless major cities.

The striking consequence of urban predominance is the contrast in economic and social standards of living between urban and rural areas. Despite individual exceptions, rural levels are substantially lower than urban in literacy rates, health and sanitation measures, food consumption, housing, and clothing. Living levels are gradually sinking even lower in those countries in which productivity is falling behind the increase in population. In all countries except Argentina, Chile, and Venezuela, the majority of the labor force is engaged in agriculture. For Honduras, the figure reaches 75 to 85 per cent. In Argentina and Chile, this figure drops 25 to 35 per cent, but even this is still several times the figure for the United States. In the Andean countries and Guatemala, a majority of these rural dwellers are isolated from the national money economy. The productivity of other parts of the agricultural sector and of small-town craftsmen is extremely low. In addition, the domestic market for their products is limited by the generally low purchasing power of the bulk of the population, thereby discouraging efficient large-scale production. Declining or widely fluctuating world prices for many agricultural and pastoral products have discouraged output for export.

Probably more than half the rural dwellers of Latin America are living at a level of mere subsistence, without any real hope of improvement. In Mexico, the revolution led to considerable capital investment in agrarian reform both in the *ejidos* and in irrigation projects for villagers and private owners. In the last two decades, the majority of the rural population, still constituting more than half the total, has not enjoyed an appreciable increase in real income commensurate with the growth of the GNP. Brazil has large poverty-stricken *campesino* groups in the Northeast, and, to a lesser degree, elsewhere in the country. Chile, where almost no attention has been given to agricultural development, must now import food, despite ample areas of good agricultural lands. (It must not be forgotten that the Castro revolution built its most loyal following among the disinherited peasants of eastern Cuba.)

For several decades, development plans have stressed industrialization as a panacea for Latin America's economic problems. Recently, a number of economists have begun to recognize the new problems created by neglect of the rural sector. Some, however, still insist that industrialization will eventually solve the agricultural problem by drawing excess labor from the countryside and creating a larger demand for farm products. Some types of carefully planned industrialization will no doubt ease the rural pressures somewhat, but it is highly questionable whether industry alone will provide a solution. The economists who argue for industry point out, correctly enough, that in recent years most of the increase in GNP has come from industry, with the benefits accruing chiefly to urban managerial and labor groups. They assert that these urban groups, by pumping their increased earnings into the economy, help other sectors, including the agricultural. Unfortunately, in Latin America a disproportionately great share of the income thus generated has been going to the upper classes, who use it to maintain high consumption levels, including luxury imports. In addition, worker purchasing power is rarely sufficient to create an appreciably higher consumption rate for farm products or for the fruits of his own labor.

As a result, it can hardly be expected that farm incomes will rise, or that new job opportunities will open rapidly in a society whose industrialists prefer high-unit profits on small-scale production, rather than low-unit profits on mass production. Capital outlays from government or foreign sources can provide no ready solution for industry either, because of the adverse ratio of investment to the creation of additional jobs. To increase the number of workers in industry and related services by 10 million would require several billions in new capital investment. Even with this increase, unemployment would not be liquidated, and population growth in five years would add 10 million new people to the working force. Finally, installation of the most efficient machinery and application of the most modern management methods offer no solutions in this respect. Instead, these possibilities might well further aggravate the problem—at least in the short run. Many industries in Latin America already employ more workers than are needed because of plentiful quantities of cheap labor, low worker productivity, and inefficient utilization of labor. Many plants use outmoded machinery precisely because it does not pay to update the equipment while labor costs are low. Modernization, on the other hand, would lead to greater unemployment and additional social and political unrest.

Obviously, what is urgently needed in Latin America is more emphasis upon capital investment in rural regions. Unfortunately, the ruling groups are narrowly urban-oriented. Although the wealth of the elite was originally based to a large extent on agriculture, upper-class families are, in fact, primarily urban dwellers, with their social, economic, and intellectual life centered in the larger cities and towns. Neither they nor the growing middle class has a pragmatic understanding of rural problems or rural needs.

AGRARIAN REFORM

The term "agrarian reform" is capable of several definitions. The narrower, and more traditional, meaning confines the concept to the redistribution of land rights for the benefit of those who work the land. This may mean the confiscation or purchase of private *latifundia* by the government for parceling out among cultivators as an outright gift, a long-term purchase, or a grant in return for improvements to be made on the land. It may also mean the distribution of government lands under similar terms. The particular type of ownership or right-in-land that results may assume various forms—fee simple, village or community ownership, collective farm or state farm. Latin American countries have experimented with all types.

In recent years, however, "agrarian reform" has come to take on meanings beyond the simple redistribution of rights-in-land to include a broad range of changes and improvements in a wide variety of agricultural practices and institutions, from credit and taxation to irrigation and fertilizing. Although the problems of tenure and development are frequently related, they involve different approaches and ramifications. Development, for example, could just as well be, and sometimes is, undertaken on *latifundia;* and while production and profits soar when capital is applied judiciously to land, the social and economic status of the rural worker may remain unchanged. For some, their status may indeed be worsened if a smaller labor force is required than before.

LAND TENURE

The *latifundia,* the great estates, are still the most common type of landholding in Latin America. Considering the area as a whole, the *latifundia* hold a commanding lead in terms of percentage of total land in farms, with about 90 per cent of the land belonging to 10 per cent of the owners. Not all *latifundia* are alike. The hacienda, a livestock or grain enterprise, normally operates inefficiently, with a minimum of capital investment and a maximum of labor usage. The plantations, on the other hand, producing export crops such as bananas or sugar, are more efficient in their use of labor and capital. The net result of both types, however, is the same with regard to the maldistribution of income, the restriction of the social and cultural opportunities of the labor force, and the concentration of political power in the hands of the managers and owners. Really a part of the *latifundia* is the *colono* system, in which landless, rural workers are given the use of plots of land and other specified benefits in return for labor and services on the great estates. Little cash is exchanged in these arrangements, which may last indefinitely. Except for Argentina and Uruguay, cash rentals for agricultural lands are not important in Latin America.

A second type of holding according to size is the *minifundia,* a plot of land too small to give an adequate standard of living to its owners or to contribute to the national economy. *Minifundia* often surround the great estates, and the small holders supplement their incomes by working on them as seasonal or day laborers. A third type is the medium-size farm, usually located away from the *latifundia-minifundia* complex.

Land tenure is both individual and communal. Communal village holdings cannot usually be alienated to outsiders but individual plots may be exchanged within the group and are frequently reallocated. They are usually *minifundia* in size. These communities are almost entirely outside national life in the Andean countries, but the Mexican *ejidos,* a re-creation by the Mexican revolution of former Indian communal holdings, play an important role in Mexican political, social, and economic development. In Mexico a few *ejidos* are large holdings equal to the *latifundia* in size.

Revolutionary Cuba has been experimenting with a farming system not previously used extensively in the Western Hemisphere: the state farm, which includes close to half of the arable land in Cuba. About half of Cuban farm land is still privately owned, but Castro is threatening to convert this into cooperatives, which today include only about 12 per cent of the land.

Land-tenure reform has been carried out, or is presently under way, in Mexico, Bolivia, Venezuela, and Cuba, and is being launched in Colombia. It is under serious consideration in Brazil, Chile, and Peru, but the future of these programs still remains in doubt. Guatemala had a crash program in 1952–54 but has rolled back the reform and relied on a small colonization program since the ouster of the Communist-influenced Arbenz regime. Haiti is plagued by *minifundia,* for which land-redistribution schemes offer no remedy. Argentina and Uruguay, with their large urban populations, and Costa Rica, with a fair distribution, are not facing critical rural problems, though some reform is called for in all three countries. The remaining countries of Latin America are discussing the problem, and a few have taken some minor and halting steps. The time appears far off, however, when the current power groups in these latter countries will consent to tackle the agrarian problem at its roots.

Land-tenure reform involves not only the exchange of property rights, but also the shifting of economic and social positions and the rise of new power groups in the political structure. In many respects, any general reform in land tenure has revolutionary aspects about it, particularly since the historical force driving it on has been the hatred on the part of the landless or the near landless for the *latifundia* with their ostentatious display of wealth and power. Understandably, the ruling elite is fearful of opening the floodgates by land-tenure changes. In its initial stages, at least, such reform has been not primarily economic but rather social and political. The creation of an independent, politically conscious peasantry with its land demands satisfied has served to stabilize the Mexican Government, and is coming to provide basic support for the moderate government of Rómulo Betancourt in Venezuela.

RURAL DEVELOPMENT

Ideally, reform in land tenure should be accompanied by rural development with heavy capital investments in irrigation, seed, fertilizers, and credit. Certainly development programs must follow shortly thereafter, or the political and social gains, to say nothing of the economic, will be lost. Although economic development is still primarily urban-centered, a number of countries are beginning to recognize the dangers inherent in the rural-urban imbalance. Several have begun to act to correct the situation. Venezuela has a rural-development program already under way, in addition to its land-reform program. Brazil now appears ready to invest a large amount of domestic and borrowed U.S. capital in the stricken Northeast, and Colombia has recently enacted agrarian legislation that if properly implemented will improve rural life. The Chilean

Government currently plans to spend about one-fifth of its available development funds on the rural sector. Cuba has set out to equalize urban and rural living standards by cutting down urban consumption and rural development.

The same long-standing social, economic, and political conditions that have everywhere hindered land reform also impede rural development. The large estates held by government or private owners, with extensive tracts of unused land of varying quality; tiny farms; *colonos* and day laborers ignorantly clinging to their traditional ways, and sometimes to the low-level security that the estate offers; inability to use machinery for lack of technicians and cheap labor; and the communal holdings, with their rigid and inflexible patterns—all have combined to prevent the efficient application of modern capital and technology to Latin American farming. For the most part, land in Latin America is cultivated with an excessive number of workers using simple tools, perpetuating a condition of underemployment. Because rural areas have failed to grow economically while population has expanded, rural underemployment and unemployment have increased, explosively in some regions. The cities have been able to absorb some, but not all, of this surplus population.

Capital-intensive agriculture in Latin America is limited to a few areas such as northwestern Mexico, coastal Peru, the grain and pastoral areas of Argentina and Uruguay, and southern Brazil. In Central America and in a few other areas, foreign-owned and foreign-developed farms or plantations, such as those of the United Fruit and Standard Fruit companies, have made heavy capital investments. Production of these exportable, dollar-earning crops has reached a high degree of efficiency, with attendant marketing, financing, and transportation facilities developed far beyond the standards for the general economy. In recent years, changing social and political conditions have discouraged investment of most foreign-based capital in agriculture. United Fruit, for example, is shifting from operating its own farms to contracting for bananas grown by small local producers. One result of this changeover has been the shift from fruit to cattle production in some areas. Another has been the loss of high wages and fringe benefits for the former plantation workers. Truck farming for the cities has been developing, with some application of capital, but in most areas (southern Brazil and the environs of Montevideo being notable exceptions) production and distribution are not efficient enough to provide the lower classes with a wide variety of foodstuffs at a price low enough to permit balanced diets.

Serious difficulties face government or private agencies concerned with capital investments for developing rural areas. To be effective, such programs must have competent personnel to administer the assistance, as well as peasant cooperatives, rural credit institutions, and other organizations to mobilize and direct the rural workers. Frequently, the persons in charge of such development projects are urbanites, who share few of the values and fewer of the customs of rural life. As a result, the administrators, whether politicians or technical experts, often assume attitudes of superiority toward rural people, and seldom take up residence under primitive rural conditions—a necessity for effective field work. Even the technical experts, imbued with the typical Latin American value system, find it distasteful to work with their hands, or to demonstrate new procedures to the peasantry. Rural organizations, for their part, reach only a small part of the population. Peasant leagues, cooperatives, school boards, and Church-led social-action groups, however, do provide nuclei in a number of countries for practical and democratic socio-economic development.

Government extension services, often aided by U.S. funds or Peace Corps workers, have enjoyed some successes. To date, these programs have been too limited to have a mass impact, but they represent an advance over other more traditional government aids to agriculture. Agronomists and other specialists, some of whom have been trained in the United States, actually work in the countryside rather than in city offices. However, throughout the eighteen countries offering such programs, a total of no more than 2,000 employees are so dedicated to rural improvements. The Ford and Rockefeller foundations and the Catholic Church have also devoted themselves to such projects, but again on a limited scale.

One further problem remains to be considered. The introduction of labor-saving machinery and tools, rural electrification, fertilizers, hybrid seeds, and improved techniques of cultivation will certainly increase agricultural production. But just as improved methods in industry have created employment problems, improvements in agricultural practices may well produce rural unemployment. (In northern Mexico, for example, commercial agriculture has swelled the number of *braceros* seeking seasonal employment in the United States.) To avoid such unemployment, these strictly economic projects must be accompanied by other socio-economic innovations to make rural life more diversified and attractive. The promotion of small-scale, semiskilled trades and home industries, and the building of hospitals, roads, and community centers, will provide not merely more attractive living conditions but also increased job opportunities for rural people.

INFLATION, CREDIT, AND FINANCING

Economic theorists everywhere disagree over the effects of inflation on economic growth. In Latin America, the so-called monetarists argue that inflation is destructive of economic growth, producing distortions and bottlenecks in the economic system. To halt inflation, they advocate the adoption of monetary and fiscal controls, as well as outside financial aid. The "structuralists," on the other hand, insist that it is precisely because an economy is growing that inflation results, and resist the "sound fiscal policies" of the monetarists. Certainly a mild inflation has accompanied the booming Mexican economy, but near disaster has occurred in Chile, where inflation has raised the cost of living more than twenty times since 1950. Brazil, with an inflationary spiral akin to Chile's, may have suffered less than the latter, though the damage resulting from inflation may become apparent only later. In Bolivia, the cost of living rose more than 1,000 per cent between 1952 and 1957, when a stabilization program began to have partial success.

Apart from their economic effects, inflation and monetary controls have had important political effects. The failure of the Ibáñez government to control inflation in Chile unquestionably contributed heavily to the success of businessman Jorge Alessandri in his candidacy during the 1958 presidential election, but Alessandri's anti-inflationary measures of reducing government expenditures and holding the wage line proved harmful to the already suffering lower classes. These difficulties could perhaps have been mitigated either by a more equitable tax structure, which would have permitted government expenditures to continue, or by a round of wage increases followed by more stringent price controls. But the government, dominated by the business and landed elite, has failed to hold down the wage-price spiral, or to reform the tax structure. The inequities continue, and the political pot continues to boil. Frondizi, in Argentina, faced the same problem. His early popularity eroded with his adoption of anti-inflationary measures similar to those of Alessandri. Frondizi placed his hopes on alleviating lower-class dissatisfactions through a rapid development of the Argentine economy that would permit granting wage increases and benefits out of increased production, rather than through inflationary printing of currency for public works and other government expenditures. Unfortunately, the economy did not respond as quickly as he had hoped. In the March, 1962, elections, popular dissatisfaction contributed to the heavy Peronista vote—which in turn led the military to step in and oust Frondizi. Conditions have worsened in succeeding months, with payless days for government workers and a political mortality rate for finance ministers and presidents that serves as an index of the economic crisis.

Vitally involved in the future of Latin American economic development and its ability to help keep inflation within reasonable bounds are the area's financial, credit, and banking institutions. The basic problems are not only shortages of funds but use of available funds for nonproductive real estate and other investments. Only a few banks, primarily foreign institutions, have substantial reserves for lending or investment. The Mexicans permit investment of certain bank reserves, but only in those sectors of the economy where they will be productive. In general, such activities are based on the rediscounting of paper at the central bank, whose funds are limited only by the restrictions set by government policy. The shortage of funds results from (1) the generally low level of savings, which in turn reflects the low level of income; (2) the unwillingness of people to deposit in savings facilities for fear of a decline in the value of money; (3) the lack of such institutions at hand.

Although some funds are attracted to savings banks, mortgage banks, and other specialized institutions, the commercial banks are the only type of financial house that has been successful in obtaining a fairly steady flow of funds, despite political disturbances or inflation. Even here, however, the quantity has been insufficient to meet credit demands, so that the commercial banks have resorted to the central bank for further assistance. Obviously, the quantity of capital available affects the contribution that the financial system makes to the economic progress of an underdeveloped area such as Latin America. Two other factors, however, are at least as important, if not more so. One is the complexity and orientation of the system. The origin of a credit institution frequently influences the direction of lending and investments undertaken. Many have been created to meet the needs of certain groups or activities, such as agriculture, foreign trade, or a specific industry. The sum of their activities does not always meet what are believed to be the country's over-all banking needs. The other factor, the use to which all funds are put, is of course related. Small-holder agriculture has never fared well, despite the fact that in most Latin American countries, this is the sector that needs the greatest credit assistance and development. Bankers, being for the most part conservative, are reluctant to lend or invest money in something so unpredictable, or to aid someone they believe to be a poor credit risk. Even more important, scarcity of capital gives rise to high interest rates and stimulates use of available funds in rapid-turnover loans, rather than in long-term, slow-yield investments. Moreover, the *personalismo* that pervades Latin American society makes a banker wary of embarking upon new ventures unless he has had some prior relationship with the would-be borrower. There are some entrepreneurs who can borrow on their existing wealth and prestige for new undertakings, but they are few in number and limited to the more advanced countries, like Mexico and Brazil.

Several factors dry up funds that could be used for economic development. First, a number of well-established and profitable firms resort to bank loans for expansion and replacement, rather than selling their securities on the market, because they wish to avoid sharing their profits with new stockholders. Inflationary spirals, when government-controlled interest rates make bonds unsalable, have aggravated the situation. Inflation and inequitable distribution of wealth have also encouraged speculative use of funds in luxury buildings, with a relatively low ratio of increment to output. The government, however, cannot be held solely responsible for either the income inequality or the inflation. Some of the pressure for inflation comes from the upper class. Other pressures come from government efforts to carry out development and welfare projects through the credit system rather than through increased taxation. Political pressures from the elite have effectively prevented necessary tax reform in all but a handful of countries.

One other problem remains. Private credit institutions will make at best only limited investments in high-risk, slowly amortized enterprises and those producing for mass consumption. As a result, many Latin American countries have established public financial institutions and development corporations to meet this need. They have undertaken social-development projects (such as low-cost housing), public-utility construction, and basic industrial development (such as steel mills). In general, these institutions have had a broader outlook on economic development than in the fields mentioned above; they have taken greater risks, and they have initiated basic research. Thus far, there has been little conflict between public and private financing, because these two sectors tend, in general, to invest in different fields.

COMMODITY STABILIZATION AND THE PAYMENTS PROBLEM

To avoid ever more severe political and social crises, Latin America not only must achieve a better distribution of wealth, but must create an economy with a substantial and sustained growth rate. Future growth, however, depends in large part upon the area's ability to expand exports, in order to import the capital goods and other materials needed for development. Domestic production of import substitutes eases the pressures for certain imports, but the process itself creates demands for other kinds of imported goods. Foreign capital, as loans or direct investments, financed about 10 per cent of Latin America's imports during the 1950's, but these funds can only serve as temporary measures, since they create servicing obligations that must eventually be met. In the long run, Latin America can pay for the imports necessary for her continued growth only by expanding the volume and value of her exports. Export difficulties are one cause of payment problems that either impede importation of needed goods or require extensive foreign borrowing to finance development. Estimates prepared by the United Nations and the General Agreement on Tariffs and Trade (GATT) indicate that Latin American exports outside the area will increase to the mid-1970's at an annual rate of between 2 and 4 per cent. The most optimistic estimate is well below the cumulative rate of growth of imports (6.5 per cent) during the 1950's. Economically speaking, Latin America's best hope of reducing this gap lies in increased intraregional specialization and trade, but political pressure for national self-sufficiency may well defeat the rational aims of a "common market."

Raw materials from mining and agriculture account for 15–20 per cent of the GNP and more than 90 per cent of the exports of many countries. In most countries, one or two commodities account for 75 per cent or more, by value, of all exports. The world market for many of these products is noted for its instability, based upon the vagaries of nature or politics, pressures for protectionism, and stockpiling. Markets for these primary commodities have expanded more slowly than world industrial production, and in recent years, the price of these goods has generally risen less than the prices of imported manufactures. Since Latin America depends on primary commodities to finance her imports, and often to supply government revenue through taxation, many Latin American countries have demanded international agreements to protect their economies against these marketing adversities.

International commodity agreements are not new. They covered a variety of products in the 1930's but collapsed with the changing market conditions produced by World War II. Today, there are only four such agreements, covering sugar, wheat, tin, and coffee. The United States adheres to the sugar and wheat agreements, and provides the chief support for the coffee agreement by a quota system for the U.S. market. Coffee is the major export of six Latin American countries, and a secondary export of four others. Brazil alone produces about 60 per cent of the world supply. The important Latin American producers, joined in 1959 and 1960 by the African producers of cheaper grades, have made an international marketing agreement under which they control about 95 per cent of world coffee production. In 1959 and 1960 about 50 per cent more coffee was produced than consumed, but by holding excess stocks off the market, the producing countries maintained reasonably profitable prices.

Economists are not agreed as to the value of commodity agreements. Those who oppose them argue that they tend to control competition, protect high-cost producers, discourage cost-cutting innovations, and reduce incentives to diversify output. Those who favor the agreements point out that individual national policies already interfere with the free market and that international controls could well rationalize such interference. Whatever the objective merits of the argument, Latin Americans have seen in commodity-stabilization agreements a means of assuring themselves a stable inflow of dollars to meet a substantial part of the cost of the imports they must have for economic development.

FOREIGN INVESTMENTS

Foreign capital, private and public, has supplied part of the capital needs of Latin America. Such capital, representing up to 15 per cent of annual capital investment in the area, is especially significant because it has undertaken many large, high-risk investments, and is accompanied by modern technology. From 1950 to 1959, the net flow of long-term capital from all sources totaled nearly $10 billion, of which almost 60 per cent was U.S. private capital. Indirect U.S. investments have been small, as a result of the widespread bond defaults during the Great Depression, but direct U.S. investments in Latin America in 1959 had a book value of $9 billion. About one-third of this total was invested in Venezuela, principally in petroleum and iron ore. Cuba, Brazil, and Mexico ranked next in order, and with Venezuela, accounted for well over two-thirds of U.S. direct investment in the area. Although the Eisenhower Administration firmly advocated private capital as the primary source of Latin America's needs, the Kennedy Administration, recognizing the political hostility to U.S. business in much of Latin America, has favored a more even balance between public and private capital in the Alliance for Progress program. The $20 billion of official and private investment expected to flow into the area over a ten-year period will ease, but not solve, Latin America's capital shortage. In Cuba, the Communist bloc can be expected to furnish the external component of the funds necessary for that country's development, as long as its present international policies continue. Some other countries may receive at least minimal assistance from the Sino-Soviet bloc.

The weight of Latin American opinion favors government-to-government loans for assistance to public-service enterprises, social overhead activities, and resource-exploiting enterprises. Although international funds from such institutions as the International Bank for Reconstruction and Development (IBRD, better known as the World Bank) or the Inter-American Development Bank (IDB) are preferred, it is probable that the United States will provide the bulk of the area's foreign technical assistance and economic aid, with lesser amounts coming from Western Europe and the Sino-Soviet bloc. At the present, most governments prefer U.S. to Soviet assistance, because of existing economic ties and a basic ideological commitment to the West. The ability of the Sino-Soviet bloc to become an alternative to the United States depends heavily on the bloc's capacity to finance social and economic development of the scale and type that will satisfy mounting demands and expectations. The attractiveness of Soviet overtures will increase if the Soviet Union can present Cuba as a glittering showcase of Communist economic cooperation. At this writing, however, it is not clear to what extent members of the Sino-Soviet bloc can become regular markets for Latin American exports. The bloc had made heavy purchases of Cuban sugar through the 1961–62 *zafra* (harvest), even though the U.S.S.R. is the world's largest sugar producer and Eastern Europe is a significant exporter of beet sugar. The declines in Cuban sugar production in 1961–62,

1962–63, may make it impossible for the Cubans to sell as much sugar to the bloc as they wish to so that they can sell the usual amount to free-world markets to obtain badly needed dollars. The primary motivation for bloc purchases of Cuban sugar is political, but the cane sugar has permitted increased domestic consumption in the U.S.S.R. and some diversion of sugar beets for feeding livestock. The goals of the rest of Latin America are so ambitious, and would require such massive investment, that it is unlikely the bloc will underwrite the economic development of any country other than Cuba. But it will offer assistance on a more restricted basis, dangling the prospect of purchases of local commodities in return for diplomatic relations or other ties.

POPULATION PROBLEMS

The population explosion in Latin America has been overemphasized in recent literature published in the United States, but the fact remains that the average annual rate of increase has been high. It has been estimated at over 2.5 per cent for the area as a whole, but reaches as high as 3.5 per cent in a few countries, and drops below 1.5 per cent in several. For mid-year 1959, the U.S. Census Bureau estimated Latin American population at 192,938,-000—compared to a combined total of 192,545,000 for the United States and Canada; before the end of 1962, the Latin American figure passed the 215,000,000 mark. Brazil, Mexico, and Argentina have about 60 per cent of the Latin American total; Colombia, Peru, Chile, and Venezuela have another 20 per cent. The population of the area has doubled since 1920, and can be expected to increase by 40–50 per cent in the next twenty years. However, this growth will be spread unevenly: At roughly 4 per cent, the annual rate of increase in Costa Rica is about three times that in Haiti, Uruguay, and Bolivia, and double that of Argentina. (For a detailed breakdown, see Appendix A.) This rapid growth has altered the age composition of the population, with half the total number of persons under fifteen years of age. Life expectancy is increasing but does not yet approach the U.S. figure of sixty-seven years for males at birth; comparable figures are, for example: Argentina, fifty-seven; Chile, fifty; Brazil, thirty-nine; Mexico, thirty-seven; Haiti, thirty-five.

In developed countries, high rates in population growth are associated with high rates in GNP growth. In Latin America, however, the formula is not applicable because of low worker productivity and inefficient use of capital. As a result, the estimated average annual increase in GNP has held steady at about 3.5 per cent for Latin America as a whole for the past five years; but it has lagged behind the rate of population growth in about one-third of the countries of the area, producing in these areas stagnation, if not actual reduction, in per capita income.

More striking than the rate of population growth is its shift in character from rural to urban. Urbanization has proceeded so rapidly in the past few decades that almost half the total population now lives in cities and towns. With ten cities of more than 1 million inhabitants (nine of which are national capitals), Latin America is the most heavily urbanized region of the world, after the United States and Western Europe. Labor surpluses in rural and semirural areas, the bright lights and supposed comforts of city life, and the belief that employment in cities is plentiful have produced this wave of internal migration to the large cities. The cities, however, have not been able to absorb all of these often illiterate, disorganized, and uprooted rural families. Unemployment and underemployment, slums, and crime plague the big cities, adding fuel to the pressures rapidly mounting for economic development and social reform.

ECONOMIC AND MANAGERIAL LEADERSHIP

Latin America, particularly the South American continent, has an adequate supply of natural resources for economic development. Their utilization, however, has been limited by political divisions and geographic barriers, which have prevented efficient development on a region-wide basis. Equally important as a factor in Latin America's failure to develop its resources is a tradition basically unfavorable to the creation of entrepreneurial leadership. The value system inherited from Spain has tended to favor stability over change, traditional practices over new ways of doing things. Capital has flowed most readily into land, including urban real estate, because of the security of land investments as a hedge against inflation and palace revolutions. The acquisition of wealth through one's own physical efforts has not, of itself, granted higher social status, though wealth and the perquisites that accompany wealth eventually permit entry into the elite. The class system, however, has confined opportunity for the acquisition of wealth largely to the elite, who already control both politics and the economy. The upper class has often favored limited industrialization but always feared, and therefore sought to avoid, the political and social consequences of increased political and economic strength among the working classes.

The leadership for economic development has come not from the old, landed aristocracy, but rather from government officials and urban industrialists and businessmen, many of whom have risen in the past three decades from immigrant and other middle-class elements. Government concern for the economic advancement of the lower classes has increased as the newer urban interests have achieved political representation. The government, by assuming many of the paternalistic functions of the landed *patrón,* has become the leading force for developmental planning. In addition, it is often the major source of employment for the kind of technical and managerial experts who in the United States find their best career opportunities in business and industry. Industrial and financial leaders seldom enter political life, preferring instead to support the political parties and candidates who can best protect their interests. The economic outlook of businessmen arises directly from their own economic concerns. Protective tariffs, government controls to limit the numbers of producers in given fields, and subsidies of various kinds are their major objectives. Because of their power and technical expertise, businessmen must play an important role in national planning, and must assist in giving their countries a sense of economic direction.

Foreign businessmen in Latin America have usually focused their attention on exportable primary commodities, public utilities, and transportation facilities. Only in recent years, and primarily in response to nationalistic pressures, have they entered more readily into production of consumer goods for the local population. Because of growing popular hostility and increasing government pressure, foreign entrepreneurs now employ substantial numbers of nationals, even at managerial levels, usually deal fairly with labor unions, and pay wages that are high by local standards. The favorable image thus created is partially clouded, however, by the socially exclusive and negative attitude that the foreign (especially the U.S.) entrepreneur all too frequently adopts toward the local community. In the coming years, this element, too, must concern itself more with economic solutions for the host country's problems.

EDUCATION

Latin America's shortage of managerial skills stems in large part from its educational deficiencies, particularly the lack of facilities for manual and technical training. Population growth has placed added pressure upon a system ill prepared to handle the problems of mass education in a developing society. Simple literacy has become a prime requisite, even for unskilled labor, in modern industry and commerce; and rapid expansion of per capita productivity depends upon a labor force that is both literate and skilled. In this situation, an investment in education is an investment in economic development. Much of the present educational system in Latin America, however, is geared to the education of an elite, in the professions of medicine and law and in the arts of philosophy and literature. In a few countries, some technical schools have been founded, but in most parts of the area, needed skills are acquired by on-the-job training whether in government service or in private enterprise.

In most of Latin America, the schools have failed to provide adequate curriculums and levels of literacy. Official estimates of literacy are generally overgenerous, judging literacy to consist of little more than the ability to read a simple primer and to write one's own name. A fair estimate is that, on the average, about one-third of the children in rural areas and perhaps one-half in urban areas receive some education, but the great majority of these drop out after only one to three years of primary schooling. There are significant variations by country, however: The literacy rates of Argentina, Uruguay, and Costa Rica are above 75 per cent; those of Guatemala, Nicaragua, and Haiti are below 25 per cent. Nor are the curriculums geared to fit the most pressing requirements. Rural and urban lower-class children (and adults) need fundamental education, including basic personal hygiene, simple agricultural techniques, home economics, and the inculcation of national awareness and loyalty. Mexico is almost unique in having imparted this kind of education, for about the last forty years—both through special cultural missions to the back country and through the regular schools. In most other parts of Latin America, the continued emphasis in the primary grades upon traditional academic disciplines has limited the schools' effectiveness, no matter what the percentage of school-age children attending. As a result, the family has retained its almost exclusive role as educator among much of the lower class.

Education above the primary level also fails to meet the needs of the area. Although secondary education (only roughly equivalent to the U.S. high school) has expanded rapidly in certain urban areas, it is grossly inadequate in most countries. Moreover, as with primary schools, the curriculums are oriented almost entirely toward middle- and upper-class students. A few technical secondary schools exist, but again, they are entirely inadequate in number and training facilities. University education traditionally emphasizes the humanities, medicine, and law, although in recent years engineering has grown sharply in importance. A characteristic of many Latin American universities, virtually unknown in the United States, is the presence of professional students preparing themselves for careers in politics through extracurricular activities. Some may remain enrolled for as long as ten or twelve years, achieving fame and notoriety as leaders in student political life. These activities present opportunities, especially for lower-class students, for entry into political-party work, government service, and even business enterprise. Unfortunately, students frequently contribute to political instability on a national scale by their political irresponsibility. Their privileged position in Latin American society, the autonomy enjoyed by the university, and the immunity of university grounds from police action make student politics difficult to control. Except in Catholic universities, student political attitudes are predominantly far-leftist and even Marxist, loosely defined, and normally clash with moderate or conservative governments. However, these students seldom carry their radicalism beyond their sojourn at the universities. Unless they contemplate revolution, the force of circumstances in government service, business, or politics and the improvement of their own economic situation make moderates, or even conservatives, of most of them in a few years. The political involvement of the student body, however, contributes to academic standards that are low by comparison with those in good U.S. universities. Lack of funds, and indiscriminate enrollments, means, in this case, part-time students, part-time faculty, poor equipment, and the dead weight of a mass of students unprepared for university work.

It is obvious that Latin America needs to revamp its educational system and philosophy from top to bottom. The schools need to be geared to the stage of economic development of each country and, perhaps, each region. Rural schools cannot be copies of urban schools, just as Mexican schools cannot be copies of French, English, or U.S. schools at any level. Latin America is a rapidly developing area. Its schools must be prepared to train its people in the skills necessary to keep their economic programs moving ahead at a rapid rate, for the betterment of the masses, not just the privileged few.

CONCLUSIONS

Latin America has already achieved a significant degree of economic development, but the rate of current growth is too slow and the pattern of wealth distribution inadequate to satisfy the needs and desires of the lower classes. Development and distribution must proceed simultaneously to avoid radical political adventures. With development come skilled technicians and unionized labor, a new political force to challenge the interests of the present trade associations of managerial and propertied groups. The middle class can be expected to expand, and social mobility, in general, to increase. With social change and economic progress, existing practices in agriculture and handicrafts may be seriously disrupted, and even destroyed.

Social and economic change inevitably involves political change. Increases in per capita income and consumption do not, of themselves, guarantee political stability or an easy transformation in social customs and political institutions, but without the former, the latter are hardly possible. Democratization must be based upon a social and economic structure that permits the mass of the citizenry to participate freely and effectively in the political process. The degradation of abject poverty can mean only the destruction of democratic institutions. The question remains, however, whether the basic fabric of Western Christian society can be renovated, as it was in the United States during the 1930's, to meet the needs and demands of the newly arising power groups and their followers. Or will dissatisfaction blaze into blind radicalism, as in Castro's Cuba, with the destruction of many existing social, political, and economic institutions?

The Alliance for Progress envisions the modernization of existing institutions to expand production and income, and to redistribute profits more favorably for the mass of the population. Achievement of these goals would carry much of Latin America to the point of economic "take-off," and propel some of the countries firmly toward economic maturity and a mass-production, mass-consumption pattern. The Cuban formula, on the other hand, demands the junking of both the good and the bad in the existing structure, and a continuation of the arduous task of development under a "dictatorship of the proletariat." Up to the present, the Alliance has fallen short of many of its stated goals, but more tragically, it has failed to arouse widespread support.

4. Interest Groups

We have had occasion to observe earlier that the complexity and variety among the twenty countries that constitute Latin America virtually defy broad generalizations. We have, therefore, eschewed attempts to establish over-all classifications that would simplify comparison of its social, economic, and political institutions with those of the United States. Such schematic comparisons can be misleading, especially without knowledge in depth of the area's history, culture, and socio-economic organization. Accordingly, in approaching Latin American political life, we shall examine the major interest groups before becoming involved with more explicit forms of political organization.

The more urbanized and industrialized countries of Latin America approximate the complexity of U.S. and West European societies, although most have a far smaller and less cohesive middle-income group and a far larger poverty-stricken, and often illiterate, rural peasantry. The more rural, economically undiversified, and technologically primitive countries have a more undifferentiated social structure, and therefore reveal a greater contrast with our own society. When we add unassimilated Indian cultures to the potpourri, we are at times strongly tempted to classify some countries as non-Western. It is a basic assumption of the authors, however, that the dominant interest groups of Latin America are Western oriented and aspire to—although they have not yet attained it—a type of social, political, and economic organization comparable to that of the more advanced countries of Western society.

HISTORICAL EVOLUTION

Interest (or pressure) groups have existed in some shape or form in Latin America since the colonial period. The Church, the military, and the large landowners—three major socio-political seg-

115

ments—consolidated their power early in the national period and fought a hard, bitter, and sustained—but losing—battle against the forces of change. Opposing them were intellectual liberals, urban professional and business groups, anticlericals and antimilitarists from various walks of life, as well as ambitious provincial leaders and segments of the military who were disgruntled about their fortunes and hoped to rise to power and wealth by overturning the ruling faction. Once their individual goals had been attained, the two latter groups often made their peace with the old ruling families.

Very few of these groups were institutionalized prior to the twentieth century. Rather, they tended to form around a *caudillo* or cacique and, for the most part, proved ephemeral in nature. An obvious exception was of course the Church, which, of the major colonial institutions, made the transition into independence with its basic structure least changed. Although liberal and conservative divisions appeared among the clergy during the wars of independence, and continued for a decade afterward, the clergy closed ranks in the early 1830's, as the liberals took positions that increasingly attacked Catholic theology and philosophy, as well as clerical privileges. Almost everywhere in Latin America during the remainder of the nineteenth century, and well into the twentieth, the Church as an institution identified itself with the forces of conservatism and fought with all the resources at its command, material and spiritual, not only against the rising tide of secularism but against basic social and economic reform. Papal social encyclicals to the contrary, the Latin American clergy, with only a few exceptions, rejected the profound changes that were sweeping through Europe and North America, and tried desperately to shore up a social system infested with the dry rot of corruption, inequity, and obsolescence—in the belief that the Church's position and the salvation of souls depended upon the preservation of this system. New political alignments finally modified the social system in the twentieth century. In Mexico, where the hierarchy was most adamant against accepting revolutionary changes, the clergy and Catholic laity suffered most grievously. In Chile, where the bishops came to terms with more moderate reformers, the Church continued its mission in peace. The hierarchies of the other Latin American countries fell somewhere between these two extremes; but until the past decade, the bishops, clergy, and lay Catholic leaders continued to be clearly conservative in their political, social, and economic outlook.

The Latin American military, which had its roots in the colonial militia, was forged in its modern shape during the wars of independence. Officers who had risen rapidly during the decade and more of conflict attempted to preserve their privileged status by demanding that the various new governments incorporate the Spanish *fuero militar* (special legal military status) into the national laws. The new armies and their leaders, however, were hardly professional in any sense, and lacked a tradition of national, much less universal, cohesiveness such as the Catholic clergy possessed. Loyalties belonged to the leader rather than to the abstract corps, and the *caudillo* who could raise troops and lead them with success decimated the ranks of his military opposition, since he felt no bonds of attachment to them as fellow officers. In Venezuela, for example, no army as such had existed for more than 100 years prior to 1935. In some other countries, however, a sense of solidarity was occasionally apparent when nonmilitary elements threatened or attacked the military as a group. Curtailment of clerical and military *fueros* in Mexico in the 1850's brought about a coalescence of army officers to stave off reforms. Not all joined the rebellion, and the bloody civil war that raged for three years resulted in victory for the proponents of change, whose armies were led, of course, by members of the officer corps. The army obviously was badly split; officers felt no overriding loyalty to the corps and, for reasons of either personal advancement or personal conviction, disregarded whatever little feeling of attachment they may have had.

The rural *patrón,* the least well-organized member of the conservative trinity, has proved to be the most durable in maintaining his position. Landholding patterns, illiterate dependent labor, and inefficient methods of agricultural production have deep roots in the Spanish and Indian past. The nineteenth-century liberals in Mexico, having despoiled the Church of its lands, were soon indistinguishable from their erstwhile lay enemies not only in the extent of their lands but in their value system as well. Only in the twentieth century, in Mexico, Bolivia, and Cuba, have the basic land systems been attacked; but only in Cuba has the hacienda completely disappeared. Some observers claim that it is reviving in Mexico, with the rise of a *nouveau-riche* class of former revolutionaries.

Since land was the primary source of wealth, power, and prestige, ambitious persons of all philosophies and areas aspired to its possession and, once having attained it, supported any *caudillo,* under whatever title he chose, as long as he seemed capable of protecting and defending the economic and social *status quo*. In the final analysis, the landholder was the dominant element in the *ancien régime,* although the bishop and the general were more frequently in the limelight. The latter now appear sometimes to have been the front men, and sometimes the scapegoats, of the *patrón,* whose primary end was to serve his own well-being, and who showed few qualms about abandoning his erstwhile allies when he felt it expedient to do so.

The early opponents of the ruling elite were even less organized in recognizable and permanent factions, parties, or associations. Their very fluidity militated for years against their chances of success in gaining entry into positions of power, and their lack of a truly revolutionary social and economic program denied them the mass support of the lower classes that could have toppled the old order. In some instances, the most powerful economic opponent of the *hacendados,* namely, the growing commercial community, was absorbed into the ruling elite, as in Chile, through political compromise and intermarriage. In Mexico, this community forced its way to power and wealth after a series of civil and foreign wars, and then promptly made peace with its enemies, with hardly a ripple in the social system. This commercial elite, frequently at odds with the hacienda lords over economic policy, was at one with them in maintaining the social *status quo.* By the end of the nineteenth century, the commercial groups were beginning to form various types of trade associations, which soon established legal contacts with the government. Once this had been achieved, their direct influence on government increased appreciably. Díaz' Mexico well exemplifies this alliance of dominant rural and urban interests for purposes of mutual protection and aggrandizement.

The anticlericals and the antimilitarists (usually more anticlerical than antimilitarist) were a completely unorganized band of intellectuals in most countries. Imbued with French Revolutionary and postrevolutionary ideals, with perhaps a seasoning of Anglo-American political philosophy, these dedicated intellectuals sought to substitute an individualistic society for their corporate society, a democratic government for their tyrannical regime, and a secular state for their religion-oriented state. Not all were anti-Catholic; some were practicing Catholics. By themselves, they were generally ineffective, but their program gave ideological support and justification to more materialistic men and movements dedicated to overthrowing existing regimes. It is ironical, but revealing, that in Mexico, Juárez, Ocampo, and their associates had to rely on a provincial *caudillo,* Juan Álvarez, to oust Santa Anna; and in Argentina, Sarmiento, Mitre, and Alberdi had to rely on the provincial *caudillo* Justo José Urquiza to oust the gaucho dictator Juan Manuel de Rosas.

Obviously, such people as disgruntled army officers and provincial *caudillos* who aspired to greater things than the government of Oaxaca or Entre Rios neither belonged to nor formed a club or association of any permanence. Perhaps a clique, a personal following, an army—but not an organized pressure group. The *caudillo* and his followers may well have supported, and been supported, by broad economic interests, but the organization that formed behind such a leader had its end-all and be-all in the person of the leader, the *caudillo.* When he suffered defeat or loss of prestige, or died, the organization melted away, perhaps to coalesce around another popular figure. Such passing groups often proclaimed adherence to a program of high-sounding principles that usually proved meaningless. The primary aim was too often self-advancement.

Because the societies were so primitive, the Latin American bureaucracy of the nineteenth century was a body without power or influence; it was small and performed only a few, relatively unimportant tasks. The permanent employee's primary skill was that, in a population largely illiterate, he could read and write. Officers and lower-echelon chiefs were frequently replaced with every change of administration, so that there was little permanence and leadership. Only with the growth of a complex society, and an increase in government services, did the bureaucracies begin to exert some influence on the course of policy. Technical experts were needed and could not be readily replaced, and although top positions continued to be distributed under the spoils system, the political leadership became more and more dependent on the experts in the bureaucracy. When this situation fully ripened, as it did in the twentieth century, with the enormous increase in social services in Mexico, Brazil, Argentina, and Chile, the bureaucracy became a force to be reckoned with.

For more than a century following independence, the lower classes, both urban and rural, were unorganized. Overwhelmingly rural in the nineteenth century, the lower classes today still live primarily off the land, but millions have moved, or are now moving, to the large cities. Sunk in poverty, illiteracy, and disease, these masses—many Indian by race and culture—had known nothing better, had worked for nothing better, and had hoped for nothing better. From time to time, a local or national *caudillo* could stir them to action or impress them into his army, but their enthusiasm soon waned, and they deserted en masse as it became obvious that their sacrifices would profit them little. No leaders appeared to offer them an escape from their lot. These conditions have changed in the past half-century. A few leaders have arisen from their own ranks, but most have been persons of middle-class origin who have seen in the masses an opportunity to rise to, or to hold onto, power through means other than the normal channels offered by the old elite. Perón used his *descamisados* in this fashion. Vargas before him, and Castro after him, operated in the same manner, and various second-generation Mexican revolutionaries built up labor and farm organizations as the foundation stones of new revolutionary institutions to replace earlier ones that had been destroyed. By these means, Cárdenas gave stability to the Mexican revolution.

THE TWENTIETH-CENTURY PATTERN

During the nineteenth century, Latin American struggles involved primarily political conflicts between liberals and conservatives—over the possession of wealth and power and over the relation of the citizen to the state. In addition, there was the problem of the position of the Church in society. For the most part, the contending factions belonged to the same upper social class, with perhaps some participation, on both sides, of the small middle class, who aspired to upper-class values. To some extent, this conflict carried over into the twentieth century, but it has so radically changed course that the very nature of the political conflicts today in Latin America cannot in any sense be equated with the nineteenth-century battles. The latter, for the most part, appear rather tame affairs compared with the titanic struggles for power and status currently being waged.

As French and English political philosophies accompanied the movement for independence from Spain, so Marxist and socialist philosophies accompany the drive for industrialization and economic development. Factories have fostered an urban working class and speeded up a rural-to-urban migration, which in turn has created new and dire social and economic problems. Until recently, demands for change went largely unheeded by the ruling elite, but the oppressed found leadership in those urban intellectuals who were themselves excluded from enjoyment of the fruits of the new economic system. In some countries, such as Argentina, political palliatives and bright promises staved off revolt for many years; in others, such as Mexico, ever-tightening repression led to the most bloody revolutions, the most deep-seated structural changes, and the most shattering experiences ever felt in Latin America prior to Fidel Castro. Only Uruguay and Costa Rica, favored by small and culturally integrated populations, have carried out broad social-reform programs without violence.

Although this revolutionary movement, which has been sweeping through Latin America now for several decades, has touched almost every country south of the Rio Grande, it has come earlier in some areas than in others, and still others have barely felt its effects. Furthermore, its pace has been uneven, and its effects have been varied. Not only was the Uruguayan experience one of the most peaceful, in bringing new elements into the power structure, but it was the earliest. Mexico, despite its revolution of 1910, did not achieve comparable results for more than twenty years, when labor, farm organizations, and the bureaucracy were finally organized and given official recognition in the government. These groups were granted limited political recognition in Brazil and Chile, after disturbances that accompanied the Great Depression, but without the violence of the Mexican revolution. Their Argentine and Guatemalan counterparts did not achieve these same ends until the following decade, under Perón and Arévalo respectively.

Elsewhere in Latin America, change has been slower in coming. Venezuela did not break the traditional power structure until 1958, and Cuba until 1959, despite earlier but unsuccessful revolutions in both countries. In other lands, such as Panama and Honduras, the old families remain entrenched. Although here, as in almost all of Latin America, some gestures have been made to improve the living levels of the lower-income groups, progress thus far has not matched popular demands. El Salvador experienced one *coup d'état* in late 1960 and a second in early 1961. The present regime is attempting to institute moderate reforms against the opposition of the elite. Disturbances of various intensities have shaken several other countries during the past year as the dispossessed demand to be heard. Renewed and continuous threats of upheaval are to be expected as Castro exports his revolution through propaganda and subversion.

Even in the countries in which new groups have gained a share of power and participate in policy-making, the process has been uneven. In Mexico, the old landholding aristocracy and the army have been removed from power, and although a few revolutionary families have acquired extensive tracts of land, their power does not rest on this factor alone. In Uruguay and Argentina, the landed gentry have been virtually untouched in their own domains, but must share power on the national level with urban-based commercial and industrial groups, labor organizations, and the bureaucracy. In Argentina, the military, although much divided, remains the decisive power factor; in Uruguay, the army is virtually apolitical. In Brazil, the conservative alliance of the coffee aristocracy, the urban industrial and banking elite, and the military has, at least until very recently, effectively restricted the political role of the middle- and lower-income groups, despite the prominence given to labor by Vargas and his supporters from 1930 onward.

The results to date of this revolutionary ferment have been complex in the extreme. A few countries have experienced a veritable overturn, not only of their basic political, social, and economic patterns, but also of their long-entrenched value systems. In Mexico, of course, the results have been most spectacular. The revolution catapulted to power middle-class intellectuals, who emphasized that the masses, including the long-despised Indians, constituted the best elements in society. At the outset, they discredited the old aristocracy by accusing it of selling out the country to foreign interests; later, they destroyed it through an agrarian-reform program. The new leaders also attacked the idea that the holder of family tradition and lineage was automatically entitled to power and status. As a result, social mobility has grown appreciably, and wealth and power can now be attained by a successful rise through the new revolutionary institutions. The politically articulate sector has increasingly been swelled by those who have risen from modest, or even humble, origins. Currently, Mexico has reached a position of political stability and balanced economic development that is unequaled elsewhere in Latin America. It is based in large part upon new interest groups, such as the bureaucracy and farmer-labor organizations, as well as upon a revised, enlarged, and reoriented business and financial community.

Argentina, in contrast, continues to be shaken badly by periodic political crises and grave economic dislocations. The social and economic revolution begun by Perón has never been completed. Although he showered benefits upon the lower-income groups, particularly urban workers, he did not confer responsible political positions upon bona fide labor leaders but subordinated them to his hand-picked political associates. The bureaucracy was enlarged, and industry and commerce were encouraged. Opposition to Perón was so divided, however, that only the military, despite its divisions, could supply the needed leadership when the dictatorship was overthrown, in 1955. The landed aristocracy, damaged politically during the Perón era, has now revived. Labor has not only been denied a role in post-Perón political life, but its material benefits have been reduced, and quarreling factions have arisen in its ranks. The urban elite of commercial and industrial leaders quickly asserted themselves after Perón's overthrow and challenged the military's monopoly of power. The urban leaders, however, have a common cause with the military in preventing the rise of Peronist labor leaders. President Arturo Frondizi (1958–62) maintained himself only by a continuously dexterous, and at times delicate, juggling of these powerful opponents. When he miscalculated Peronist strength in the 1962 elections, the military and the conservatives toppled him.

Between the extremes of Mexico and Argentina, such other "advanced" countries as Brazil, Chile, and Uruguay have experienced changes in their systems, though perhaps not so profound as those in either of their neighbors (in other words, they have neither achieved the stability of Mexico nor suffered the instability of Argentina). In none of these three has the position of the lower classes been so enhanced as it has been in Mexico, and in none of these is the power of the military so decisive as in Argentina, although the military is far stronger in Brazil than in Uruguay or Chile. In all three, the power of the landed aristocracy persists, but it is shared with industrial and commercial groups, and some recognition is given to the lower-income groups, especially in the cities.

Bolivia's revolution, beginning in 1952, resembles Mexico's earlier upheaval in several important respects. Many radical measures have been achieved, and in much less time. Like Mexico, Bolivia has destroyed its old army, and created a new revolutionary military force, supplemented in this case by a civilian militia of miners and farmers. It has also nationalized its major mining industry, and has carried through an agrarian reform. Bolivia, however, does not approximate the potential of Mexico in human, geographic, or natural resources. Its governmental stability depends on a yearly subsidy from the United States and will continue to do so for the foreseeable future. Nor do the new power groups that have emerged present an exact parallel to the Mexican movement. With little or no industry, powerful labor activity is confined largely to workers in the mining industry; furthermore, the *campesinos,* organized into militia bands, exercise an influence on the government that Mexican *campesino* groups seldom if ever enjoyed. Both groups—in Mexico and Bolivia—were, and are, led by urban intellectuals and politicians, few of whom have risen through the labor unions.

MAJOR GROUPS

Having examined interest groups in general terms, and sketched some of the most significant variations among countries, we are now ready to proceed to a more detailed consideration of the most important of the interest groups that play a key role in the area's rich political life: the Catholic Church, propertied interests, students and intellectuals, organized labor, and the ever-present military. For illustrative purposes, we shall cite developments in specific countries, but the systematic country-by-country treatment will be reserved for Chapter 6.

THE CATHOLIC CHURCH

By the very fact of its supranational character, the Catholic Church presents a high degree of uniformity in its goals and policies. Although the clergy have often fought for their own material well-being, and Catholic lay leaders have attempted to use the Church as a springboard to political power, nevertheless the Church's stated primary goals have always been spiritual. Since the battles for clerical privileges have been fought and lost everywhere, the clergy's major concern today is their freedom to teach, govern, and minister to the Catholic laity on matters of faith and morals. At times, these activities have, indeed, strong political overtones, and still bring occasional conflicts with government in such matters as education and marriage laws, but except in Castro's Cuba, most of these conflicts are subject to arbitration and compromise. Of secondary but growing interest is the Church's concern with social welfare and political justice. The response of the clergy, however, varies from country to country, depending on such factors as the influence of the Church over the laity, the strength of the government, and the organization of civic groups.

In some countries, the hierarchy has taken a short-term view of its interests in relation to the political situation. For example, in the Dominican Republic under the late dictator Rafael Trujillo,

the bishops occasionally raised their voices in protest against viola-
tions of basic human rights, but they were careful not to push the
Church into conflict with the state. With the first signs of conciliation from the government, they were ready to make a truce
with the authorities, who would promise—but not necessarily
guarantee—a minimum of security to the populace, and a minimum
of freedom of operation to the Church. This attitude was almost
universal in Latin America up to a decade or two ago, and in
many instances, there was little or no opposition to any degree
of political or civil oppression if it was not coupled with restrictions on religious worship and activity.

After World War II, and noticeably in the 1950's, the hierarchies
in several countries began to take a broader view of their social
and political roles in the community, and a longer view of the welfare of the Church and its doctrine. In many countries, members
of the hierarchy withdrew their support of dictators, criticized
tyrannical actions, and thereby lent support to the opposition. In
Brazil, in recent years, the influence of the Church has been used
not only against Communism, but also in behalf of constitutional
government, even when the bishops are out of sympathy with the
regime. In Argentina, Colombia, and Venezuela, some bishops
have viewed the drive for social, economic, and political reforms
with unconcealed approval, and have lent their support to the
new governments that succeeded the dictatorships, even when the
successors were not notably friendly to the Church. In a few countries, such as Colombia, Mexico, and Argentina, individual clergymen—priests and bishops—have vigorously taken up the cause
of social reform, at times in collaboration with the government,
while the Catholic laity, notably in Chile and Venezuela, have attempted to organize Christian democratic or Christian socialist
movements. In some instances, the reforms have been motivated
by the negative purpose of combating Communism, but more and
more frequently, the motives seem to have sprung from a sense of
responsibility to improve the lot of the lower classes.

One cannot generalize easily, however, about the power of the
Church in Latin America today, except to say that nowhere is it
the dominant group. The Church retains two distinct but related
sources of strength among the people: (1) their attachment to the
Church and its doctrine in spiritual terms, and (2) their willingness to follow their spiritual leaders on economic and political
matters. Although where the first situation prevails, the second
often follows, there are exceptions. Estimates by U.S. Catholics,

lay and clerical, on the extent of religiosity in Latin America uniformly indicate a weakness of practice and belief. Estimates on practicing Catholics in Chile and Argentina run as low as 5 or 10 per cent, and of these, most are women and children. The faith appears strongest in Colombia and Mexico. The Church's political influence, however, is weak in Mexico and Chile, and strong in Colombia and Argentina. The Church in Costa Rica, little known for its influence in the nineteenth and early twentieth centuries, has more recently established the strongest labor organization in the country, Rerum Novarum, in collaboration with a reformist political movement.

In some countries, the Church appears weak or disorganized; yet it exercises political influence of considerable magnitude when it opposes the existing regime. The reason for this anomaly is that in such cases as Haiti and the Dominican Republic, the Church is the best organized, if not the only, effective opposition group. It cannot be destroyed with the same ease as political parties, student organizations, and civic groups—not only because of its greater complexity and deeper historical roots, but also because of the powerful sentimental attachment that it still exerts even on many persons whose religious faith is virtually nonexistent. By a tradition that amounts to little more than a cultural vestige, physical attacks on the clergy are still viewed with revulsion and horror. As a result, governments must tread warily lest they provoke rebellion among the discontented, whose anxieties are complex, but who see in the Church a rallying point for overthrowing the regime. Trujillo, prior to his assassination in 1961, followed this type of policy, as did Duvalier, in Haiti, until the last months of 1960. It remains to be seen whether the latter can sustain himself in the face of the growing hostility of the local Catholic populace, who are bolstered by a decree of excommunication that has been pronounced against all members of the government associated with the expulsion of clergymen from Haiti.

Everywhere in Latin America, the forces of conservatism within the Catholic Church appear to be on the defensive. Few, if any, clergymen can be found to speak openly today in behalf of the old-style regimes embracing authoritarian government, grave economic inequity, and the landlord-peasant relationship. On the other hand, few have reconciled themselves to the secular state, and most would like to see some sort of formal cooperation between the Church and the government. Almost all desire the teaching of religion in the public schools (Mexican Catholics, at present, would be content with the legalization of Catholic schools at all levels in addition to higher education), the outlawing of divorce, and some restraint on non-Catholic criticism of Catholic teachings on morals and dogma. Again, these feelings vary in intensity from country to country, as does the expression of opinion on these subjects. For the most part, the Catholic reactionaries are quiet; the vociferous Argentine group that publishes the extremely nationalist *Azul y Blanco* is the exception rather than the rule. The Sinarquistas of Mexico and the Integralistas of Brazil have long been in decline and have little open clerical support. Even in El Salvador, the Catholic conservatives are fast losing ground. Copying a successful Colombian Catholic movement to educate the masses by radio, a group of prominent Catholic laymen in El Salvador has purchased a radio station and is distributing several thousand receivers in an attempt to reach about 20,000 rural people, as a start. With the aid of a teacher having at least the rudiments of an education, and a few teaching materials, the group hopes to instruct the illiterate in reading, writing, civics, sanitation, and home economics. Although the Colombian group teaches courses on the Catholic religion, the Salvadorans plan only a more general course in morals.

In a few countries, almost nothing is heard from the Church. The Catholics of Nicaragua, Paraguay, and Bolivia play virtually no role as pressure groups. In some instances, it may be presumed either that they support the present, or past, dictatorial regimes, or that they do not feel obliged, or able, to take a public position. Certainly any conservative clergyman would not be wise to oppose the Bolivian revolution today. The future appears to rest with the liberal elements within the Church, but their final victory over those who hold the older viewpoints will be long delayed in several countries; in others, it has already arrived. Elsewhere, the pace falls somewhere in between.

THE MANAGERIAL AND PROPERTIED GROUPS

In every country of Latin America except Bolivia and Cuba, private entrepreneurs who control or provide services for the means of production, urban or rural, constitute a major force in government policy-making. In some countries, such as Panama or Peru, an alliance of landowners and urban merchants and industrialists enjoys a virtual monopoly of power. In Argentina, Venezuela, and Brazil, these same groups must compete for power with the emerging middle class, labor, and the military. In Mexico, the urban elite share power with labor and the bureaucracy; in Honduras, the rural elite vie with the military; and in Haiti, the urban elite and the military constitute the power groups.

The power struggles of the late nineteenth and early twentieth centuries between the emerging urban elite groups and the land-holding aristocracy were more or less resolved in a series of compromises—some violent, some peaceful. In Mexico, Bolivia, and Cuba, however, the second phase of social and political conflict, i.e., lower-class revolt, has also occurred. The Mexican revolution of 1910, the Bolivian revolution of 1952, and the Cuban revolution of 1959 (middle class led and mass supported) destroyed the hacienda pattern of agriculture, as well as the political power of landed families upon which it rested. In Mexico and Bolivia, these revolutions also eclipsed the power of the urban elite, temporarily at least. Although the Cuban revolution has proved far more socialistic and radical than the Mexican or Bolivian, all three have had a common result in enhancing the political importance of the lower classes. Cuban reforms are still under way; the Mexican and Bolivian are in the process of gradual expansion, consolidation, and institutionalization. The struggle in Cuba revolves around further changes; in Mexico and Bolivia, it centers on extending the improvements won by the lower classes and fending off the thrusts of the *nouveaux riches* and a reviving older urban elite.

The current conflict elsewhere in Latin America involves a demand for recognition and a share of power, not by a new elite, but by lower-income groups who have found leaders among middle-income intellectuals and reform-minded nationalists; this has already taken place in Mexico, Bolivia, and Cuba. The problems of the ruling groups have been enormously complicated during the past two decades by a rapid increase in population that, in the past few years, has outstripped the rate of economic growth. To the drive for power has been added a drive not only to maintain, but also to improve, present living standards. Faced with this crisis, the elite of Latin America have been willing, in many instances, to make some specific concessions (especially with the specter of Castro hanging over all), but they have generally proved adamant against any basic social and political restructuring of their countries. Such reorganization would entail a decline in their relative power position and in their economic well-being. The lower classes will be satisfied with nothing less, and should the ruling classes prove unwilling, in the long run, to institute such changes peaceably, the lower classes, led by ambitious middle-class intellectuals and politicians, will eventually achieve their demands— with violence. The only questions remaining are whether or not the masses will be satisfied with evolutionary, rather than revolutionary, change; and if not, whether the traditional forces of society will prove strong enough to hold back these demands long enough to effect their own program. There is, however, a further consideration: Can these deep-seated changes be accomplished without a scapegoat for the masses to destroy?

Compared with their counterparts elsewhere in Latin America, the Mexican and Venezuelan propertied classes exercise limited power relative to other groups in the society. Of the major interest groups in Mexico, the industrial and commercial classes alone enjoy no official recognition in the dominant government party, and the landholding groups have not yet sufficiently revived to play a vital political role. Nevertheless, since 1940, the Mexican business community has exercised increasing influence upon the government. The personal and business contacts of Mexican industrialists, bankers, and merchants with leading party politicians have assisted in the attainment of business objectives. Through the various chambers of commerce and industry, the Mexican propertied groups also collectively exert their influence directly on high officials of the government. The direct line of business into party and government is checked, however, by the equally well-organized bureaucracy and labor unions, which, unlike the business groups, form integral parts of the official party. The urban elite is flourishing, but it must compromise its interests with these other powerful pressure groups.

The Venezuelan business community, including foreign capitalists in the oil- and mineral-extractive industries, supports the regime of Rómulo Betancourt, together (but not necessarily in alliance) with a majority of the labor force and most of the military. Businessmen in Venezuela have been pleased with Betancourt's moderation and have expressed their satisfaction with his rejection of a Castro-like program for their country. Many recognize that their fate rests in his hands, and that his regime, in turn, depends not on their support but on that of the military and the lower classes. Consequently, a large number of businessmen and industrialists joined with the Confederation of Venezuelan Workers (CTV) in August, 1960, in petitioning the government for assistance to both labor and management. Their program included requests for higher credit grants and faster processing of requests, a public-works program, agrarian reform, a tariff, and exchange controls. They opposed the government's austerity program, recommended by the International Monetary Fund, which advised budget balancing and tight credit. In the present fluid and often tense political situation in Venezuela, a change in regime and program could constitute only a break to the left, not to the right.

If a judgment on the influence of a pressure group can be made on the basis of government policies favoring that group, one can conclude only that from Frondizi's inauguration, in 1958, until his overthrow, in 1962, the business elements in Argentina had the confidence of top government officials. Frondizi's major policies were to make the country self-sufficient in oil and to restore order to its finances. First, in the face of bitter nationalist resentment, he invited private capital to participate in oil development under favorable contracts with the government oil monopoly. Secondly, he clamped on an austerity program that finally halted inflation (after a rise of about 150 per cent in the cost of living, with no equivalent rise in real wages). The results were impressive to the business minded, but hardly palatable to the wage earner. To stem violence, strikes, and growing lower-class unrest, his Administration used the army on several occasions. Furthermore, Frondizi, for several years, relied upon businessman Rogelio Frigerio, the celebrated *éminence grise* of Argentine politics, as one of his principal advisers. Frigerio, a leftist in the early 1930's, later rejected his youthful radicalism, apparently out of fear of the Communists and lack of confidence in the socialists. During the Perón era, he remained politically inactive and concentrated upon his various highly successful business activities. Having joined Frondizi after the fall of Perón, he is credited with engineering Frondizi's election through a pact with the Peronists. He is also credited with persuading Frondizi to abandon his ultranationalist oil policy, and to sign contracts with foreign oil companies for petroleum exploration and extraction. Frigerio, in addition, pushed hard for economic stabilization and industrial and agricultural modernization and development. He never held a Cabinet post, probably because of the opposition of the military due to his alleged friendliness to the Peronists. His basic probusiness policies were carried out, however, by businessmen in the Cabinet, such as Alvaro Alsogaray, Minister of Economics from 1959 to 1961. Alsogaray, unlike Frigerio, supported the army position for a strong stand against the Peronists.

The ouster of Frondizi by the military in March, 1962, does

not seem to have affected business interests adversely. Some businessmen, such as Dr. Alberto Gainza Paz, Argentina's leading newspaper publisher, supported the military intervention, and Alsogaray returned temporarily to the Ministry of Economics. Other anti-Peronist and antilabor conservatives were most happy to work hand in glove with the new Administration set up by the military chiefs. Despite the favorable position occupied by the business community, it must be remembered that the military is the arbiter of power, and that business interests will be heeded only as long as their interests do not conflict with those of the armed forces. Although Argentine landholders cannot be ignored politically, their influence has declined appreciably since the pre-Perón era. Since 1955, they have been assisted principally by the removal of the economic restraints placed upon them by Perón.

In Uruguay, power is divided between the urban industrial and commercial groups and the old landholding aristocrats. The former dominate Montevideo and the surrounding truck-gardening areas; the latter, the northern rural provinces. To some extent, the urban elite has come to terms with the laboring groups, conceding to them an extensive social-welfare program. It is unwilling to share political power, however, and has set itself up as arbiter of the frequent conflicts. The landholders have remained in peaceable possession, politically and economically, of their own areas, and until after World War II, the central government made little effort to extend social-welfare legislation into the rural provinces. Enforcement is still sporadic and uneven, and the rural workers have made few economic or political gains.

Chilean political parties, at least those now in control, operate in an atmosphere of political liberalism, but they represent almost exclusively the urban and rural elite groups. This is in striking contrast to the situation in Mexico, where opposition parties cannot expect impartial and free elections, but where the all-powerful official party gives heed to the interests and aspirations of all major groups in the country, albeit not equally. The primary goal of the Alessandri Administration, in Chile, is to check a disastrous inflation that has plagued the country for years. To this end, the government is composed of men from private business, or directors of state corporations who support a philosophy of private enterprise and market competition. Congress, somewhat responsive to organized labor, however, has granted moderate wage increases; and administration spokesmen blame them for the continued inflation. Despite these wage increases, the lot of the urban worker is far from enviable. Too frequently, he and his family live in slums and subsist on a diet that keeps them in a constant state of malnutrition. The lower classes, as a whole, are disunited and poorly led, and have made no major political or economic gains since the 1930's. The lot of the rural worker is worse, at least from a political point of view, since his position has scarcely changed since the time of independence.

With the army nonpolitical, and the bureaucracy and intellectuals politically in eclipse, the upper- and upper-middle-class propertied families govern Chile, permitting only minimum concessions to prevent outright revolt. The *hacendado* participates actively in the Conservative Party, and in pressure groups that promote agricultural interests. He has successfully prevented, by law, the formation of rural unions, limited agrarian reform and can easily evade paying his taxes. The business, industrial, and commercial groups in the cities belong to the Liberal and Radical parties, but recently have worked closely with the Conservatives in elections and in Congress. Wages remain low, profit margins high, and goods all too often inferior. Few political and economic leaders have any sense of social responsibility. Chilean democracy, however, does present an alternative to revolution, since the lower classes, if properly led and organized, might be able to overturn the oligarchy peaceably. Whether the changes that followed would be evolutionary or revolutionary would depend upon who had organized the masses: the Christian democrats and democratic socialists, or the Communists. The question is still very much open.

INTELLECTUALS AND STUDENTS

Everywhere in Latin America, intellectuals and students, in so far as they engage in politics, are identified with the forces struggling for change. The vast majority of the politically active students and intellectuals have been nurtured on a nationalist creed, reinforced by Marxism, in their approach to the solution of Latin America's ills. Their facile use of Marxist terminology, their hostility to private-business enterprise, their aversion to "imperialism and colonialism," their endorsement of the concept of class conflict, and their advocacy of broad and deep government control over the social and economic life of the nation attest to this intellectual formation. Many are impressed with the Soviet methods that developed a backward country—which Imperial Russia was—

into one of the two most powerful and technically advanced countries of the world, in the space of forty years. They are seeking a formula for themselves, and some hope to emulate the Soviet Union in the economic development, social reforms, and political changes that they advocate for their own countries. Most of these people are not Communists, but many are willing to work with the Communists toward the achievement of supposedly identical goals. Frequently, they are in the forefront of the battle, the mature intellectual furnishing the ideology and program content, and the student the vanguard of the rioting or rebellion that often results from their sustained agitation. Everywhere, too, except in Mexico, they are a potent political force that no government can ignore. But in no country are they the most powerful interest group, as is the army in Argentina, the propertied class in Chile, or the bureaucracy in Mexico.

Mexico has not always been an exception to the general rule that student groups and intellectuals can exert important political pressure on the government. Intellectuals actively participated in the formulation and early development of the revolution, and enjoyed positions of prestige and power from the outbreak of the revolt, in 1910, to the end of the Cárdenas Administration, in 1940. Intellectuals wrote the social program of the Constitution of 1917, counseled semiliterate military leaders such as Villa and Zapata, expounded the ideological direction of the movement, and directed the revolutionary education program of the 1920's. In the next decade, they organized and directed the labor movement, and occupied positions in the Cabinet. With the achievement of major reforms by 1940, a new and more conservative business-oriented leadership, which aimed at the consolidation of changes already achieved, emerged in Mexico. Since these new men were not eager to try additional social or political experiments, the intellectuals found themselves shunted aside. Some unrest manifested itself during the 1940's and 1950's, particularly among reform-minded students. The culmination of this unrest came in 1956, when students rioted through the streets of Mexico City, and popular indignation against the students rose to unprecedented heights. The government ended the riots and, with police and troops, broke the back of the most powerful student organizations. In 1961, minority student efforts to defy the new rector of the National University, whose program called for a cessation of student political activities, ended in complete failure. The lack of support for, and even outright popular opposition to, student disturbances in Mexico points up the degree of progress that country has made in stabilizing its political institutions, improving its economy, and achieving a more equitable distribution of its wealth and production.

Pro-Castro and anti-U.S. student demonstrations have been widespread throughout Latin America during the past three years. In such stable countries as Chile and Uruguay, students have led what little agitation there has been, directed against the United States and in behalf of Castro's revolution in Cuba. President Eisenhower's trip to South America early in 1960 was the occasion of remonstrances in both countries. Several Chilean student organizations were highly critical of the visit and addressed a letter to the U.S. Chief Executive, urging him not to intervene in Cuba. They did not, however, demonstrate. In Uruguay, students perched atop one of the buildings of the University of Montevideo waved a banner proclaiming, "Yankee, Hands Off Cuba," and shouted, "Death to Yankee Imperialism!" From another building, jeering students threw tin cans along the route of the Presidential motorcade, but police dispersed the rioters with tear gas before the dignitaries had arrived.

More serious and frequent student disturbances have shaken Haiti, Panama, and Paraguay, and students played a major role in the revolutionary movement of El Salvador from its inception in October, 1960. Educational opportunities in the two or three major cities of Panama are good to excellent by Latin American standards, largely because of the influx of U.S. capital. Unfortunately, the undeveloped and undiversified nature of the Panamanian economy offers little outlet for the education imparted. As a result, the university is a center of considerable bitterness and political radicalism. The primary targets of these pent-up emotions are, quite naturally, the U.S. citizens in the Canal Zone, with their rights, privileges, and snobbery. Furthermore, Panamanian politicians, by appeals to nationalism, deflect student animosities away from the actual source of many of their problems—the internal backwardness of the country—toward the alleged outside aggressor. As a consequence, students are in the forefront, making demands of little, or no, material benefit to themselves or to the country, such as the right to fly the Panamanian flag in the Zone and concessions for Panamanian businessmen in the Zone market. Logical arguments have made little impression on these hotly nationalistic students.

In Paraguay and Haiti, student groups, though small and impotent in the face of their dictators' military might, comprise the

most cohesive and determined opposition forces to the present regime. In mid-1959, Paraguayan students demonstrated for the
ouster of the Chief of Police in Asunción, and attempted unsuc-
cessfully to organize an insurgent youth and student group within
the ruling Colorado Party. As a result of these activities, the President, General Alfredo Stroessner, clamped on a state of siege.
At year's end, the exiled student organization—The Fourteenth of
May (named after Paraguay's independence day), with a membership of about 200—attempted to launch an invasion from Argentina, proclaiming a program based on Castro's reforms in Cuba.
The rebellion was easily crushed, and severe repressions followed.
As a result, Paraguay has been relatively calm, despite a worsening
economic crisis.

Student unrest in Haiti seems to stem from President François
Duvalier's conflict with the clergy, who control much of the educational system of the country. Duvalier claims the clergy are dis-
loyal to the government. Haiti, like Paraguay, has been experiencing economic difficulties, and the students have attempted to
capitalize on growing discontent to win over labor and other groups
in Port-au-Prince. Although the upper classes look with favor
upon student propaganda and agitation activities, these have
not yet won broad-based backing. Early in 1961, the student
movement began to acquire an anti-Yankee tinge, because of U.S.
support for the government. Pro-Castroites are becoming more
prominent, although the majority of students belong to Catholic
youth organizations. Duvalier has, so far, remained calm in the
face of student boycotts against the schools, on the grounds, first,
that the students are hurting only themselves, and second, that the
laboring class, and the "blacks" in general, are basically sympathetic to him rather than to their traditional enemies, the mulatto
elite, from which most of the students are drawn. Student violence,
which began to erupt early in 1963, has, however, frightened
Duvalier into taking extraordinary personal-security measures, including the arrest, torture, and execution of student opponents. In
Haiti, as in Paraguay, the final outcome seems to depend upon the
military, who must be kept satisfied or divided. Empty treasuries
could overthrow both dictators.

Student agitation in El Salvador led to the rebellion in October,
1960, against President José María Lemus, only the most recent
of a long line of military semidictators. Colonel Lemus' attempts to
remove the students from political activities, and his curtailment of
civil rights, provoked a coup of military and civilian leaders. Pro-

Castro students strongly supported the new government, and leftists of varying degrees initiated a program to organize the *campesinos,* and to lead them in a movement for land reform reminiscent of Cuba's. However, in January, 1961, more moderate elements in the military and in the upper classes became alarmed over the leftward drift, and overthrew the government in a second coup. There was no thought of restoring Lemus; in fact, the second junta, and the constitutional regime that succeeded it in the spring of 1962, continued the earlier reforms, despite the vigorous protest of the oligarchy. Nevertheless, student leaders at the National University remain distrustful of the government, and form a vital sector of the opposition.

Of all the countries of Latin America, Venezuela faces probably the most serious problem of student unrest. The Venezuelan revolution of 1958 and the subsequent Betancourt Administration have had, and still have, a tremendous reservoir of good will toward the Cuban revolution's announced goals for social and economic reform, if not toward its political and international policies. There is much identification between the overthrow of dictators and the introduction of a reform program in both countries. During most of 1959, Betancourt and Castro, and their respective governments, were on the best of terms. By the end of 1959, however, the Venezuelans began to show concern over the virulence of Cuba's anti-U.S. position, and its *rapprochement* with the Soviet bloc. Betancourt's counsel of caution was greeted by Castro with vituperation, and since early 1960, the two have been estranged. Diplomatic relations were broken late in 1961.

The Venezuelan revolutionary program has proceeded much more slowly and moderately than the Cuban. Most Venezuelans, although not satisfied with the progress made, are not yet sufficiently discouraged to turn against the regime. However, certain impatient student groups, egged on by left-wing politicians, have harried the Administration since early 1960, when it became apparent that a break with Castro was in the offing. In March of that year, 2,000 demonstrators, many of them students, tried to arouse popular support by marching through the streets of Caracas shouting, "Death to Yankee Imperialism!" and "Cuba, Yes! Yankees, No!" Organized labor and the lower classes in general did not respond, and in comparison with other political rallies, the turnout was considered poor.

Student radicalism showed up simultaneously in university elections held that same month. Of the 6,000 university students, fewer than half belong to political parties, but this minority controls student affairs at the university and exerts great influence on university administration. The student political parties are directly dependent upon the national political parties, although the students are somewhat more given to violence and precipitous action. In the election, the Communist Party won full control over student affairs in two faculties, and in five others shared control with President Betancourt's Democratic Action Party. In April, however, student support rallied behind the regime, in the face of a right-wing military rebellion that was promptly crushed. Student agitation then died down until late in November, when a group of radical students, led by left-wing politicians, rioted in support of striking telephone-company workers. The government quickly settled the labor dispute, but the students (from high schools as well as the university), now armed and shouting pro-Castro slogans, continued their agitation for the overthrow of Betancourt. Only a few workers joined them. Fortifying themselves on the university grounds, the students referred to their defense positions as Stalingrad, but the appearance of army tanks brought their surrender within a few days. Since early 1961, the political power of the leftist intellectuals has declined. They were able to muster only weak opposition to President Kennedy's visit to the country in December, 1961. Leftist military revolts in two naval bases in mid-1962 were easily crushed, and aroused virtually no response in Caracas, the seat of major left-wing opposition to the government. To the present, they continue to inspire terrorist activities, but they pose no immediate threat to the Betancourt regime.

LABOR

In only one country of Latin America today, Bolivia, is organized labor, urban and rural, the leading pressure group; in another, Venezuela, labor is probably as important as the military; and in two others, Mexico and Costa Rica, labor plays an important, but somewhat lesser, political role. In other countries that are undertaking industrial development—such as the ABC powers and Uruguay—urban labor can force wage increases (at times, however, insufficient to keep pace with the rising cost of living) and make its voice heard, if not heeded, on a variety of issues. But in none of these can it be said that labor has an important share in political power. In several of the Central American countries, labor organizations are just beginning to exert some pressure; in others, there is hardly the semblance of a labor union.

The Bolivian revolution of 1952 destroyed the regular army, removed power and wealth from the old mining and landed aristocracy, and conferred power upon the workers and peasants by organizing them into unions, arming them as militia, and incorporating them into a political party that has maintained a monopoly of the reins of government. Following the revolution, the government expropriated the tin mines and other industries, until today more than 80 per cent of industry is in the hands of the state. This close union of labor with politics, however, has not augured well for either side. The moderate leaders of the official party recognize the need for an austerity program, a stable financial position, and greater discipline in the labor force—in order to obtain the foreign capital necessary to increase production in many lines, and thus to create a viable economy. Such a program would entail a decrease in consumption for those workers in state-owned enterprises who have tasted the fruits of victory in the form of increased purchasing power. Their appetites have been whetted for more, not less, and modest attempts to reduce their benefits have already been bitterly resisted. Thus far, their leaders have held their loyalty, but the rank and file cannot be pushed much further before they turn to more radical leaders, who will promise them what they want.

In Mexico, as in most other parts of Latin America, rural labor is the weakest of the numerically large interest groups. *Campesinos* are organized into a national confederation and form one of the three sectors of the official party. Agrarian leaders hold a few posts in the government and seats in the legislature. Government economists have long understood the need for a balanced economy, and several past administrations have tried to provide for some of their most basic requirements. Accomplishments have not kept pace with demands and needs, however, and millions of *campesinos* still live in the direst misery. Urban labor has fared much better. After reaching the height of its power in the 1930's, it began to decline, relatively, in the 1940's, as business interests revived and the bureaucracy gained power. Labor, of course, constitutes another sector of the official party, and its leaders occupy government positions and legislative seats. Their primary job appears to be liaison work between the government and the labor rank and file. Well organized and concentrated as it is, Mexican labor today occupies a power position just behind the bureaucracy and the business groups. Its counsel must be heard, and an approach must be made toward meeting its demands for wage and benefit increases.

Labor in Argentina today, whether Peronist or not, feels betrayed. Arturo Frondizi, while campaigning for the Presidency in 1958, promised the labor unions a prominent place in determining the country's course. However, in his four years in office, he followed a program of austerity, budget balancing, and wage controls that worked to the immediate detriment of the lower classes. Many of his leading Cabinet officers were drawn from the business community, and to contain labor's drive for power, he was forced to apply army pressure behind the scenes at all times, and openly on occasion. As President, he appeared to be unable or unwilling to buck these conservative and traditional forces in order to improve the lot of the laboring classes, whose political support he needed. The purchasing power and living standards of many families were substantially reduced. Members of labor unions forced through some wage increases, but they were not sufficient to keep up with the continued inflation. Others, such as pensioners, teachers, and civil servants, were unable to exert effective pressure to raise their incomes.

The labor movement itself is split into three main parts: the Peronists, the anti-Peronists, and the independent unions. As a political force, the Peronist unions and their sympathizers have long been a floating mass without political attachment. Frondizi's refusal, until early 1962, to sanction the formation of a Peronist-type political party alienated them from his Intransigent Radicals, and their 2 million votes were often cast in blank or on behalf of more nationalist and radical politicians. Frondizi's failure not only to win over the Peronists, but also to retain what labor strength he originally possessed, was evident as early as February, 1961, when a by-election to a Senate seat from Buenos Aires Province was won by a Socialist candidate with Peronist and Communist support. In an attempt to force a showdown with the Peronists— and apparently overestimating his own popularity with labor— Frondizi authorized the legalization of the Justicialist Front, a neo-Peronist party, for the March, 1962, elections. The Justicialists won a series of smashing victories, polling about 2.5 million votes, with strong labor support. Frondizi's misjudgment cost him the Presidency, since the military insisted on his deposition and labor refused to stir itself in his defense.

In Venezuela, although labor must share its power with the military, and to a lesser extent with business, its political position is infinitely better than that of labor in Argentina. The Betancourt government has engaged in a reform program that is much more moderate than Cuba's, and even though it is interested in financial stability, it has not had to impose the degree of austerity that prevails in Argentina. Although the economies of both countries were harmed by their respective dictators, Venezuela's greater wealth per capita has permitted a development program with less financial stringency. The powerful Venezuelan Confederation of Labor is intimately linked with, though not subservient to, the official Democratic Action Party, and most of the rank and file, as well as the leaders, have continued to support the regime, despite criticism from students and the political left. Labor refused to join the student riots of November, 1960, and in the following month supported leaders who demanded a diplomatic break with Cuba. Betancourt demurred at that time, on the grounds that he wanted to keep the Venezuelan Embassy in Havana open as an asylum for those fleeing the regime. In striking contrast to group relations in Argentina, Venezuelan labor cooperates rather well with business interests and the military. With the former, labor negotiated a new three-year oil contract without a strike, or even the threat of one, in February, 1960; and with the latter, they cooperated in quashing the attempted rightist revolt the following April.

In the larger, more industrialized, and more developed states, organized labor as a political force is almost entirely urban. (In Brazil, however, a radical peasant-league movement is in process of organizing and expanding.) In some countries, such as Chile, rural labor is prohibited by law from organizing. In others, it may be organized, but exerts little or no political power. By way of contrast, in the smaller, more underdeveloped countries—as for example, in Central America—labor groups, where organized, are often stronger in rural than in urban areas. In these countries, rural workers are employed by foreign enterprises such as the United Fruit Company, and therefore can obtain government support more easily, both in organizing and in obtaining wage increases and fringe benefits.

Labor organizations are virtually nonexistent in Nicaragua and, until late 1960, were illegal in rural areas of El Salvador. In the latter, however, between the coup of October, 1960, and that of January, 1961, organizational efforts were carried on by pro-Communists and *Fidelistas*. Since that time, moderate reform groups appear to be leading the rural labor movement in El Salvador. Urban labor is fairly well organized, but the Directorate of the countercoup of January, 1961, did not invite this group to participate in the plans to restore constitutional government.

More typical are the cases of the four other Central American republics. In all four, United Fruit and/or Standard Fruit have large land concessions, and employ hundreds to work their plantations. The governments, to counteract growing nationalist criticism, have supported improved wages and living conditions for the nationals who work for these foreign-owned companies. President Mario Echandi intervened to settle a strike early in 1960 on United Fruit Company lands in Costa Rica, and Panamanian President Roberto Chiari stepped into similar contract negotiations in his country early in 1961 to prevent a work stoppage and possible violence. Wage increases were won in both instances. Of these two countries, Costa Rica is more responsive to labor demands. A Catholic labor union (the strongest in the country) was formed following the revolution of 1948, and social-welfare legislation was passed. In Costa Rica, labor is a political force to be reckoned with by any government. In Panama, on the other hand, labor is virtually excluded from political power, although it can gain economic concessions from business. Indeed, organized political groups constitute only about 10 to 15 per cent of the population. This political phenomenon was emphasized by the fact that in the Presidential election of 1960, none of the candidates addressed himself to the interests of the 85 to 90 per cent of the population that comprised the lower-income groups.

THE MILITARY

The military in Latin America is composed largely, but not exclusively, of the national armies. Most countries have at least token air forces and navies, and some—notably those of Brazil, Argentina, and Chile—are of sufficient strength to be seriously considered in terms of their political power and influence. Naval officers, continuing a tradition of long standing, usually come from old families, and represent the conservative political tradition. Army and air-force officers, sons of middle- and upper-class urban families, more often reflect the new drives toward nationalism and, increasingly, toward social and economic reform. Motivated at times altruistically, the "reforming" military have more frequently used the lower classes simply to catapult themselves to power. On other occasions, once in power, they have abandoned their reform program, fearful of opening a Pandora's box of labor and *campesino* organizations (and consequent social complexities) that they felt they could not control. Perón tried to control the forces that he released; Pérez Jiménez tried to slam the lid shut. Both were destroyed by their inability to govern a modern nation with all its social, technological, and economic problems.

Today, the armed forces exercise political influence, in widely varying degrees, in almost every country in Latin America; but in only a few of the more primitive does this entail obvious, and almost singlehanded, control of the government. Examples of the latter type are Paraguay and Nicaragua, whose armed forces are kept well content by their respective *caudillos,* through liberal budgetary allotments and special privileges and perquisites. On the other hand, the military in several countries have become highly professionalized, and to a large degree nonpolitical. Costa Rica and Bolivia virtually abolished their old regular armies after World War II, but Bolivia subsequently created a rural militia and a new army to support the government and the official party. Uruguay and Mexico have subjected their armies to civilian control. In all four countries, budgetary percentages for defense expenditures have been substantially reduced.

Cuba presents a unique situation, in that a radical revolution is still in the process of developing. The old army was destroyed, and a new revolutionary army was created. However, since the new army itself proved untrustworthy in the light of the regime's radicalism and ties to the Soviet bloc, Fidel Castro created a mass militia, armed and partially trained by the Soviets. A later reorganization of military and semimilitary forces merged the most professional elements of the militia with the army. The remaining militia units were largely relegated to police duties. Soviet military personnel in Cuba as of January, 1963, totaled about 17,000, as compared with some 15,000 present on the island during the October, 1962, missile crisis. Though most of the Soviet troops are there for the purpose of training, some 5,000 are combat troops whose functions are not entirely clear. All armed forces are under the control of Raúl Castro (Fidel's brother), Minister of Defense, and constitute one of the primary institutions supporting the revolutionary government.

In Chile and Colombia, the military operate with at least semi-autonomy from the civilian government. After unhappy experiences with their excursions into political affairs, however, both have retreated to their former professional status. President Alessandri, of Chile, with little open opposition from his own military, is today one of the leading exponents in Latin America for an arms-reduction agreement. In late 1959, highly critical of Peru's purchase of warships from Great Britain, he proposed that the Inter-American Conference scheduled for the spring of 1960 consider plans to halt what he turned the "arms race" in Latin America, and to use these resources for economic development. When the Quito Conference was indefinitely postponed, he sought to promote a special conference on the arms issue. Although Alessandri's ideas have met with sympathetic verbal responses, both in the United States and elsewhere in Latin America, his proposed conference has not materialized, and little concrete action has been taken to implement his proposals.

In most of the remaining countries of Latin America, the military are deeply involved in partisan political activities, but the officer corps are deeply split over a number of major issues. The 1961 governmental crises in Brazil and Ecuador brought the issue of constitutionality of succession to the fore. Among the military in both countries, the issue aroused dissension, but the predominant group in both countries opted for adherence to legal and constitutional procedures. Similarly, the coup attempted in January, 1962, by General Rodríguez Echavarría in the Dominican Republic failed when his subordinates refused to support him. In the Peruvian and Argentine crises of 1962, the results were different. The Peruvian military could not accept the victory at the polls of their hated political enemy, APRA. The army nullified the elections, overthrew the government, and established a military junta in July. Significantly, the junta promised the re-establishment of constitutional government as quickly as possible. In Argentina, the military had been seriously divided since 1958, but the moderate elements in the army prevailed in their support of constitutional government until the Peronist political victories of March, 1962. The balance then shifted to the rightist *"gorilas,"* who joined with the more conservative navy officers to overthrow President Arturo Frondizi. The most interesting aspect of those confusing weeks in late March was the attempt of the military to preserve at least the outward semblance of constitutional procedure in transferring power from Frondizi to his successor, José Guido. Again, during the rebellion in the spring of 1963, the military tried to maintain the constitutional framework.

In addition to being divided on the issue of nationalism, the military of Latin America disagree among themselves over the role of government in the economy; some advocate a high degree of socialization; others speak out for private enterprise. Furthermore, they are split, to some extent, on the Cuban issue. The dominant voice in Argentina has pressed the government for a strong anti-Castro position, but some of the leading officers in Brazil support efforts to use the Castro issue to pry further aid from the United States. Recognizing their lack of unity, realizing their political limitations in a complex society, and understanding the strength of new civilian groups, the military—in the more developed countries —hesitate to seize power openly except in the gravest crises. They have no stomach for street fighting against labor, students, and other urban opposition groups.

François Duvalier controls Haiti by his appeal for "black" support against the mulatto elite. This division in Haitian society carries over into the military—the National Guard. By playing upon these animosities, Duvalier has thus far been able to control the National Guard and obtain the acquiescence of the business community of Port-au-Prince, the center of political activity. Student and Church opposition to his regime erupted in 1960, but during 1961 was successfully quelled. Discontent among numerous groups has been rising so rapidly since early 1963 that Duvalier's regime is seriously threatened for the first time since he took office in 1957.

Rómulo Betancourt of Venezuela has been the subject of repeated attacks from extremists since he assumed office, in 1959. Although the military has been traditionally hostile to reform, most of the officers supported the move to overthrow Pérez Jiménez in 1958, and accepted the election of Betancourt, a moderate leftist. Extreme right-wing elements in the army attempted revolt early in 1960, and there were uprisings in some leftist-led marine and naval units during 1962, but the bulk of the military rallied overwhelmingly behind the government. Student disorders at the end of 1960 met with similar loyal troop support. Labor's solid backing of the regime and the continued government sympathy toward military requests have probably contributed to the military's acceptance of Betancourt. In addition, the President has adopted a moderate program and his anti-Communist and anti-Castro position appears to offer the strongest barrier to a Castro or crypto-Communist regime in Venezuela. With the lesson of the failure of the military regime of Pérez Jiménez, the Venezuelan armed forces obviously feel that they cannot go it alone, but would probably try it again, if necessary, to prevent an extreme leftist victory.

Of the larger, more populous, and more highly developed countries of Latin America, Argentina unquestionably has the most politically influential military forces. Well organized and well armed, the military, despite some internal differences, are the single most powerful political group in Argentina. They cannot, however, totally ignore such other pressure groups as businessmen, landholders, and workers—who are also organized, and determined to maintain their economic interests.

The military's current position stems from developments of the recent historical past. When Perón came to power, in the mid-1940's, he built his political edifice on labor and the military, and played them off against each other and against his political opposition. He ruthlessly suppressed hostile members of the managerial class, whether urban or rural, and though he did not intentionally destroy them as a class, he drastically weakened them politically. Labor, once unified, was reduced to subservience under hand-picked leaders. Perón's material benefits to labor, by way of wages and fringe benefits, were supplemented by his arousing in them a sense of importance, as well as participation in the political life of the country (something the lower classes had never before experienced). Millions were won over to him in this way, and many remained loyal despite the obvious economic decline and the growing political tyranny evident by the mid-1950's. However, other segments of labor had begun to lose confidence in their leader, so that by the time the army revolt occurred, in 1955, labor was split. Consequently, when the dictatorship was overthrown, the military possessed not only power and a 'degree of unity, but great prestige, as the principal force in Perón's downfall. Almost by default, the Argentine military controlled the new provisional government and prepared the country for its return to constitutional government.

Both the actions and the many pronouncements of the Provisional President, General Pedro Aramburu, make it obvious that the army command did not feel qualified to govern Argentina. Aramburu, as quickly as possible, set up a schedule for Presidential and congressional elections, and proceeded most cautiously in adopting domestic and foreign policies that might bind or embarrass the constitutional administration that would succeed him. So anxious were the military to surrender political control that they accepted the candidacy and election of Arturo Frondizi, of the Intransigent Radicals—supported, as he was, by Peronists and Communists—and ensured not only his installation as President, but also the installation of his followers as the dominant party in Congress. In his farewell address, President Aramburu warned the military to uphold constitutional order, but to refrain from active participation in political life. Some months later, Aramburu urged that the Peronists be permitted to organize a legal party, and that labor unions be freed from the obligation of belonging to a Perón-style central labor organization.

After Aramburu's retirement from the Presidency, control of the armed forces passed into more conservative hands, and his advice was for a time disregarded. Not only did the army not remove itself from politics, but for about two years, it immersed itself progressively deeper. Though somewhat tolerant of Peronist voters and their political aspirations in 1958, the military were adamant in their opposition to a Peronist recovery of power, either through its own political organization, or in coalition with acceptable political parties or groups. On numerous occasions, the armed forces pressured Frondizi to adopt anti-Peronist measures.

Obviously, there were splits in the armed forces, and they have deepened since 1958. Only a small minority are pro-Perón. When a handful of army officers attempted rebellion in November, 1960, in three provincial towns, there was no response elsewhere. All other troops and their officers remained loyal, and the uprising was suppressed with little difficulty. On the extreme right of the officer corps, there is another minority, larger than the pro-Perón group, that would like to assume direct control of the country for an indefinite period of time. It is opposed by the great majority of air force officers, but finds support among naval officers, who are traditionally conservative and fanatically opposed to Peronism and labor unions. The majority of army officers, however, believe that the proper role of the military is one of stabilization and moderation.

The extremists, personified by the former Provisional Vice-President, retired Vice Admiral Isaac Rojas, violently oppose the readmission of the Peronist rank and file into active politics, and tend to support those business interests that advocate holding the line on wages and other labor benefits. The moderates, long led by Aramburu, believe that the Peronist rank and file must be assimilated into Argentine political life to promote national stability. For as long as these rivalries split the armed forces, President Frondizi was able to outmaneuver his military chiefs; when they united, as they did in demanding the diplomatic break with Cuba, they were able to force the President's hand.

The elections of March, 1962, with their startling demonstration of the strength of the Peronists, after they had been outlawed for more than six years, upset the delicate balances of forces within the military establishment, as well as within the larger context of

Argentine politics. Frondizi's archfoe, Vice Admiral Isaac Rojas, demanded the President's resignation, and when Frondizi proved obstinate, Rojas gathered support from all the services to effect a *coup d'état*. Aramburu's last-minute plea for the preservation of constitutional order evoked little favorable response from his fellow officers when civilian elements refused to rally to Frondizi. To preserve a façade of constitutionality, the armed-forces leaders prevailed upon the presiding officer of the Senate, José Guido, to accept the Presidency. But once Guido was sworn in, the military demonstrated their control of national politics. Guido was swiftly forced to nullify the March elections, to dissolve Congress itself, and to order all political parties reorganized. During the rest of 1962, the military were in thinly veiled and unchallenged control of Argentina, with the right-wing extremists maneuvering to establish a military dictatorship. Moderate elements in the army, supported by the air force, successfully challenged the bid for power in September. Early in 1963, the moderates, who seemed firmly in control, were preparing for the return of constitutional government. But fear of the Peronistas precipitated still another uprising, in April, led by naval forces. With the army extremists tightly contained by the moderate majority, the navy rebels were forced to come to terms. By virtue of vetoing certain Peronist-backed candidates, the military leaders were able to hold elections on July 7, which paved the way for the re-establishment of constitutional government, under President Arturo Illia.

CONCLUSIONS

It is obvious that the power structure in Latin America, in terms of pressure groups, is one of enormous variety and complexity. It is also in process of change. Only a few countries have had so thoroughgoing a social revolution (bloody or bloodless) that new groups have been brought to power and the old elite, with its traditions reaching back to colonial times, has been displaced. In several countries—particularly, but not exclusively, in the larger, wealthier, and more populous ones—some innovations have been introduced into the system; but these have consisted, for the most part, of concessions by the old elite to the newer groups, which have only whetted their appetites for more. In none of the countries of this second group have the lower classes approached even relative satisfaction. The question remains whether or not the elites are willing, and able, to make the required further concessions to prevent Castro-type revolutions in their own backyards. In grossly underdeveloped and nondiversified economies, the danger is great, but not so immediate. At the same time, however, there is little inclination on the part of the ruling families to abet the erosion of their power position, social status, and economic holdings.

Although Latin American interest groups, new and old, display considerable similarity from country to country in their political and economic philosophies—as well as in their specific goals and objectives—there are significant variations in the pattern. Furthermore, the power and influence that each exercises varies tremendously. In every country, virulent nationalism crosses group lines, economic independence is a national goal, and improvement in living standards for everyone is at least piously proclaimed. The policies advocated to achieve these goals, however, are frequently seriously divisive factors in most countries. A few have worked out compromises; a few have solved the problem by revolution.

Propertied groups, a powerful factor in most countries, are reluctant to change the basic socio-economic organization of their societies, although many pursue economic policies that will, in turn, force basic changes. Organized labor and other lower-income groups, as well as students and certain leftist-inclined intellectuals, are driving for sweeping change. Churchmen and the military are split—some reformist, some traditionalist—but the trend in both is against direct involvement in politics, and toward rapid economic development and social change (albeit with some misgivings). The middle-income groups are still too small and too greatly divided internally to constitute by themselves the determining political force in any country. Nevertheless, they are of great political significance in such key countries as Mexico, Argentina, and Chile. The middle-income groups in Brazil are in the process of rapid development, and this is having an important effect upon the political system. In all these countries, the middle class exercises greater influence on policy-making than on the choice of officeholders, chiefly because of its role in manning the burgeoning government bureaucracies.

5. Political Parties

The power groups that quickly manifested themselves in all parts of Latin America, with the achievement of independence from Spain, soon began to form themselves into political factions. Unstable and poorly organized at first, they slowly evolved into recognizable political parties, with leaders, platforms, and programs of action. Because of the limited number of politically active individuals in nineteenth-century Latin America, the interest groups were few in number, and those with common bonds formed the nuclei of the political parties. By and large, the clergy and the members of upper-class families who wanted to preserve their traditional social patterns furnished the leadership for the conservative parties. Their opponents—urban intellectuals, small businessmen, and professional people—organized and led the liberal parties. The lower-income groups, in both city and countryside, had no political party that represented their interests.

LIBERALS VERSUS CONSERVATIVES

Party goals of an earlier day reflected the interests of the politically active minority in the population. During the wars for independence, both conservative and liberal patriots used the words "liberty," "democracy," and "equality," but interpreted them for their own interests and ends. To the landed aristocracy, they meant freedom from Spanish overlordship and Spanish monopoly of political power and position. They did not mean improved living conditions, land, and suffrage for the peons. Once independence had been achieved, one heard less of these terms, but they never entirely disappeared from the conservative lexicon. The churchmen in this alliance seldom if ever used these terms. Identifying democ-

149

racy with political liberalism and the French Revolution, they abhorred and condemned these words, but tolerated their use by their landed allies as simple political jargon. The conservative parties of the nineteenth century also sought to preserve the traditional role of the Church in society, and supported the many rights, privileges, and immunities that the clergy had enjoyed from Spanish times. Moreover, the conservative parties pledged themselves to protect Catholic doctrine and religious practices against hostile criticism, both domestic and foreign, and to keep education primarily in accord with Catholic principles and teaching. Finally, the conservative parties attempted to hold the military leaders within their ranks by supporting military privileges as they supported Church privileges. Army officers of upper-class antecedents easily allied themselves with lay and clerical conservatives, but ambitious officers from all classes often found it personally advantageous to support liberal parties from time to time. This switch in allegiance is particularly noticeable in countries in which a strong military caste system did not develop, or developed slowly.

As the conservative parties represented tradition, except for political ties to the mother country, the liberal parties represented change—the thrust of new groups for power, social position, and wealth. The liberals were almost always anticlerical, sometimes anti-Catholic, and frequently antimilitaristic. Since the Church and the army represented institutions of the old order, the liberal parties sought not only the curtailment of their privileges, but strict government control and limitation over their members. Often, this meant specifically the expulsion of the clergy from politics, the expropriation of Church lands, the reduction of the size of the armed forces, and the removal of clerical and military judicial privileges. It should be noted that while the liberals demanded the distribution of land in the name of "progress," they attacked only the *latifundia* of the Church, even in countries where private estates were entailed. For them, as well as for the conservatives, land alone could bestow social position, and wherever the liberals achieved political power, they soon acquired land—by purchase from impecunious landholders, by expropriation from the Church, or through intermarriage with landed families.

Other issues besides the urban-rural struggle for power, the position of the clergy and the military, and the quest for social recognition by urban groups marked the liberal-conservative conflicts of the nineteenth century. Many of these, however, reflected local conditions as they affected the primary groups in the contest.

In Mexico, for example, the conservatives were centralists, and the liberals federalists; in Argentina, conservatives were at times federalists, and liberals at times centralists, but not consistently throughout the nineteenth century. In most countries, the conservatives supported strong executive authority, while the liberals generally supported legislative supremacy. However, the Chilean liberals under Balmaceda supported a strong executive against the legislature, and on numerous occasions, liberals elsewhere supported thinly disguised or outright dictators. Party platforms seldom revealed an adequate picture of the practices of the party in power.

Since the conservatives were firmly in the saddle in virtually every country of Latin America within a few years of independence, the liberals were frustrated in their initial efforts to carry out their reform programs. Having no past experience with electoral practices and customs, the populace in most countries acquiesced in the seizure and maintenance of power by brute force. Chile and Brazil, once the turmoil following independence had abated, were two noteworthy exceptions. In both countries, the reigning conservatives made accommodations, and eventually shared power, with their liberal opponents. Elsewhere, the liberals fought their way to power through civil war. In the latter cases, the Church conflict often embittered the struggle, and many years elapsed before accommodations could be made between the contending groups. However, as the liberals established themselves in one country after another, by force or by vote, the once-quarreling factions found not only that they could coexist, but also that, at times, they had to work together to preserve what the one had gained, and what the other had salvaged, from their controversy. A new political specter was rising to haunt them both: lower- and middle-class drives for power that had been created in the major countries by growing urbanization and the beginnings of industrialization. By the turn of the century, most liberal parties represented the urban elite, and most conservative parties the landed elite—and both groups were under pressure to broaden the base of political power, and to share more equitably the fruits of developing economies.

PERSONALISM AND NATIONALISM

Before considering the rise of the new reform parties that have dominated the politics of Latin America during the twentieth century, two further points must be made concerning the traditional parties. First, despite their formation around group interests, they were seldom firmly institutionalized, and more often than not bore the imprint of a powerful leader or leaders. The liberal party of Mexico in the 1850's and 1860's reflected the ideas of Benito Juárez and his followers, but that same liberal party, from the mid-1870's, was the creature of the dictator Porfirio Díaz, who eventually killed it. The conservative party of Ecuador in the mid-nineteenth century reflected the religiosity of García Moreno; the conservative party of Chile reflected the more secular views of strong man Diego Portales and his successors. So completely did the parties come under control of popular *caudillos,* at times, that their roles were reversed, the conservatives advocating change and free elections, the liberals upholding the *status quo.* Party labels became meaningless. Perhaps the most conspicuous of these aberrations was the "liberal" dictatorship of Antonio Guzmán Blanco, in Venezuela. His only claims to liberalism were his exile of the Archbishop of Caracas and the implementation of an anticlerical program similar to those elsewhere in Latin America, from Mexico to Chile. Ironically, the latter deed was prompted not so much by party principle or conviction on the part of the dictator as by his personal quarrel with the Archbishop.

Second, the traditional and personalist parties and factions, primarily concerned with their internal struggles for power and wealth, were concerned with foreign affairs only intermittently throughout the nineteenth century. Nationalism seldom went beyond the bounds of simple patriotism and devotion to country. In its earliest manifestations, it was directed against the mother country for the attainment and protection of political independence. Even before the separation had been successfully completed, nationalism moved into a second phase, the disruption of the large Spanish kingdoms into their component parts. Nueva Granada, despite Bolívar's efforts to maintain unity, split into three countries before the Liberator's death. So too did the viceroyalties of Peru and La Plata. Mexico held together, but attempts to assimilate Central America failed, and the area eventually disintegrated into five quarreling and backward states. Border disputes troubled the whole of Spanish America and led to several serious wars. In these internal and international difficulties involving nationalist issues, party labels meant little. Portuguese America attained its independence with a minimum of hostility to the mother country, and experienced relatively weak separatist movements, which were easily suppressed. Once independence had been attained and unity assured, it turned its interests, in the nineteenth century, to rounding out its borders and provoking quarrels or disputes with virtually every one of its Spanish American neighbors. On these questions, party and factional differences were negligible.

The widening commercial contacts of Latin America, coupled with the growth and expansion of U.S. power and territory, introduced a third stage in the development of Latin American nationalism. To counter the overwhelming influence of the United States in the Caribbean area, and the economic dependence on European powers in South America, the traditionalist elite in a number of the larger countries began to espouse economic developments such as industrialization, modern communications systems, and modernized agriculture. They expected not only to gain personal profit, but also to strengthen their countries economically and politically, and thus, by avoiding colonial dependence upon a greater power, ward off absorption. To this end, they invited foreign private capital, often with privileges and concessions, to invest in their countries. At times, they encouraged investors from several European countries, as well as from the United States, so that no one group could dominate the economy of the nation. The governing elite usually profited from these enterprises either directly, through sinecures in the foreign companies, or indirectly, through tax relief, since the companies in time bore the major part of the host's financial burden.

THE EMERGENCE OF REFORM PARTIES

The response of the traditional parties to the new pressures from below, largely urban, varied considerably in the different countries at the turn of the century. The conglomeration of factions that supported Díaz of Mexico (they could hardly be called a political party) resolutely turned their faces against concession, whether political, social, or economic—with the result that they and their radical opponents, the new liberal party of the Magón brothers, were all swept away in the violence of ten years of civil war. More stable and permanent political parties did not emerge until the 1930's, but these were products of the revolution, with few roots in the past. At the other end of the political spectrum stands Uruguay, culturally homogeneous and small in population and territory. Uruguay's Colorado (liberal) Party gained dominance toward the close of the nineteenth century, and maintained it in the face of repeated Blanco (conservative) Party uprisings. In the first decade of the twentieth century, the parties began to reach a political compromise, in which the Colorados controlled Montevideo and the national government, while the Blancos retained control over their rural strongholds. The former, under the enlightened leadership of José Batlle y Ordóñez, undertook the reorientation of traditional Uruguayan liberalism toward modern reformism; this included strong doses of socialistic experiments, but with a minimum of class conflict. Batlle pumped government money into the economy, bought out foreign capitalists, and introduced a far-reaching social and economic reform program that placed Uruguay in the vanguard among the nations of the world. Two significant points stand out. First, the reform was achieved without violence or dictatorship (in fact, at the very moment that these phenomena were ending). Second, the reforms applied largely to the urban population, particularly to that of Montevideo. Until after World War II, virtually nothing was done to assist the rural proletariat in the domains of the Blancos.

Some countries did not respond at all to the demands of new groups. They did not experience, and have not yet experienced, this period of transition, though reform-minded political parties have been formed almost everywhere in Latin America. In the Dominican Republic, they were in exile until the assassination of the elder Trujillo, in the spring of 1961. In Paraguay, they have operated both within and outside the country. In Nicaragua, they have been ineffectual. In Haiti, they have been, at best, personalist factions that have followed a leader who promises a new deal. In several of the larger countries, such as Venezuela, Colombia, and Peru, reform parties, or reform-minded factions of the old parties, had brief tastes of power in the 1940's, but until recently, they have had little hope of implementing their social program. The traditional power groups, sometimes under new party labels, firmly controlled the political situation to the middle of the twentieth century.

Among the remaining larger countries of Latin America, some compromises were effected. New stirrings in Argentina could be detected as early as the 1890's, when a group of immigrants' sons banded together with small merchants in Buenos Aires to form the Radical Civic Union (UCR), a mildly liberal group that demanded fair elections and the broadening of the suffrage. For years, fraudulent voting and ballot counting prevented a Radical victory at the polls. Following an initial flirtation with the resort to force, the Radicals, after 1905, under the leadership of Hipólito Yrigoyen, turned to a policy of abstaining from the polls. This tactic apparently paid off, in an Argentina that was becoming more and more proud of its political maturity and stability, its economic prosperity, and its growing status in the community of nations. In 1912, a conservative President, Roque Sáenz Peña, forced through the conservative-controlled legislature a secret compulsory-voting law affecting all males from eighteen years of age. The next three Presidential elections were won by Radical candidates. Though composed largely of urban- and middle-class elements, the party attracted lower-class support by promises of labor and welfare legislation. Unfortunately, the party promised more than it was able or willing to provide. By 1930, it had lost prestige by the corruption it had permitted, by its lack of performance on social and economic issues, and, particularly, by President Yrigoyen's inability to govern in the face of the grave economic crisis of the time. A military-backed conservative coup swept the Radicals from power. Despite continued conservative control throughout the 1930's, President Ortiz, a onetime Radical elected in 1937, demonstrated the growing awareness among the traditional party leaders of the pressures from below. His Administration espoused improved housing for workers and a homestead loan program to promote land settlement. Little was done to implement the program, and nothing at all was said of higher wages, the organization of labor, or the breakup of the *estancias*. The next step forward would be taken by Perón.

In Chile, the political problems facing the newly conscious political elements were simpler than in Argentina. By Latin American standards, Chile had long enjoyed a high degree of regularity at the polls. The question was primarily one of organization, program, and a candidate who would appeal to lower-class voters. These conditions were met by 1920, a Presidential election year. A young lawyer of lower-middle-class origins, Arturo Alessandri, had put together, some years before, a new political organization, the Liberal Alliance. Elected as a senator from the northern mining districts, he had made a national reputation by promoting a program for the benefit of the middle class and the labor groups in the country. In the face of this threat, the traditional liberals and conservatives—who not only were still fighting each other for office, but also were splitting into factions among themselves—merged, for the election, to form the National Union. Alessandri, declared winner by one electoral vote in a closely contested race, peacefully assumed the Presidency as the leader of the new groups. Although he was balked in much of his social program by a conservative-controlled legislature, his social reform for urban workers was ultimately carried through in the 1930's. Agrarian reform has yet to be instituted in Chile; nor has political organization of rural workers been achieved, although moves have been made in this direction.

Brazil was unique among the nations of Latin America in attaining its independence under a member of the royal house of the mother country (Dom Pedro), and for almost seventy years, Portuguese royalty ruled an independent Brazil. The second Emperor, Dom Pedro II, though favoring the conservatives, alternated them in power with the liberals during his long reign of almost fifty years, thus conditioning Brazilian politicians to a peaceful transition of power from one group to another. The growth of republicanism, especially in the armed forces and among the urban populace; the unpopularity of the heir to the throne, and the weakening of his support through the abolition of slavery (which alienated large landowners); and the development of Church-state quarrels led eventually to the abdication of the Emperor, in 1889, and the establishment of a republic. After a brief military rule, civilian government was re-established, but the first forty years of the republic were marked by few, if any, concessions to the growing industrial population of São Paulo and Rio de Janeiro, much less to the poverty-stricken masses of the backlands and fazendas (plantations). The economic depression of the late 1920's, combined with the political blunders of the incumbent Administration, sparked a revolt with tremendous consequences. Out of the chaos, Getúlio Vargas, Governor of Rio Grande do Sul, emerged as military victor and President. As head of the Liberal Alliance, Vargas not only centralized authority in his own hands, but started to implement the economic and social program of his organization. He began cautiously by establishing a Department of Labor and instituting educational reforms. Once he had consolidated his political position, however, he imposed an urban social-welfare program and permitted neither the recipients nor his political opponents to have any hand in shaping it. By 1937, Vargas had assumed dictatorial powers based not only on the military, but also on urban lower-class popularity. A new element had been introduced into Latin American politics: authoritarian social reform. Others soon emulated Vargas.

THE NEW NATIONALISM

A factor common to all the reform movements and parties of the twentieth century has been the shift to, and new emphasis on, an old sentiment—nationalism. Middle-class political and intellectual leaders, identifying foreign entrepreneurs with the political and social system they were bent on reforming, preached a doctrine of economic national self-sufficiency, to supplement the political self-sufficiency that the elite had sought to ensure. The response was immediate, and cut broadly across class lines. Expropriation of foreign interests appeared as a panacea to lower-income groups. It also seemed to offer new business opportunities, and perhaps to some members of the propertied class—especially those who had profited only marginally from foreign investment—a relaxation of pressure for internal reforms. The pace, scope, and manner of the attack on foreign holdings has varied from swift, complete, and uncompensated liquidation to mild murmurings of dissatisfaction. Cuba stands at one end of the spectrum, Colombia at the other. The Mexican and Bolivian revolutionary parties launched violent attacks on foreign holdings simultaneously with their attacks on the ruling elite. Today, economic nationalism is well entrenched in all major parties in both countries, but foreign capital has been permitted to return under certain restrictions and limitations.

The early decades of the twentieth century also marked the rise of antiforeign nationalist fervor among the traditionalists. The causes, here, however, were political rather than economic. Following its victory over Spain in 1898, the United States moved rapidly and deeply into the Caribbean—militarily, politically, and economically. The repercussions of this power display were felt from Mexico to Chile. While the reformers stepped up their attacks on the interventionist policies of the "Colossus of the North," the traditionalists launched their own campaign—in international conferences and diplomatic exchanges—to extract a commitment of nonintervention from the United States. The combined forces of the traditionalists and the reformers finally prevailed, in 1936, at the Buenos Aires Convention. The high-water mark in U.S.–Latin American relations was reached in the late 1930's and in World War II.

Since World War II, the reformers and traditional party leaders have renewed their attacks on U.S. investments and trade policies, charging the U.S. Government and its citizens with responsibility for the economic colonialism of the area. Today, nationalism, in both its political and its economic aspects, runs deeply and strongly through Latin American society, across class and party lines. Variation in attitudes and activities may be detected from country to country and from group to group, but no political party or faction in Latin America today can afford to call itself other than nationalist, or appear overly friendly to foreign investors and the U.S. Government. All must maintain some position of independence, or risk the charge of *"entreguismo"* ("selling out") and resultant political death.

A few political elements have begun to move into another stage in the development of Latin American nationalism—one in which pride in national achievement comes to the fore. This new sentiment is most noticeable in the Mexican official party, where wide sectors of the population, including government officials, stress the positive accomplishments of the revolution: land reform, increasing food and industrial production, construction of new enterprises, solution of the oil problem, improvement of the transportation system, and achievement of political stability. Despite pride in these accomplishments, the Mexicans have not abandoned their fear and distrust of the United States. The survival of sentiments of inferiority with respect to the United States indicates that Mexican nationalism has not yet fully matured. Elsewhere in Latin America, there are only glimmerings of this kind of positive nationalism. Some elements in the industrial sector of Brazil, and some political leaders in Costa Rica, have given evidence of this sense of security in accomplishment. Uruguay seemed to be achieving it, but economic deterioration and overexpansion of welfare measures have brought forth renewed querulousness. Most other Latin American reform leaders today are more concerned with their national problems than with their national accomplishments. They blame the United States for their ills and insist that the United States remedy them, but they appear reluctant to engage in the necessary but painful self-help that the United States is demanding under the Alliance for Progress.

POLITICAL PARTIES

In recent years, the majority of people of Latin America have experienced, at best, only a modicum of improvement in their material and cultural well-being. Many have no sense of improvement whatsoever, but have awakening aspirations for a better life. Even in countries that have experienced social revolutions, the lower classes are not satisfied; and although they may not, as in Mexico, be prone to revolution, the political leaders of the country cannot ignore their strivings. As a result of chronic misery, poor health, and high illiteracy among the masses; of high hopes, frustration, and anxiety among middle-class intellectuals; and of suspicion, conservatism, and fear among the ruling elite, there have emerged in modern Latin America three types of political parties, reflecting the various aspirations, philosophies, and socio-economic statuses of their members.

Most easily categorized are the traditional parties—sometimes under new names, and sometimes with slightly revised programs— that have survived from the nineteenth century. A few are still called liberal or conservative, but whatever the names, they repre- sent the managerial and propertied groups of their societies; they are interested in the protection of property, and therefore are least hostile to foreign capital. Another survival from the past century is the "personalist" party, formed to support the political aims of a hero-leader.

The second type of party of the mid-twentieth century is one that has been on the scene for at least half a century. It derives from the semisocialistic movements that base their strength on so- cial and economic sectors of society other than the aristocracy. In general, it demands a more equitable distribution of wealth and power, and some curtailment of foreign enterprises. Three dis- tinct subtypes, and a bewildering variety of programs, render this a less cohesive inter-American movement than it might appear at first. The newest of the subtypes are the Christian democrats, who take as their models Christian democratic parties of postwar Europe. The oldest are the secular democratic reform parties, such as the Radicals of Argentina, whom we have already reviewed in their early stages of development. The third subtype is the authoritarian reform party, of the kind that Vargas promoted in Brazil, Perón in Argentina, and Arbenz in Guatemala.

The third category of current political parties includes the radi- cal, or revolutionary, movements, which envisage not only the broadening of the base of the political structure, and a more equita- ble sharing of the economic and cultural fruits of society, but also the elimination of the elite as a political and economic force in the nation, and the expulsion of U.S. influences from the area. The Communist, and Communist-front, parties throughout Latin America, the Castro organization in Cuba, and extremist wings of other leftist parties (which tend to split off and become new par- ties) have these goals in common.

TRADITIONAL (LIBERAL AND CONSERVATIVE)
AND PERSONALIST PARTIES

Few among the present-day traditional parties of Latin America
are dominated by reactionaries, though they include reactionaries
in their ranks. It is true that they are conservatives, but most have
managed to move somewhat with the times and to strive for attainable goals (at least in the short run) for their members among
the upper class. Seldom do they blindly oppose all participation of
other groups in politics, though they do struggle to hold it to a
minimum, in order to protect their social and economic domination. For the most part, too, the Church-state struggle that divided
liberals and conservatives in the nineteenth century is a dead issue. True enough, the conservative parties in Chile and Colombia
draw much of their strength from militant Catholics, and the liberals tend to attract those of the elite who are suspicious or fearful
of a revival of clerical power. Nevertheless, this problem has not
been of sufficient magnitude to prevent the parties from forming
alliances to protect their material interests. In like manner, the
issues of centralism versus federalism have been solved in compromises that are now acceptable to all factions.

What, then, is the modern program of the traditional parties?
Foremost among their aims is the curbing of social-welfare programs and the accompanying rapid inflation that threatens their
profits and their political power. In Chile, for example, they have
successfully enforced a severe austerity program for the past two
years at the expense of the laboring class. The conservative Blancos
of Uruguay rallied around a similar call for the 1958* general
elections. Criticizing the reformist opposition for overextension of
welfare measures, government deficits, and decline in foreign trade,
the Blanco campaign stressed the need for firmness toward inflation and labor demands. The party also called for foreign financial
assistance, from both international and U.S. lending agencies, to
rebuild the cattle industry and to strengthen the national currency.
Following its victory at the polls, the party, despite a long series of
strikes, has held largely to its original plans for austerity and
monetary stabilization. It has also welcomed U.S. assistance to set
its economic house in order, in line with orthodox economic doctrine. Traditional parties drag their heels even more on the sub-

* The Blancos won by a comfortable majority in 1958 and by a very
slender margin in 1962.

ject of agrarian reform than on the subject of urban welfare. The former official party of El Salvador, dominated by the landed magnates, successfully opposed all attempts to legalize the organization of rural workers prior to the revolution of October, 1960, and the Blancos of Uruguay successfully opposed such organization, in practice if not in law, until after World War II. The peasants are still not well organized politically, leaving the Blancos supreme outside Montevideo.

Personalist parties, as a subtype, have survived the social and economic turmoils of the twentieth century. Like the old liberal and conservative parties, they have for the most part been forced to change, in so far as they have given recognition, to the new pressures. Only in the few remaining dictatorships have the parties remained the purely personal organization of the cacique. At the very least, most have had to present a program of intense nationalism, and some, because of the personal politics of their leader, have espoused socialistic and radical causes. In Peru, for example, the Party of National Unification was founded, in 1956, for the sole purpose of supporting the candidacy of Hernando de Lavalle for the Presidency. Lavalle was the favorite of retiring strong man Manuel Odría. On the other hand, the Popular Action Party of Fernando Belaúnde Terry, a highly personalist organization formed at about the same time, took a strongly left-wing position, with appeal to younger, middle-class people. The Peruvian Democratic Party, personal instrument of Presidential victor Manuel Prado, which appealed to traditional liberal political groups, supported fair and free elections and political tolerance (Prado legalized the leftist Alianza Popular Revolucionaria Americana, or APRA, upon taking office in 1956), but it was cautious about economic and social change. At times, personalist parties have openly adopted the name of their leader, though the party may have another formal legal designation. The supporters of former President Velasco Ibarra of Ecuador formed the National Velasquista Federation in 1952 to unite the followers of their hero. The followers of Carlos Guevara organized in 1960 to present his candidacy in opposition to Velasco Ibarra. The latter, allied with the Communists and left-wing socialists for the election of 1960, broke off these ties following the election. Although it preached social as well as political reform, appealed to the underprivileged, and stood to the left of center, Velasco Ibarra's movement bore the strong imprint of its founder.

PARTIES OF REFORM

Secular Reform Parties. The most successful parties of political and social change include the Institutional Revolutionary Party (Partido Revolucionario Institucional, or PRI) of Mexico, the Colorado (liberal) Party of Uruguay, and the Nationalist Revolutionary Movement (Movimiento Nacionalista Revolucionario, or MNR) of Bolivia. All these have profoundly altered social, economic, and political relationships in their countries. Changes were brought about in Bolivia and Mexico following revolution and/or civil war, and in Uruguay through peaceful evolutionary development. Evolutionary change, however, has primarily affected urban groups; the more violent changes have shaken traditional values and power positions in both city and country. Uruguay's reformers stand apart from the others, in fact from most other Latin American reform parties, in that a traditional liberal party, the Colorados, became the vehicle for change. Under José Batlle y Ordóñez and his successors, the party pushed through health and sanitation measures, educational laws (including agricultural, industrial, and adult programs), and labor codes that restricted child labor and provided accident insurance, pensions, maximum hours and minimum wages, and generally improved working facilities. The government also instituted a more equitable tax system, including income taxes, and involved itself deeply in the economy to stimulate production and reduce unemployment. To achieve this with a minimum of resentment from urban business, and to stop the rash of conservative rural-led *coups d'état* that plagued the country at the turn of the century, Batlle bought off the former with various economic inducements, including the expropriation of foreign companies, and the latter by leaving the countryside virtually untouched in every respect, including political control.

The Mexican reforms of the 1930's, and the Bolivian reforms of the 1950's, follow those of Uruguay in philosophy and practice, in so far as they apply to urban classes. The former, however, were able to carry the reforms into the rural areas, since in both Mexico and Bolivia the conservative landed families had suffered military defeat and lacked the strength to fight off the expropriation of all or part of their properties. Thoroughgoing land reform has been accomplished in both, and the programs of the two parties continue to state as their objectives the general improvement of the living levels of their rural populations, and their full incorporation into national political and cultural life. Both initially expropriated foreign holdings and established government-owned oil monopolies, but are currently more moderate in their expressions of nationalism. What prevents the Bolivian and Mexican parties from being included in the radical or revolutionary type is that, like the Uruguayan Colorados, they did not carry out a systematic destruction of the national elite groups, abolish productive private property, or change, fundamentally, the political structure of the nation.

Other reform parties in Latin America have not yet had the time, opportunity, or ability to alter their countries to the degree of those discussed above. The Democratic Action (Acción Democrática, or AD) of Venezuela, the Intransigent Radical Party (Unión Cívica Radical Intransigente, or UCRI) of Argentina, the Liberal Party of Honduras, and the Party of National Liberation (Partido de Liberación Nacional, or PLN) of Costa Rica have all been impeded by entrenched, and still powerful, conservative factions; the scarcity of money; and the legacy of tyrannical and wasteful prior regimes. All are relatively friendly to the United States and U.S. investors, and seek financial assistance to meet their difficulties. Progress is slow, the people are impatient, and revolutionary groups threaten to destroy them if they cannot pro-. duce the desired changes in the near future.

Still other reform parties have not yet had their day in court. The several socialist-minded parties in other parts of Latin America have yet to experience political power and responsibility since World War II. The best known of these is Peru's APRA, or Party of the People. APRA was briefly included in a governing coalition in the early postwar years, but accomplished little and was finally outlawed in 1948. The party regained legal recognition in 1956, but was denied the fruits of its electoral victories in 1962 by a military coup. Some of the others held power prior to World War II, but either carried out moderate reforms that today are no longer satisfactory, or held power under dictatorial rulers, such as Vargas in Brazil. The Brazilian Labor Party (Partido Trabalhista Brasileiro, or PTB), with its leaders claiming the Vargas inheritance, has yet to enjoy a position of dominance in perennial Brazilian coalitions, much less majority control. Vargas' own policies, as democratically elected and democratically functioning President from 1950 to 1954, were more traditionally liberal than reformist. The Labor Party today is strongly reform-oriented and nationalistic, but in word rather than deed (although there is now a sizable activist faction). Chile's political problems are in a sense similar to Brazil's. A social reform party, or rather a coalition of reform parties, gained control in the 1930's and enacted considerable labor and welfare legislation. In Chile, the process was democratic rather than authoritarian, as in Brazil. Following World War II, coalition government continued to plague Chile, as it did Brazil after political liberties were restored in 1945. Unfortunately, coalition governments and coalition-elected Presidents have not had the will or the political power to push through further programs, as demanded by the lower classes and as outlined in their own party programs. Both Chilean and Brazilian reform parties have largely ignored, thus far, the agrarian problems, and have concentrated their attention on urban lower-class demands and needs. In Guatemala, the Revolutionary Party (Partido Revolucionario, or PR) founded in 1957, has not yet been able to win political power, and its future is uncertain.

Religious-Oriented Reform Parties (*Christian Democrats*). Newest among the types of Latin American political parties are the Christian democratic groups. Unlike the traditional parties or the secular reform parties, the Christian democrats have begun to forge ties across national boundaries, both on the basis of their common inheritance from similar parties in Europe, and on the Catholic Christian principles that form the philosophical base of their platforms. Broadly, these parties are in agreement with the reform and Aprista-type parties discussed above, calling for improved social and economic conditions for the lower classes through democratic political action. On certain specifics, they may disagree with the secular reform parties, particularly where questions of faith and morals are involved, e.g., birth control, abortion, or divorce. The Christian democrats are not clericalists, as were the old conservatives, and try assiduously to demonstrate that they are neither supported nor controlled by the local hierarchy. They insist that they are a lay political movement, devoted to the political, social, economic, and cultural welfare of all citizens, but at the same time, a movement based upon the moral and social teachings of the Catholic Church.

Despite some international ties, the Christian democratic groups in the various countries develop their own specific programs according to the needs of their country as they see them. Their position in the political spectrum, therefore, varies with the state of local politics, but almost everywhere, they may be considered moderate nationalists and reformers. In Paraguay, however, the movement is virtually revolutionary in its attitude toward the dictator, and in Mexico, it is considered conservative and right of center, in a country that has experienced a far-reaching revolution. In most other countries, it is left of center, either in support of reform governments or in opposition to traditionalist or personalist parties. The strength of these Christian democratic parties varies considerably. In most countries, it has no seats in Congress; in four or five, it has a small minority; in Chile it ranks among the leading contenders for power; and in Venezuela, it forms an important part of the coalition government of President Rómulo Betancourt. Still relatively small in Brazil, it is by far the fastest growing party. In May, 1961, the Christian democratic parties of the Caribbean zone held their First Congress, in Caracas, with several hundred delegates from twenty-two nations and territories in the Americas. In its political and economic resolutions, this conference covered all aspects of Latin American development, and prepared the way for the holding of the Third World Conference of Christian Democrats, which met in Santiago, Chile, July 27–30. At the latter conference, the first of its kind to be held in Latin America, the Christian Democratic World Union was organized as a permanent association. In addition a number of congresses have been held in various cities of Latin America over the past decade that have concerned themselves not only with the activities of the Christian democratic parties but also with affiliated youth and labor groups.

Authoritarian Reform Parties. The earliest of the authoritarian reform movements originated in Brazil, under Getúlio Vargas, who, as we have noted, seized power in 1930, hard upon the heels of a political dispute traditional in origin but concealing more deep-seated political unrest and economic discontent. Though nominally heading a political organization then called the Liberal Alliance, Vargas did not utilize this group or create a new party in the years of his dictatorship. This is not to say that he did not put together a political organization. Rather, he based his regime on the armed forces, who supported his desire for order and acquiesced in his social reforms, since they affected only urban elements. Labor, though denied the right to strike, benefited materially, and at least was not worse off politically than before. However, the denial of civil and political rights, particularly severe after 1937, soon alienated some of Vargas' supporters, and aroused his opponents to open criticism. In 1945,

Vargas promised free elections, and the armed forces, responsive to organized civilian groups, insisted that he fulfill his promise. Following Vargas' retirement from the Presidency, his adherents formed a personalist party, first called the Queremistas (We-Wanters), which Vargas soon transformed into the Brazilian Labor Party. In his later years, however, Vargas worked through the re-established democratic processes, and his Brazilian Labor Party did not use authoritarian political techniques, openly or covertly, to attain their ends.

Perón of Argentina began his political career in a manner reminiscent of Vargas, and his reform measures closely paralleled those of the Brazilian dictator. Similarities between the two regimes have frequently been pointed out. They differ, however, not only in style but in essentials. Perón rose to power during the mid-1940's, in a time of social ferment, economic discontent, and political disorientation. Unlike Vargas' career, though, Perón's was chiefly military, and his assumption of political duties, particularly as Minister of Labor, resulted from a military coup and a disinclination of his fellow officers to take the post. Perón recognized the political potential of organized labor and set about not only to encourage further unionization, but to bring about the subjugation of these elements to the government, specifically to himself as Minister of Labor. So successful were his efforts, that the attempts of his superior officers to remove him from power brought his labor following pouring into the streets of Buenos Aires, demanding his return. Besides returning to his ministry, Perón soon seized unchallenged command of the country, ratifying his position by election to the Presidency in 1946, in large part through nationalistic appeals to his countrymen to resist the U.S. Government, which opposed his policies.

Perón, like Vargas, concentrated his reform program in the cities. He aroused opposition from political liberals because of his fascist tendencies, and from urban managerial groups, who had to pay the costs of the welfare programs. He soon alienated the landed conservatives by imposing rigorous government controls over Argentine wheat and beef, the country's two major exports, and by initiating a program of social welfare for rural workers. To consolidate his position, Perón soon organized his followers, largely urban and rural labor-union members and ultranationalists of many types, into the Peronist Party.

Again like Vargas, Perón did not push his reforms to the point of revolutionizing Argentine society. There was no mass nationalization of property, no systematic attempt to destroy the elite classes, and no effort to destroy old institutions such as the army and the Church. In fact, Perón based his power in large measure upon the army, and attempted for a time to use the Church to strengthen his regime.

By the mid-1950's, opposition emerged openly, as a result of Perón's political oppression and economic failures. All important groups, except labor and some extreme nationalist middle-class elements, had abandoned him by mid-1955. The army was split, and elements of the Church were in rebellion. The end came for Perón in September, but his party has continued after him. Unlike the Brazilian experience, Argentine popular support of the authoritarianism of the Perón era has continued with the restoration of constitutional order. In subsequent balloting, the Peronistas, even when outlawed as a formal political organization, represented from one-fourth to one-third of the total electorate. One of the primary political goals of democratic, reform-minded political parties in Argentina, such as the Radicals (both wings), the Socialists, and the Christian Democrats, has been to convince the Peronistas that their welfare can be protected without Perón, and without dictatorship. The Communists and left-wing Socialists are assiduously trying to convince them that it can be assured without Perón, but not without dictatorship—the dictatorship of the proletariat. The Peronists are biding their time.

The Arévalo and Arbenz administrations, in Guatemala (1945–54), present a third, and quite distinct, example of reforms imposed by a dictatorial executive. Juan José Arévalo captured the popular imagination in the electoral campaign of 1944, which followed the overthrow of the traditionalist dictator Jorge Ubico. Elected democratically, with the support of a variety of newly formed "revolutionary" parties, and installed constitutionally in office in March, 1945, Arévalo strengthened his political position to such a degree during his first years in office that by mid-1949, he was able to impose press censorship and to stifle political opposition almost as rigorously as had Ubico. The head of the army, a political rival, was assassinated, and the revolt that followed was crushed. In the 1950 election, Arévalo's hand-picked successor, Colonel Jacobo Arbenz, won easily. Social and economic change, begun with Arévalo, picked up momentum under the more radical Arbenz. Important positions in labor organizations and the government were opened to the Communists. The Western alliance and the United States were severely criticized, and economic assistance was sought from the Soviet bloc. In addition, both urban and agrarian reform programs were implemented. It is impossible to prophesy exactly how far the Guatemalan course would have gone had it not been overthrown in 1954, at the hands of a U.S.-supported military revolt; it was not then fully Communist controlled, though it was very heavily Communist infiltrated and influenced. The regime's public program did not call for class warfare, expropriation or nationalization of all private property, or other measures usually associated with radical reform. Arbenz' unconditional support of the regime of Castro (whose guest he has been) is indicative of his final goals. Even in power, Arbenz was never able to unify his supporters, and they remain divided among a flock of insignificant splinter parties. Arévalo, rather than Arbenz, is the symbol to whom the Guatemalan masses appear to be turning. Thus nothing resembling the Peronistas of Argentina has appeared in Guatemala, nor has a political group such as the Brazilian Labor Party arisen to claim his inheritance. The Revolutionary Party, which was founded in 1957 and has attracted the democratic left, claims no connection with Arbenz, his Administration, or his programs. Arévalo, whose return to Guatemala in March, 1963, to run for the Presidency touched off a military coup, has at least publicly rejected Communism and Castroism.

RADICAL REVOLUTIONARY ORGANIZATIONS

Today, there are two basic types of extremist revolutionary political movements in Latin America: the Communist and the Castrista. The Communists have been in evidence since the early 1920's, but the Castro-type organizations have sprung up only since 1959. Prior to World War II, there appeared semifascist ultra-nationalist groups that might be considered in this radical category. The two best-known were the Sinarquistas of Mexico, and the Integralistas of Brazil. The latter were militarily crushed by Vargas in the late 1930's, and the former were disbanded as a political party by President Camacho during the war. With the defeat of the Axis, fascist organizations in Latin America lost their importance on the political scene.

Following the introduction of Communism in the area, during the early 1920's, the Communist Parties grew, but slowly and not without some serious reverses, such as being banned and persecuted in Mexico in 1930. In many countries, they have long been illegal, but illegality has not in the past, and does not now, constitute an insuperable obstacle to the implementation of important aspects of the Communists' program. Communists have infiltrated trade unions, intellectual and professional groups, and farm organizations; have continued to operate the Party presses; and have successfully organized front groups to castigate the United States and the West, to promote peace and disarmament, to create closer ties with the Sino-Soviet bloc, and to fight "colonialism and imperialism."

In most cases, Communist political activity has been carried out by overt Party organizations, whether it be the Communist Party of Ecuador, of Venezuela, or of Brazil. In several countries, there are dissident Communist or Communist-front parties, such as the Revolutionary Workers Party (Trotskyite) in Bolivia, and the Socialist People's Party in Mexico. The Cuban orthodox Communist Party is called the Popular Socialist Party (Partido Socialista Popular, or PSP), and this type of nomenclature has been used elsewhere in the Caribbean and Central American countries to escape the results of Communist illegality. In Haiti, and in the Dominican Republic prior to Trujillo's assassination, repressive governments successfully stamped out all organized political opposition, including the Communists.

The Communist apparatus in Latin America has made significant progress in the last two or three years. Communist organizations show a higher degree of self-confidence and optimism now than at any time since World War II. The official Communist Parties have not grown substantially over the past several years (with the exception of Cuba), and over-all membership remains at about 230,000 plus the Cuban Communists, who have become part of a mass Marxist-Leninist organization. The progress experienced by the Communist organizations consists, rather, of better linkage with the international Communist apparatus and of the improved environment for operations in many countries. The establishment of Cuba as an appendage of the Sino-Soviet bloc provides a regional headquarters well equipped with hotels and bourgeois tourist comforts. Here, Latin American Communists meet with European and Asian Communists, and with like-minded leftists and neutralists from many countries of the world, as well as with official bloc representatives. The Communists of Latin America have also traveled more frequently to the bloc countries, notably to Moscow conferences, which have been held annually for the past several years.

On the national scene, the Communists are enjoying their greatest success since World War II in finding political allies. Until recently, they were able to make *ad hoc* alliances on specific issues with influential non-Communists, but never continuously over a broad front. There was a promising flare-up over the Guatemalan issue in the mid-1950's, but the issue lost appeal as the Arbenz-Communist cause was defeated. Now, with the demonstrated ability of the Castro regime to maintain power and to get necessary support from the Sino-Soviet bloc, many indigenous leftist and nationalist groups are ready to make common cause with the Communists on the Cuban or "national liberation" issue (although the October, 1962, missile crisis led to a temporary setback in this field). Their willingness to work with the Communists is permitting the latter to effect new and wider penetration into political parties, the press, student and professional organizations, and to a lesser degree, the trade-union movement. Despite Castro's extremely deep involvement with the Cuban Communist Party, and his heavy dependence on bloc support, he still appeals to many Latin leftists and ultranationalists as one of them, and as a worthy leader of the cause. Many Latins, especially among the intellectuals, still do not equate Castroism with Communism, in spite of all that happened during 1962. Moreover, it is widely asserted by leftists of all hues that Castro was forced to turn to the bloc in early 1960 because of U.S. refusal of aid, and for protection against U.S. aggressive designs. Even if allied to extremist opposition groups, the Communists may be treated tolerantly by the authorities as long as they refrain from direct attack on the government. Thus, the Communists were allowed to operate freely in Venezuela until they joined forces with extremist groups in November, 1960, to stir up mob action, and the Betancourt government did not move vigorously against them until after the May, 1962, revolt.

In rural areas, the Communists have stepped up operations, and are active in trying to organize and to seize organizations created by non-Communist leaders. Here, they have advantages in the poverty, the pressure for land, and the newly roused hopes for change that make the rural population vulnerable to irresponsible leadership. However, the authorities may also be especially touchy in this area, and in many countries, they have hastened to put up defenses against Communist penetration.

One of the most potent appeals of the Communist apparatus to extremist opposition groups is its ability to finance them and to provide other material support. This aid can be provided to selected Communist-penetrated groups by way of Cuba, avoiding embarrassment to the Soviets. While spokesmen of the Castro regime—and of the Chinese Communists—may incite guerrilla action in Latin America, the Soviets can thus stand aloof and deny responsibility for Communist-supported subversive operations in the area.

Communist Parties, whatever their official names, have faithfully followed the twists and turns of the Soviet line, in both internal politics and international relations. Stalin has been downgraded, collective leadership exalted, and the creation of anti-imperialist and anticolonial fronts proclaimed. Peaceful coexistence, an end to atomic testing, and restraints on the "Western warmongers" have all been consistently preached. Despite the militance of the language, and the occasional violence attending their agitation, the Communists have not tried seriously since the uprisings in El Salvador and Brazil in the 1930's to capture control of a country directly by armed assault, although they have frequently collaborated in overthrowing governments by force. In Guatemala, between 1944 and 1954, they appeared content to influence the course of events from behind the scenes, rather than as the acknowledged wielders of power. In Cuba, until the summer of 1961, they played an even less open role, leaving all major government positions to friends and sympathizers; by mid-year, however, they began to assume more overt control, and from then on they have further exploited their commanding positions.

It appears, nevertheless, that in most of Latin America today, the primary goal of the Communists is not the open seizure of power, but the political and economic disruption of the Inter-American System, and the creation of ties of all types to the Communist bloc. In Cuba, they have achieved their greatest success, since Castro not only has switched economic dependence from the United States to the Soviet Union, but has forced a break in diplomatic relations with the United States, and has caused serious dissension within the OAS. Similar ends are being pursued throughout Latin America, the Communists working closely with ultra-nationalists and leftist extremists who desire to follow the Cuban lead. Communist success or failure will depend in large part upon how far, and how quickly, present regimes can proceed to satisfy the increasingly loud and urgent cries for reform. Peru and Ecuador, along with several of Cuba's small Caribbean and Central American neighbors, are among the most critical areas. In a few countries, repressive dictatorial regimes are sitting tightly on powder kegs. Their overthrow is a matter of time, and the Communists are preparing for that day. Mexico, Costa Rica, and Uruguay seem the safest of all, having experienced their reform, and having the material wealth to satisfy minimum demands. The

Communist movements in these three countries are the weakest to be found among the politically tolerant regimes of Latin America.

The Castro-type movements and political parties are more dangerous than those of the Communists, not only for U.S. interests, but also for the cause of civil rights and political tolerance within the Latin American countries. Castrista agitation has gained more popular support, and enjoyed greater respectability, since 1959 than has the Communist movement in more than forty years. Thousands of Mexicans still identify their revolution with the current Cuban internal reform, and drive for national independence despite the many and obvious essential differences between the two. Frustrated liberals and reformers of various types look to Castro and Cuba as models for what can be done in a static or slow-moving nation, even under the shadow of its powerful neighbor. Elections, legality, and respect for opponents seem to these persons calculated obstacles to impede or defeat plans for change. The more frustrated they become, the more willing they are to brush aside democratic procedures for authoritarian, revolutionary methods—governing with mob support and decreeing change by executive order.

Some Castrista movements are not far different, in a number of their basic demands, from many of the more moderate reform groups. The familiar programs of land reform, improved wages and working conditions, pensions and insurance, honesty in government, and controls and restrictions on foreign enterprises are all there. Other plans are more radical, calling for general land expropriation without compensation, socialization of property, and class conflict. These parties may well prove to be the Trojan horse by which the Communists gain entry. Like the Communist movements, they advocate violence, dictatorship, and armed terror to achieve their programs. In Venezuela, for example, the Democratic Republican Union (Unión Republicana Democrática, or URD), one of the original coalition parties, broke with Betancourt in 1960, specifically on the Castro issue and on the use of force by the government to quell extremist agitation. Since then, the URD has attempted to lead a leftist coalition, including the Communists, strongly opposed to the Betancourt Government.

In depressed and poverty-stricken Northeast Brazil, the Peasant Leagues of Francisco Julião not only demand agrarian reform, but advocate forcible seizure of land and the institution of strong national leadership, in emulation of Cuba's Fidel Castro. Late in 1961, Julião openly announced that he was a Communist, but his relations with both the orthodox and dissident Communist Parties have frequently been strained. Support of Castrismo can also be found among the nation's university students. In Recife, "capital" of the Northeast, students at the federal University of Pernambuco invited the mother of Ernesto ("Che") Guevara to address them in the spring of 1961. Riots followed the banning of the meeting by the Dean of the Law School, and troops were sent in to restore order. A group of law students at the University of São Paulo, 2,000 miles to the south, supported their fellows at Recife by breaking street lights and dumping garbage cans. No basic issues have since been solved, and the unrest of the peasants and the students can be allayed only by introducing the necessary changes —quickly. Jânio Quadros, President Goulart, and even the U.S. Government have promised aid to the Northeast, but the Peasant Leagues continue to grow, to arm, and to threaten.

In many other parts of Latin America, the Castrista or pro-Castro movements are not well organized politically. In Peru, for example, pro-Castro sentiment is strong among university students, but has just begun to move into labor circles. The peasantry is becoming restless but, except for certain areas, is not yet contaminated by pro-Castro sympathizers. The elements are all present in Peru for a revolutionary upheaval, but so far, organization, leadership, and opportunity are wanting.

CONCLUSIONS

It is the authors' contention that in Latin America the best hope to avoid violence, bloodshed, and a Castro-Communist-type take-over lies in the accession of power of political parties of the non-Communist left—the social democrats and/or the Christian democrats. Where they have already achieved power, these parties have had impressive success in staving off radical solutions to national problems. The PRI in Mexico has long and thoroughly undercut Communist appeal in that country; and the Colorados of Uruguay and the PLN in Costa Rica must be given much credit for the scant success of radical movements in those countries. Despite grievous sufferings and seemingly insurmountable economic problems, Bolivia, with its reform-minded MNR, has not succumbed to Communist overtures. On the other hand, in the two countries in which the Communists were able to gain their greatest influence— Cuba and Guatemala—right-wing dictatorships had for many years successfully frustrated the functioning of democratic parties and movements.

The accession to power of these parties will not, of course, bring immediate solutions to a nation's ills, eliminate radicalism from politics, or usher in a new era of good feelings with the United States, comparable to the "Good Neighbor" period of the late 1930's. Venezuela, under Rómulo Betancourt's Acción Democrática, well illustrates the difficulties of the moderate approach to reform. The grinding poverty and suffering of the masses is only slowly being alleviated, and leftist revolutionary agitation, quelled for a time, broke out during 1962 with particular fury. Despite these internal problems, President Betancourt has maintained friendly relations with the United States and with the private oil companies in his country. Late in 1961, he broke diplomatic relations with Castro. These moves have subjected him to bitter attacks by extremists, who brand him a lackey of imperialism. Betancourt and his moderate-left party (AD), in alliance with the Christian Socialist Party (Comité Organizado por Elecciones Independientes, or COPEI), have been able to ride out the storm thus far, largely because of his strong party organization—combined with great national wealth in land and minerals and a relatively small population. With the highest per capita income in Latin America, better distribution of existing wealth could bring rapid results.

Unfortunately, perhaps, Venezuela is not typical. Some countries need a drastic land reform, with at least partial expropriation and distribution to the peasantry. All countries need increased production, both in agricultural products and in industrial goods. Such measures, however, require not only large outlays of capital, but considerable redistribution of the national wealth. The traditional parties, dominated by the rural and urban elite, have proved unwilling to take the necessary measures to institute these changes. They do not wish to share the fruits of national production with the lower-income groups, and often have demonstrated great reluctance to plow profits back into national industry, preferring instead to bank their wealth abroad. Land is underutilized, profit per unit is high, and consumer goods are costly. The Castroites and Communists promise drastic changes and immediate benefits to the lower classes through authoritarian methods. The Christian and social democrats promise more moderate changes and eventual benefits through democratic political procedures. The Castroites and the Communists have already made many converts among the masses. How much longer can these masses be persuaded to remain patient and await a democratic solution? In the final two chapters, we shall try to cast further light on this question and essay tentative predictions for each country.

6. Political Dynamics

INTRODUCTION

Superficially, the countries of Latin America seem to be easily classifiable into one-party, two-party, or multiparty states. When examined in depth, however, the variations, country by country, defy virtually any rational classification. In several countries, there are currently no viable party systems, because of revolution, dictatorship, or special political arrangements among political groups. There are one-party states in the absolute sense, and there are one-party states in the relative sense, where one party completely dominates political life but permits other parties to operate with some degree of freedom. Opposition parties do, therefore, exist in dictatorial and nondictatorial countries. Then, there are two-party states with political competition, and two-party states with political cooperation. And finally, there are the multiparty states, in which government is run by coalitions of reformers, traditionalists, and/or personalists, or by some combination of these. Some states are run by traditionalist parties, some by reform-minded parties, some by personalist parties, and one by a revolutionary movement that can hardly be termed a party. In countries run by reform administrations, the social democrats control the government in all instances. In one of these, the Christian democrats are in the government coalition; in several others, they are among the principal opposition parties; and in still others, they are a minor opposition. Some sort of categorization, however, is necessary if we are to analyze Latin American poltical systems in any meaningful manner. Therefore, without denying the validity of other approaches, we have selected the following categories to study the political organizations in Latin America: traditional dictatorships, competitive party systems, noncompetitive party systems, and mass-based totalitarian regimes.

The most obvious and perhaps best-known, though not currently the most widespread, type of government is the dictatorship: one-man arbitrary and oligarchic rule supported, in part at least, by armed might—with virtually no party competition. Most dictators in Latin American history have been military men, but a number of outstanding strong men have been civilians. Normally, they pay some lip service to democratic procedures and make some feeble gestures toward reform; but basically, they rest their position upon the maintenance of the current social structures of their countries. Frequently, they are accepted by large segments of the upper class, because they maintain order, protect property, and prevent dangerous innovations. From the mid-1930's to the mid-1950's, there appeared in Latin America new forms of dictatorships that combined autocracy with limited social reform, but these have all disappeared. Dictatorship, however, has provided stability only in the short run; over the long haul, it has led instead to revolution and a high degree of instability. The longer and tighter the lid is clamped on the forces of change, the more violent is the explosion when the dictator is toppled. Díaz in Mexico and Batista in Cuba are prime examples. The Mexican revolution has not been so far-reaching as the Cuban, but it was far more violent in its early stages. Present traditional dictatorships include those of Haiti, Paraguay, and Nicaragua; the latter may soon pass out of this category.

A second grouping of political systems comprises those that permit and encourage a high degree of party competition, the type of regime that U.S. citizens normally classify as democratic, and with which they therefore easily identify. Although party competition and political stability are compatible in the United States because of the broad consensus of the population on a number of basic issues and values, they often are incompatible in Latin America because of the very lack of consensus over fundamental economic, social, and political questions. Positions are often irreconcilable, political defeats at the ballot box unbearable, and resort to arms a widely accepted alternative to acquiescence. Most of this type, Uruguay and Costa Rica being the prime exceptions, tend to be unstable, because new power groups of the middle and lower classes have not been fully accepted and integrated into the political system by the traditional ruling elite. Where moderate reform programs have had considerable impact, as in Argentina, Brazil, Chile, Venezuela, and Guatemala, the appetites of the new groups have only been whetted for more. Where they have not yet tasted power, as in Peru, Ecuador, Honduras, and Panama, they are clamoring for their rights. Promises of reform, nationalistic appeals, and some minor concessions are temporary palliatives, but the ruling elites will have to permit substantive changes in the next few years to stave off violent solutions. The Dominican Republic and El Salvador—striving today to establish constitutional governments and political competition after the overthrow of strong men —can be placed in this category, but only with the understanding that their political systems are still in flux.

The third type of political system is democratic oriented but noncompetitive. Three countries—Mexico, Bolivia, and Colombia —meet these criteria. In all three, opposition political parties are permitted to organize. In Mexico, however, only the official Institutional Revolutionary Party enjoys a national organization reaching down into the grass-roots level in every part of the country. It has complete control of the government apparatus from top to bottom, and its hegemony cannot be threatened. Bolivian political conditions resemble the Mexican somewhat, but there are important differences. An official party, claiming to symbolize the revolution of 1952, has monopolized power for ten years. Like the official party in Mexico, it has organized labor and the peasantry throughout the country, it has created a new military force to support the revolution, and it controls elections to assure its continued ascendancy. Opposition political forces, however, are better organized in Bolivia than in Mexico, and internal rumblings of discontent and divisions within the official party are a far more serious threat to the continued dominance of the party's moderate leadership. Although the Mexican official party would, without manipulating elections, win control of the national executive and the national Congress (though with reduced majorities), the revolutionary party of Bolivia would possibly lose power or disintegrate. In Colombia, competition for office between the two major parties has been temporarily set aside, in an effort to bring peace to the country after ten years of civil war and dictatorship that have cost at least 300,000 lives. The two major political parties have formed a National Front, under which they have agreed to alternate the Presidency and share equally other political offices.

Cuba, still in the throes of violent revolution, has adopted a mass-based totalitarian-type system in which opposition factions and parties are ruthlessly suppressed in the name of national unity. Like the systems of the first type, the Cuban system is dictatorial, but unlike them, it is not satisfied by the exercise of power alone.

The regime is bent not only on governing Cuban society, but in restructuring the nation politically, socially, and economically. Although the traditional dictatorships depend for support on the officer corps, the landed magnates, the wealthy business elements, and, to some extent, the church hierarchy, the Castro Administration has systematically destroyed these long-entrenched interest groups. In their place, it has founded new institutions dedicated to the revolutionary goal of creating a Soviet utopia. The Cuban experience stands alone in Latin American political experiments. The regime exercises total control far beyond that enjoyed by Perón in Argentina, or Vargas in Brazil; it is radical-reformist far beyond any Mexican or Bolivian revolutionary government.

THE TRADITIONAL DICTATORSHIPS

Of the three indigenous dictatorships remaining in Latin America, one is controlled by a military man, and two by civilians. Outgoing President Luis Somoza, of Nicaragua, a civilian, has little in common with the leaders of Haiti and Paraguay—François Duvalier and General Alfredo Stroessner. Somoza is the son and heir of a military dictator who was assassinated after two decades of virtually unlimited authority. Luis has taken a number of steps to introduce democratic changes into the regime, beginning with the dismantling of the worst features of his father's police state. He and his brother Anastasio, who heads the armed forces, promised to restore representative government following the Presidential election held on February 3, 1963. With the major opposition party, the Traditional Conservatives, abstaining, René Schick, the Administration candidate, won overwhelmingly. Schick, considered a tool of the Somozas, is threatened, however, by a revived, and sometimes irresponsible, opposition, which demands changes far faster and deeper than he or the Somozas believe can presently be permitted without throwing the country into chaos. The sincerity of their intentions, and the new President's ability to lead the country by peaceful transition to meaningful political change, remain in doubt.

Despite the civilian administration of Duvalier, Haiti is more akin to Stroessner's Paraguay than to Somoza's Nicaragua. The Haitian and Paraguayan strong men have both paid lip service to reform, but have shown little interest in any programs beyond those of keeping their political position intact and their economic position solvent. Stroessner, during the past two years, has permitted limited and intermittent operations by opposition political parties and newspapers, but Duvalier has been ruthless in suppressing all opposition. In congressional elections, farcical in both countries, Duvalier and Stroessner have packed their legislatures with their personal followers. Neither has made any serious move to establish representative constitutional government.

HAITI

Haiti has been in unending political crisis since it attained independence, in 1804. It is doubtful that anything resembling a fair and free election has ever been held there. A small elite—primarily mulatto—has controlled all aspects of Haitian development. A vast mass of illiterate and poverty-stricken Negro peasants constitutes the bulk of the population. Long-term ills contribute to chronic political instability, which shifts the country devastatingly between chaos and tyranny; and depressed economic conditions, government corruption, and racial and political factionalism plague the nation. In recent years, anti-U.S. nationalism has broken out, perhaps accentuated by U.S. economic assistance programs offered to a repressive regime. Disagreements have also arisen between the governments of the two countries over the amount and disposition of the aid. At the Foreign Ministers' Conference at Punta del Este, in January, 1962, Haiti withheld its crucial vote for the ouster of Cuba from the OAS until it had extorted satisfactory guarantees of aid from the United States.

Political parties have always been highly personalist. The current President, François Duvalier, elected popularly in September, 1957, governs with the support of a political organization, the National Unity Party, that is entirely loyal to him personally. There are no other political organizations operating at present. The Communist Party was outlawed in 1948, and the few local Communists in Haiti tend to be of the intellectual, rather than of the militant, variety. Duvalier has employed individuals widely believed to be Communists or sympathizers, and late in 1962 appointed several of these types to his Cabinet.

Following his inauguration in October, 1957, Duvalier became increasingly authoritarian. Arbitrarily dissolving the legislature in the spring of 1961, he called for special congressional elections for April 30. In preparing for the election, he reduced the bicameral legislature to a single-house Assembly and presented a single list of fifty-eight candidates, all his personal supporters. He thereby eliminated the handful of followers of his opponent in exile, Louis Dejoie, who had held seats in the previous legislature. At the same time, he had inscribed on all ballots for the legislature "Doctor François Duvalier, President," signifying, as he later explained, that the incumbent was standing for re-election for a new six-year term, to begin in May. He was duly inaugurated on May 22, 1961.

Since the elections, all political opposition has been prohibited, and Duvalier has brutally suppressed student, Church, and elitist opposition, presenting himself as the champion of the Negro masses against the mulatto minority. His power rests upon the military, which he has controlled by periodic purges of the National Guard and appointments of personal followers to key posts. He has also attempted to check the power of the National Guard by the creation of a militia that is personally loyal to him. He has furthermore used an extralegal organization, the Tontons-Macoutes, to terrorize the opposition. Although Duvalier successfully collected the various strands of power in his own hands, his use of terror to suppress the opposition provoked counterterrorist activities during the early months of 1963. Duvalier, fearing for his personal safety, constantly surrounds himself with loyal militiamen, and is carrying out a campaign of rising terror to protect his regime. In the early summer of 1963, Haiti resembles the Cuba of late 1958.

PARAGUAY

Paraguay has never experienced political democracy or stable government. Its primitive social and economic organization precludes the development of modern political institutions. The exercise of power has been highly personalist, and the two political parties, the Colorado and the Liberal—both dating from the nineteenth century—have represented the political aspirations of different factions of the social elite. The Colorado Party has held power continually since 1947, the opposition refusing to participate in controlled elections. The current President, General Alfredo Stroessner, supported by the party and the military, won the office unopposed in 1954, to fill out an unexpired term. He was re-elected in 1958, again without opposition, for a full term, to expire in August, 1963. Uncontested congressional elections, held in March, 1960, gave the Colorados exclusive representation in the unicameral legislature. When he stood for a third term in February, 1963, Stroessner's victory was a foregone conclusion; when the tally was completed, he had more than 90 per cent of the votes.

The regime is frankly authoritarian, as were its predecessors. Paraguay has been governed under an almost continuous "state of siege" since 1940. Even under normal conditions, the President has the power, when Congress is not in session, to issue decrees having the force of law. His only formal restraint is a subservient Council of State, whose approval is required. The basic power of the regime rests with the police and the military, which together absorb about 40 per cent of the budget. Secondary support comes from the civilian leaders of the Colorado Party.

The political opposition consists of the conservative and traditionalist Liberal Party, the reform-oriented Febrerista Party, and the Communist Party—outlawed since 1936. Minor opposition groups include a dissident wing of the Colorados, and the newly formed Christian Democratic Social Movement. In 1958, the regime permitted the Liberals to hold a public meeting in the capital, its first in more than a decade. In the spring of 1959, Stroessner lifted the state of siege, but student riots, civil disturbances, and general unrest led to its reimposition in less than a month. Liberal Party leaders and Colorado dissidents were imprisoned. Stroessner supporters won all seats in the congressional elections of 1960, but in the general election of February, 1963, in which Stroessner was re-elected President, the regime made one small concession toward a more representative political system. It registered a small dissident group of the Liberal Party for electoral participation, and provided by law that the first opposition party be awarded one-third of the seats in the Congress. This "democratization," however, was marred by the fact that the leaders of the two major opposition parties were imprisoned just prior to the election, and neither party was registered for inscription on the ballot. Many opponents of the regime have continued to place their hopes of overturning it by armed force, rather than by the electoral process.

The illegal Communist Party, with an estimated membership of over 3,000, has no overt organization within the country. Most of its members are in exile. It draws its primary support from intellectuals and appears to be successfully infiltrating student organizations. The Party, however, poses no immediate threat to the regime.

NICARAGUA

Nicaragua, one of the most backward and undeveloped countries of Latin America, has been dominated since 1936 by the Somoza family. U.S. intervention, including the stationing of marines in the country from 1912 to 1933, apparently had little effect in promoting constitutional government and democratic processes, despite U.S. supervision of elections and reorganization of the country's finances and armed forces. Within three years of the U.S. withdrawal, dictatorship once more took over. During the twenty-year rule of Anastasio Somoza, Sr., a frankly authoritarian regime prevailed. The laws, the constitution, and basic civil rights were flagrantly violated, and political opposition groups were permitted to exist only on Somoza's terms. At the same time, the dictator built up a personal family fortune. With Somoza's assassination in 1956, his sons Luis and Anastasio, Jr. (Tachito), took over the reins of political and military power. Luis became President, and Tachito commander of the National Guard (Guardia Nacional), which has long been loyal to the family in return for privileges and perquisites. As President (1956–63), Luis mitigated some of the worst features of his father's authoritarianism, and in August, 1959, he pushed through the legislature a constitutional amendment prohibiting election to the Presidency of any member of the Somoza family. In the balloting of February, 1963, René Schick, Education Minister and then Foreign Minister under Luis Somoza, was elected to succeed to the Presidency. Although long faithful to the Somoza family, Schick is regarded even by some members of the opposition as a man of personal honesty and integrity. It is doubtful, however, that he can remove the Somozas from power, since Tachito has insisted that he retain control of the National Guard. Schick has publicly promised to follow Somoza policies, has confirmed Tachito's command of the Guard, and has retained Guillermo Sevilla Sacasa, brother-in-law of the Somozas, as Ambassador to the United States. During Schick's Administration, the key power factor will remain the National Guard.

Pressure groups in Nicaragua reflect the domination of political, economic, and social life by a relatively small number of wealthy families. These families informally exert pressures through the exploitation of family and business relationships, and through several producers' organizations. The most important of the latter are agricultural, reflecting agriculture's overwhelming predominance in the national economy. The significance of the National Guard as a pressure group stems from the fact that its support is essential to the regime; within a few years after its creation in 1927, under U.S. auspices, it came under the control of Somoza, and National Guard members have received many favors in exchange for their loyalty. Labor groups and the Catholic Church have, on occasion, induced the government to follow courses of action favorable to themselves, but they do not constitute true pressure groups.

The primary reason that Nicaragua has failed to develop stable political institutions lies in the primitive character of its socio-economic organization. Nicaragua's elite has found political expression in two century-old, mutually antagonistic, and highly personalistic political parties—the Liberal and the Conservative—which have alternated in power for relatively long periods of time. While the leaders of these parties have professed some interest in furthering democratic practices, promoting economic development, and improving the extremely low levels of living prevalent among the bulk of Nicaragua's inhabitants, they have long been preoccupied with enhancing their personal and political fortunes. The masses are apathetic toward the continuing struggle between the two contending groups, and regard government as a mechanism for personal advancement, rather than one designed to promote the general welfare.

The Somoza-dictated Constitution of 1950 provides that all seats in the Chamber of Deputies and in the Senate be apportioned between the two principal parties, as defined by law. The official Nationalist Liberal Party (Partido Nacionalista Liberal, or PNL) receives two-thirds of the seats in the lower chamber and three-quarters of those in the upper body, and the legally recognized opposition, the Nicaraguan Conservative Party (Partido Conservador Nicaragüense, or PCN), the remainder. The PCN, however, is only a minority faction of the Traditional Conservative Party (PCT), the major opposition party in the country.

The Communist Party is called the Socialist Party of Nicaragua (Partido Socialista de Nicaragua, or PSN) and has been outlawed since 1945. Although the Somoza family has rigorously suppressed the movement and exiled its leaders, the PSN has not been crushed. Communist leaders in exile have been able to organize fronts not only in neighboring countries, but within Nicaragua itself. The party in exile has warmly supported the Cuban revolution, and has found sympathetic response among several thousand bitter opponents of the Somozas, with primary strength concentrated in student and labor organizations.

THE COMPETITIVE SYSTEMS

Thirteen of the twenty countries of Latin America have political systems in this second category. Within this category, however, there are vast differences, some superficial, some substantive. The range extends from a basically two-party system in Uruguay (with one party in power and the other a loyal opposition) to multi-party systems, with a single-party majority (as in Costa Rica or Honduras), or with a coalition government (as in Chile), or even with a coalition of coalitions (as in Panama). Costa Rica is stable, with an established tradition of democratic constitutional government and peaceful transition of power, but Venezuela, which has recently emerged from dictatorship, is frequently threatened with revolts; and El Salvador and the Dominican Republic are in the process of establishing civilian representative governments, following revolutions in 1960 and 1961. In Chile, political organization has suffered virtually no restraints; in Peru and Argentina, large sectors of the voting public (the Apristas and Peronistas, respectively) have been limited in their political aspirations by the military, who effected coups in their countries during 1962 to prevent them from gaining political power. In Brazil, the resignation of President Quadros, in August, 1961, impelled the military into action to prevent the inauguration of Vice-President João ("Jango") Goulart until a constitutional amendment had been passed that reduced Presidential power. By a plebiscite in January, 1963, however, full Presidential powers were restored. Political activities have not been controlled by means of a state of siege in Uruguay for many years, though they have been intermittently restricted by such measures in Argentina since the fall of Perón, in 1955.

Despite these great dissimilarities, all the countries in this category have attempted in recent years to meet their political and social problems through an open political-party system, in which differences of opinion among numerous political groups are aired publicly and fought out in the legislature and at the ballot boxes. Two small and culturally homogeneous countries, Costa Rica and Uruguay, have successfully met the challenge that such a system implies: responsible opposition, whatever the party or group; respect for minority rights and viewpoints; and sufficient consensus on basic issues so that political defeat does not compel resort to force or the threat to use it. The remaining countries in this category have only partially met the prerequisites for stability. Therefore, this type of system operates with difficulty, under the constant threat of insurrection or forcible basic changes in the constitutional process.

ARGENTINA

Argentine politics since the overthrow of dictator Juan Domingo Perón, in 1955, have been characterized by weak and splintered political parties that are unable to muster substantial popular support. Urban workers, strong and well organized in their labor unions, are in large part alienated from national politics, and the armed forces, accustomed for many years to political activity, have not hesitated to intervene to resist labor demands, Peronista political action, and pro-Castro activities. As a result, the Administration of Arturo Frondizi (who was overthrown by a military coup in March, 1962) was constantly maneuvering to steer a careful middle course between these powerful pressure groups, which represented only a minority of the total electorate.

The one political party that survived Argentina's time of trouble (1930–55) was the Radical Civic Union (UCR), now divided into two competing organizations. Originally middle-class-oriented, with some upper-class leaders, it held power between 1916 and 1930. Factionalism in the UCR led eventually to the formation of two parties in 1957—the Intransigent Radicals (UCRI) and the People's Radicals (Unión Cívica Radical Popular, or UCRP). Despite the split, the two wings of the Radicals have virtually monopolized political office since Perón's downfall. Peronist political organizations, as such, were outlawed until early 1962. Followers of the fallen dictator, especially strong in the labor unions, cast blank ballots representing about one-fourth of the electorate in the 1960 congressional elections, but with legalization, they polled almost 34 per cent of the total vote in the congressional and state elections in March, 1962.

The Argentine Communist Party, one of the largest in Latin America, with about 50,000 members, also has its strength concentrated among organized labor in industrial areas. Its primary threat to Argentina's attempt to return to political democracy and economic well-being lies in its efforts to gain control over the Peronistas. Thus far, the Communists, despite their support of the Peronistas in the 1962 elections, have not been able to capture this large and potentially powerful political bloc.

Argentina has seen a political monopoly by the upper class give way to the sharing of power between the upper and middle classes. The transition was achieved peacefully early in the twentieth century, and until 1930, Argentina was considered one of the most stable countries of Latin America. In that year, middle-class failure to heed the demands of urban labor, administrative incompetence by the leaders of the Radical Party, and the world-wide depression brought military intervention and a temporary return of the oligarchy to power.

The coup of September, 1930, was followed by two years of military rule. In the elections of 1932, the traditionalist Conservative Party of the landed oligarchy returned to power and, with the support of the military, remained dominant in Argentine politics until the revolution of 1943. Although the Argentine political situation was thus frozen, social and economic patterns were rapidly developing into new forms. The decade of the 1930's witnessed such rapid industrialization that by the early 1940's industrial goods equaled agricultural production in value. Social changes accompanied economic development. The middle class, of sizable proportions in urban areas as early as World War I, had further expanded with the need for white-collar workers in government and business. Although the landed oligarchy still dominated the countryside, middle-class farm tenants, independent farmers, and small-town merchants became increasingly prominent. Most of these groups chafed under Conservative Party dominance. Adding to the political discontent was the new and growing industrial labor class, whose attempts to organize met determined resistance from government and employers. As a result, when the army marched against the Conservative regime of Ramón Castillo, on June 4, 1943, few could be found to defend the Administration.

Among the officers who engineered the 1943 coup, Juan Domingo Perón was hardly the most prominent member. Installed in the minor post of Minister of Labor, in November, Perón was quick to realize that the civilian support the military regime needed could be obtained only from the neglected working class. The oligarchy had been alienated by the coup, and the middle classes were still attracted by the democratic-oriented Radical Party. For two years, Perón quietly consolidated labor support by promoting the unionization of industrial labor, insisting upon increased wages, and enforcing social-security legislation. At the same time, he ruthlessly eliminated labor leaders who appeared reluctant to accept his lead. His tactics paid off in October, 1945, when labor blocked military efforts to head off Perón's bid for election to the Presidency. These kaleidoscopic changes, between 1930 and 1946, weakened the traditional party system and diminished the power of the middle and upper classes. Labor's political role was enhanced.

Of the traditional power groups, the army alone continued to exert major influence on government, but its activities were checked by labor's determination to hold its gains. The Catholic Church, at first friendly to the Perón regime, became increasingly alienated, after 1952, on moral and political grounds.

The turning point in Perón's career came in mid-1952, at about the time of the death of his wife, Evita. Coincidentally, or not, his problems multiplied, and his support diminished from that time onward. Elements in the military displayed increasing dissatisfaction with his economic and labor policies, farm groups became restive over falling profits, and even labor's enthusiasm waned as inflation eroded its economic gains. When, in 1955, Perón turned to foreign private companies to exploit Argentine oil reserves (in the hope of thus solving his over-all economic problems), some of his closest followers bitterly assailed his abandonment of nationalism. It was his attack on the Church, however, that sparked the military revolt that led to his overthrow, in September, 1955. Like the Radicals of 1930 and the Conservatives of 1943, Perón had few to defend him when the army marched.

Following Perón's overthrow, a military provisional government ruled Argentina for more than two years. Once order had been established, the provisional regime, reluctant to cope with the complex problems of a modern nation, concentrated its energies on restoring constitutional government. It attempted, however, to destroy Peronist influence among the workers and resisted Perón's efforts to return to power. Basic remedies for the social and economic ills of the country were purposely left to the government that would be chosen by popular vote. Despite some misgivings that the President-elect was committed to the Peronists, the military authorities, under the leadership of the Provisional President, General Pedro Aramburu, permitted, in May, 1958, the inauguration of the freely elected candidate of the UCRI, Arturo Frondizi.

Frondizi, the leader of the traditionally middle-class Radical Party, advocated in his electoral campaign much of the nationalism and lower-class-oriented program that Perón had initially sponsored. As a result, he was elected by a wide popular margin that included Peronista support, and was given an overwhelming majority in Congress. However, he began to lose much of his support before the year was out, chiefly because he followed Perón's later oil policy and adopted more orthodox economic measures to combat the chaotic conditions he had inherited from the dictator. Frondizi's emphasis upon the need for austerity, increased production, and private investments alienated much of his labor and nationalist support.

Frondizi's declining popularity was reflected in the losses that his UCRI suffered in the congressional elections of 1960, when the party ran third in total votes behind the UCRP and the blank ballots of the Peronists. In early 1962, despite an impressive December victory in the Santa Fe provincial elections, the UCRI viewed the approaching congressional and state contests of March with some apprehension. The party was particularly doubtful of the two big districts of Buenos Aires Province (with 50 lower-house seats) and in the Federal District (with 35). With half the 192 seats in the lower chamber at stake, the UCRI could well lose its narrow 24-seat majority, especially since under the existing electoral law, the front-running party would gain two-thirds of the seats in a province, the runner-up taking the remainder. The opposition most feared by the UCRI was their disaffected Radical brethren in the UCRP—not the Peronists or the Communists. So confident was Frondizi that Peronist strength had diminished, and so desirous was he of destroying the "myth" of Peronist appeal, that his government permitted several pro-Perón parties, for the first time, to register and obtain places on the ballot. The most important of those was the Justicialist Front, headed by union leader Andrés Framini, who became Justicialist candidate for Governor of Buenos Aires Province. Following vigorously conducted, but violence-free, political campaigns, the electorate streamed to the polls on March 18.

Within an hour of the closing of the polls that Sunday evening, the UCRI knew they had lost their gamble on completely free and open elections in Argentina; Peronism had won a stunning and overwhelming victory. Nationwide, the Justicialists polled more than 2.5 million votes, with almost 1.2 million in Buenos Aires Province alone. The party won 9 of the 14 governorships and 47 of the 96 Chamber of Deputies seats at stake (5 of these had been elected the preceding December). By contrast, the UCRI polled slightly more than 2 million votes, with 764,000 in Buenos Aires Province. The UCRP ran third, with a total of 1.7 million. A government crisis immediately ensued.

Admiral Rojas, and the extreme anti-Peronists and anti-Communists among the army officers, vociferously demanded the ouster of Frondizi. A number of the armed forces leaders, perhaps a majority, seemed willing to permit Frondizi to maintain office, provided a coalition Cabinet of non-Peronists could be formed, and the elections canceled. General Aramburu pleaded for constitutionality, but to no avail, when the UCRP and the Conservatives refused to rally to the regime. Frondizi refused to resign, and he was arrested and placed in custody on Martín García Island. The military chiefs then prevailed upon José María Guido, President of the Senate and constitutional successor, to assume the Presidency. Despite some early attempts to outmaneuver the military, Guido could muster no strength to oppose them. Under military orders, he dissolved the Congress and ordered the reorganization of the political parties. Struggles within the military during the summer of 1962 ended with a victory for the moderates, who advocated civilian political control and a rapid return to constitutional government. The July, 1963, elections saw the UCRP candidates run strongest, with about one-fourth of the total vote, outdistancing the UCRI. The blank vote of the Peronists dropped below 15 per cent.

BRAZIL

The political-party and interest-group structure of Brazil has its origin in the aftermath of the Vargas dictatorship, which ended in 1945. Getúlio Vargas, who seized power in 1930, gave heed to urban middle-class and lower-class aspirations without destroying the economic or political power of the traditional elite. As a result, political control today is exercised by upper- and middle-class leaders who, like Vargas, are aware of urban lower-class needs. The military regard themselves as the guardians of the Constitution. They will technically violate it, or threaten to violate it, and intervene in the political process to preserve the system as they believe it should exist. The Catholic Church, as an organization, engages in political action to protect its vital interests, to resist what it interprets as the advancement of Communism, and to support constitutional order. Individual members of the clergy, moreover, hold a variety of political offices. The lower classes are poorly organized politically. About half of the adult population is disfranchised by literacy tests. Since the bulk of the illiterates are rural lower-class, urban voters have a disproportionately large voice in the conduct of national affairs. Educational advances are further reducing urban illiteracy, but they have almost no effect in rural areas.

Of the four leading Brazilian interest groups (labor, the elite, the army, and the Church), the first two operate primarily from within the political parties, the latter two primarily outside the party system. Through personal and family connections, and by the economic pressures that they can bring to bear, agricultural and industrial producers, importers, and merchants can frequently defeat proposed legislation harmful to their interests. In this manner, they have long delayed tax and land reforms, and have successfully resisted restrictions on coffee production. Business groups have also organized state and national federations to promote their common interests, and recently have established a variety of other, more openly political organizations. Labor, though partially organized since the 1930's, has not fared so well as business in achieving its goals. It is persistently more difficult for labor groups to obtain positive legislation that will introduce reforms into the socio-economic patterns of Brazilian life than for the elite to retain the *status quo*. Moreover, labor can achieve only limited gains by resort to the strike or by the threat of violence. Labor's hope of obtaining wide concessions and a real share of power through political leaders and parties, such as the Brazilian Labor Party of President Goulart, have thus far proved illusory, although events during 1963 appear to be heading in this direction.

The army and the Church are but tenuously attached, as organizations, to political parties. The armed forces believe, and the populace is inclined to agree, that the military has the duty (above the Constitution) to intervene in politics when, in its judgment, such action is necessary to preserve established institutions. In recent years, the military has intervened four times. In 1945, and again in 1954, it ousted President Vargas to restore or ensure constitutional government, and in 1955, it moved to assure the inauguration of democratically elected Juscelino Kubitschek. The military also intervened in August, 1961, after the Brazilian Congress had accepted President Jânio Quadros' resignation. This time, however, elements of the army threatened to bypass the constitutional successor, Vice-President Goulart, on the grounds that his alleged extremist leanings constituted a threat to Brazil's basic institutions. The impasse was resolved when Congress amended the Constitution to establish a modified form of parliamentary government, thereby reducing the power of the President and investing considerable authority in a Prime Minister responsible to the Congress. The military, the majority of whom were torn between distrust of Goulart and the question of constitutionality, accepted the compromise, and the crisis passed. When Presidential powers were restored by plebiscite in January, 1963, the army acquiesced—convinced apparently that Goulart was not the radical that they had feared.

The Catholic Church, too, exerts influence on major issues of vital concern to itself. As ardent foes of Communism, Church leaders have issued public protests and have privately urged the President and Congress not to legalize the Communist Party or establish closer diplomatic or commercial relations with the Sino-Soviet bloc. The Church has also been a major force for political stability at crucial moments. It openly endorsed Kubitschek in April, 1956, in a period of extreme political tension, and helped to stabilize the political situation as no partisan group could do at that time. Furthermore, in the crisis of September, 1961, Church leaders offered to accompany Goulart to Brasília for his inauguration, as a guarantee of safe conduct against military or other potentially hostile forces.

Brazilian political life is also characterized by a multiparty system that is of recent origin. All current political parties date from the end of the Vargas dictatorship, in 1945. None has any direct relation to the traditional conservative or liberal parties of the pre-Vargas era. Because of the broad popular support for the innovations of the 1930's, particularly Vargas' stress on nationalism, economic development, and social welfare, nearly all parties have broadly the same program, and attempt to appeal to all segments of society. As a result, most parties lack precise ideological differences, and appeals to the voters are generally based on the personalities of the leaders. Neither politicians nor voters feel any great sense of party loyalty, and easily shift their allegiances.

Although there are notable policy differences between the extreme left and the extreme right in the party spectrum, all but the Communists support the basic structure of Brazilian political life. Several political leaders, among them former President Kubitschek, strenuously objected to the parliamentary system in effect from September, 1961, to January, 1963. All parties advocate social reform and economic development, although the emphasis varies from party to party—one stressing health or sanitation, another education or industrialization and modernization of agriculture. All parties endorse peaceful international relations, with some members of every party advocating closer ties with the Communist bloc. All parties are nationalistic, differing only in degree, in their desire to see Brazil become a world power, in their advocacy of industrialization as a means to national growth, and in their support of state control over natural resources. All parties strongly support the government oil monopoly, Petrobrás—the symbol of nationalism. No political group with realistic aspirations dares oppose these views.

So badly is the party system factionalized that electoral and governmental coalitions are a constant necessity throughout the country. Alliances or understandings between parties at the national level, however, are not binding at other levels of party organization, even during Presidential campaigns; local issues generally predominate. Every conceivable combination is possible. The party system is further complicated by intraparty factionalism, which exists in all parties as a result of personal disputes or differences on issues, particularly nationalism.

One result of this party fractionalization has been the broad political spectrum represented in the Cabinet. During the parliamentary regime, all major parties participated in the government of Prime Minister Tancredo Neves (September, 1961—June, 1962), and the return to Presidentialism in January, 1963, has not changed the basic conditions of Brazilian political life. Goulart appointed to his new Cabinet members of parties ranging from left to right. The majority are left of center, however, with a liberal sprinkling of moderates. The only major party not represented is the centrist National Democratic Union (União Democrática Nacional, or UDN), the traditional rival of the coalition of the Social Democratic Party (Partido Social Democrática, or PSD) and the Brazilian Labor Party (Partido Trabalhista Brasileira, or PTB), which support Goulart. These three parties, roughly of equal strength, hold 80 per cent of the congressional seats and all but a few of the governorships.

Within the Congress party affiliations are not the prime indicators of the position of the legislators on many issues. Since the parties are composed of broad coalitions of varying interests, party discipline is weak or nonexistent, and individual members vote the interest of their supporters and constituents. Cutting across party lines, two rival political groupings have formed in the Chamber of Deputies: the ultranationalist Nationalist Parliamentary Front and the more moderate-to-conservative Democratic Parliamentary Action, each claiming over 150 of the 409 votes of the Chamber inaugurated in February, 1963.

The Brazilian Communist Party (Partido Comunista Brasileiro, or PCB) has suffered diminished prestige during the past few years, through its poor showing in the 1958 congressional elections and its support of the losing Presidential candidate in 1960. With an estimated membership of 25,000 to 35,000, the PCB can bargain effectively, however, in the fragmented Brazilian party system. And although it has been banned, the Party entered congressional candidates in the crucial October, 1962, elections by running them on the tickets of other parties, particularly Goulart's PTB. The PCB position is further strengthened by its alliance with the small, but increasingly vocal, Brazilian Socialist Party (Partido Socialist Brasileiro, or PSB), which numbers among its representatives in Congress pro-Castro peasant leader Francisco Julião. It has also been assisted by Brazil's renewal of diplomatic relations with the Soviet Union late in 1961, and by the new amnesty law that includes participants in the 1935 Communist revolt. The Communists also control the leading national organization of university students and some key positions in labor organizations.

In August, 1961, Brazil witnessed the breakdown of its established governmental patterns. Right- and left-wing pressure groups, with powerful support in the Congress, bitterly opposed President Jânio Quadros' plans for social and economic reforms, and his new international policy of "independence" from U.S. influence. In an attempt to muster popular support to counteract his opposition, and perhaps in a bid for absolute power, Quadros offered his resignation to Congress and awaited the reaction. However, his power play went awry, either from popular apathy or from his lack of proper preparation. The mobs did not demonstrate in sufficient strength to support their hero of a few months before, and Congress hastily accepted his resignation. As we have seen, Congress then established a parliamentary regime to appease the powerful units of the military who opposed Quadros' constitutional successor, leftist "Jango" Goulart, and at the same time, to satisfy widespread demands that the Constitution be respected.

Parliamentary government did not work particularly well. Prime Minister Neves called it a hybrid, and Goulart never resigned himself to playing a secondary role. Since the establishment of the republic in 1889, Brazil has had no experience with parliamentary government, and the people have come to expect the President to furnish national leadership. The factionalism of Brazilian politics, combined with the absence of a strong executive, produced a regime that could not develop, enact, and implement a coherent policy. Because of the deep divisions among Brazilian political leaders over method and means of tackling a worsening economic and social crisis, and because of the approaching elections in October, the government was reduced to virtual inactivity, or, as the Brazilians called it, "immovability," during most of 1962.

The elections of October 7, 1962, renewed all seats in the Chamber of Deputies for four-year terms and two-thirds of the Senate for eight-year terms. About one-half of the states elected governors. Prior to the elections, all major political figures in Brazil were maneuvering for positions of strength. President Goulart tried to satisfy both conservative and left-wing elements, and former President Kubitschek, a political ally of Goulart, agitated strongly for a return to the Presidential system. Jânio Quadros was politicking to elect a Congress favorable to his elevation to Prime Minister, while Leonel Brizzola, Governor of Rio Grande do Sul, and brother-in-law of Goulart, formed a leftist coalition, the National Liberation Front, with Francisco Julião's Peasant Leagues and the Brazilian Socialist Party. The results of the election were mixed, with some surprises everywhere. Over all, they may be interpreted, however, as a victory for the moderates and centrists. Jânio Quadros lost to Adhemar de Barros in the gubernatorial contest in São Paulo State. Pro-Communist Miguel Arrais was elected Governor of Pernambaco, but democratic candidates triumphed in the other key Northeastern states of Bahia and Ceará. Leftist Leonel Brizzola handily won a congressional seat from Guanabara State (Rio de Janeiro), but his protégé to succeed him, as Governor of Rio Grande do Sul, lost to a moderate conservative. In general, the complexion of the Congress has changed but little, with moderate conservatives comprising a majority. Goulart succeeded in his drive to restore the Presidential system. His demand was endorsed overwhelmingly by plebiscite in January, 1963. Despite this strengthening of the President's position, however, it is not probable that a coherent majority can be formed in Congress to carry through rapid economic and social reforms. Brazil's past history indicates that the government will enact some moderate changes to stave off radical solutions to its problems.

CHILE

Chile in the twentieth century has experienced a moderate degree of political, social, and economic change in urban areas, through evolution rather than revolution. The rural areas, however, have remained almost untouched. Economic development has been in progress for many years, but social-welfare programs and procedures for the more equitable distribution of wealth have lagged since the end of World War II. The elite no longer enjoy undisputed control of political processes in Chile, but they remain powerful, and currently share power with a moderately reform-minded middle-class party, the Radicals. The lower classes exert little direct political influence. Rural laborers have usually followed the lead of the landed magnates, and urban workers have split their votes among parties of the center and left, including the Communists. The military has long been disinclined to play an active political role, and the Church has remained quiet since the Radical-sponsored separation of Church and state was enacted into law, in 1925. Recently, however, several bishops, notably Manuel Larraín Errázuriz, have spoken vigorously in favor of agrarian reform.

The power monopoly of the elite, a combination of rural land-holders and urban industrialists and businessmen, was first broken in 1920, when the middle-class-oriented and labor-supported Radical Party successfully endorsed Arturo Alessandri for the Presidency. Halting and uncertain through the 1920's and most of the 1930's, the reform movement culminated in a Radical-led Popular Front coalition government in 1938. A flood of legislation for urban welfare and economic development poured from the Chilean Congress, supported by the Administration. Although the Radicals continued to hold the Presidency until 1952, the Popular Front fell apart in the immediate postwar years, and inflation eroded the gains of the urban working class. Rural laborers, little affected by the reforms, remained as before—economically depressed and politically unorganized. Middle- and lower-class dissatisfaction with the Radicals' failure to control inflation accounted for the victory of Carlos Ibáñez in 1952, but party fragmentation made it impossible to form a bloc that could command a majority in Congress. Political equilibrium between the major urban interest groups—management and labor—made it difficult to enact legislation opposed by either group.

The failure of middle-class leadership led to a revival of the traditional Conservative and Liberal parties, dominated by rural and urban upper-class leaders, respectively. In the 1958 Presidential election, they threw their support behind Jorge Alessandri, the son of former President Arturo Alessandri. The younger Alessandri ran on a platform of economic austerity and honesty in government. Avoiding party commitments, he presented himself to the voters as an independent, pledged to appoint technical experts to the Cabinet to solve the critical economic and financial problems plaguing the nation. In a hard-fought campaign, Alessandri, with a minority of the vote, narrowly edged out Salvador Allende, of the

Socialist Party, and Eduardo Frei, of the Christian Democrats. Jorge Alessandri, however, is no reformer, and thus far in his Administration, he has done little to ameliorate the lot of the lower classes.

The Radicals and the Christian Democrats, both of whom are pressing for social-reform legislation, occupy the political center in Chilean politics. To the present, the Radicals, the largest party in the Congress, have supported the Alessandri Administration, despite increasing uneasiness with its conservatism. The Christian Democratic Party, one of the largest parties, is frankly in opposition, and has not hesitated to attack the Administration in bitter terms for its failure to act on tax and land reform.

The left is composed of an assortment of non-Marxist, Marxist, and Communist parties, bound together in an uneasy coalition called the Popular Action Front (Frente de Acción Popular, or FRAP). The Socialist Party and the Communist Party, with 20 seats each in Congress, and the non-Marxist National Democratic Party, with 12 seats, constitute the bulk of FRAP strength. The Communist Party, which has a membership of over 25,000, regained legal registration in 1958. With nearly 12 per cent of the vote in the congressional elections of March, 1961, it obtained 16 seats in the Chamber of Deputies and 4 in the Senate, more than doubling its parliamentary strength. Communist influence has been strongest among industrial labor and students. In recent years, however, the Communist-dominated Chilean Workers' Central, the country's major labor confederation, has declined to little more than a paper organization. In addition, the Christian Democrats have cut into Communist strength among university students.

Presidential elections are scheduled for September, 1964; Congressional, for March, 1965. The Chilean political situation is in such flux that prediction is extremely hazardous. The Conservatives and Liberals, who lost strength in the April, 1963, municipal elections, are backing a Radical, while the Christian Democrats, now the country's first party, are again going it alone. If the FRAP holds together, growing popular dissatisfaction with Alessandri's conservatism could give it victory in 1964, and thus bring the Communists into the government. Furthermore, Communist influence on the choice of a President could be considerable, since Chile's multiparty system makes it possible to elect a President with as little as one-third of the total popular vote. However, some Socialists are growing increasingly restive about their alliance with the Communists in the FRAP. They are threatening to withdraw, possibly to form an alliance with the Christian Democrats. Such a coalition would have an excellent chance of electing the next President, achieving a coherent majority in the Congress, and pushing through Chile's much-needed economic- and social-reform programs.

VENEZUELA

Venezuelan political developments in the twentieth century have been marked by vigorous attempts to transform a traditionalist society into a modern democratic, representative nation. In the process, national parties and pressure groups have arisen, authority has been increasingly centralized in the national government, and political integration has been achieved under the pressures of economic nationalism.

Prior to the revolution of 1958, Venezuela had made only slow and halting steps in transition from upper-class domination to more modern social and political complexities. Throughout the nineteenth century, the national government fluctuated wildly between near anarchy and periods of prolonged tyranny. The central government frequently exercised little control outside the capital city and environs, with local *caudillos* ruling their petty domains. With the coming to power of dictator Juan Vicente Gómez (his regime lasted from 1909 to 1935), the authority of the national government was extended for the first time over the whole country.

Serious rumblings of discontent from lower- and middle-class groups were first heard in the 1930's. As a sop to these groups, the ruling elite enacted some reform legislation, but were slow to enforce it. At the end of the decade, middle-class intellectuals and professionals organized a revolutionary reform political party, Democratic Action (Acción Democrática, or AD), which has since come to resemble the social democrats of Western Europe. In 1945, AD, in cooperation with dissatisfied military elements, seized power by a *coup d'état,* but soon alienated not only the upper class, but also the Church, the military, and other reformist parties by its radical reform program and monopoly of patronage. As a result of AD imprudence, the military was able to carry out, in 1948, a countercoup with broad civilian support. Military rule soon disillusioned the important civilian groups, including the Christian Democrats, that had supported the revolt of 1948. The next nine years were marked not only by graft and corruption but also by extreme brutality, murder, and sadism in the regime's attempts to suppress opposition. Oil wealth poured into the government's coffers, but was wastefully expended in gaudy and extravagant construction projects and public-works programs, to the neglect of educational and welfare projects. In January, 1958, dictator General Marcos Pérez Jiménez was deposed by an uprising of virtually all sectors of society, including the military. A civilian-military junta under Admiral Wolfgang Larrazábal assumed authority, permitted free scope to political activities, and prepared for the return to constitutional government.

With the overthrow of the dictator, most Venezuelan interest groups rapidly formed political movements. Because of their association with the discredited tyranny of Pérez Jiménez, some members of the elite refrained from organized political activity, but a group of leaders in business, law, and cultural affairs organized the Republican Integration (Integración Republicana, or IR) Movement and participated in the 1958 elections. Although they polled only 2 per cent of the vote, their influence on government policy has far exceeded their voting strength. The IR itself has since been disbanded, but many of its former leaders have held public office, and many members occupy the nation's leading professional and managerial positions. The stress of the current Administration on social and economic development has enhanced the position of industrial and business leaders, and their influence has grown with their founding of employer associations. The outlook of these groups has been moderate to liberal. They support the reform government of Rómulo Betancourt, advocate the maintenance of constitutional order, and decry the resort to violence of both right- and left-wing extremists.

The urban middle classes have been growing in numbers, competence, and power since the mid-1930's. Middle-class elements have predominated in the new political parties of the past two or three decades, and have furnished the bulk of the leadership for the drive toward political democracy and stability, economic development, and social welfare. They have also supplied leaders for the organization of rural and urban labor, and have tied these lower-class groups tightly to their political organizations. Although politically to the left of the business groups, most of these middle-class leaders are moderate in their political action, reform programs, and nationalistic sentiments.

Organized labor, rural and urban, has been an important force in Venezuelan politics since the mid-1940's, and has played a major role since the overthrow of Pérez Jiménez, in 1958. About half the labor force of the nation belongs to the Confederation of

Workers of Venezuela (Confederación de Trabajadores de Venezuela, or CTV), almost equally divided between rural and urban elements. The majority of both the urban and the rural labor class supports the present governing coalition. Only a minority has succumbed to extreme left-wing appeals to violence and radical reform. Most Venezuelan workers are, thus far, at least minimally satisfied with the pace of the reforms that have been implemented since 1958, although they would like to see it stepped up.

Students and intellectuals have made up a major segment of leftist extremism, but their failure to unseat the government, or to attract broad popular support, has diminished their influence and prestige. At the other extreme, rightist military elements have been easily crushed in several attempts at revolt. On the whole, the prestige of the military has grown appreciably since 1958, as the vast majority of officers have refrained from political action, and have firmly supported the government and the Constitution in the face of revolts from the right and the left. The Church, seldom an important factor in Venezuelan politics, has also gained stature by its support of constitutionality and moderate reform.

Party activities blossomed with the fall of Pérez Jiménez. The three major parties revitalized their national organizations, agreed on a broad reform program, and cooperated in preparations for a coalition government. The Venezuelan Communist Party (Partido Comunista Venezolano, or PCV) resumed overt activities, expanded its membership, and attempted to associate itself with the parties of the coalition. Since the non-Communist parties could not agree on a joint candidate for President, each party presented its own nominee for chief executive, as well as candidates for congressional seats and state offices. In one of the very few free and honest elections in Venezuelan history, Rómulo Betancourt, the nominee of the AD, won the Presidency, and his party won a majority of seats in both houses of Congress. Betancourt immediately invited the other two major parties, the Christian Democrats (Comité Organizado por Elecciones Independientes, or COPEI) and the Republican Democratic Union (Unión Republicana Democrática, or URD), to participate in his government. The Communists, though excluded from the Cabinet, agreed to support the governing coalition. Betancourt was inaugurated in February, 1959, and a tripartite committee was established in May to settle points of conflict among the cooperating parties. Despite these efforts, the coalition began to weaken by mid-1960. Marxist elements within the AD left the party in May and formed a new party, the

Movement of the Revolutionary Left (Movimiento de Izquierda Revolucionaria, or MIR). Shortly thereafter, the Communists announced their withdrawal of support of the government, and by November, the URD formally left the coalition. These three groups joined forces in attacking the government for alleged delays in reforms, and participated in the leftist agitations in October and November. President Betancourt then reorganized his government to include AD, COPEI, and some independents.

AD, with an enrolled membership of about 800,000, and 89 seats in the Congress, is Venezuela's largest political party. At present, however, it is split into two factions, one of which, known as the ARS, has aligned itself with the leftist opposition to organize the Chamber of Deputies. AD strength is concentrated primarily among laboring groups in small towns and villages. Almost unchallenged, the party controls the Federation of Rural Workers of Venezuela, with about 500,000 members. It controls a smaller percentage of urban workers in Caracas than in other cities, but possesses considerable urban middle-class appeal everywhere. The party program is nationalistic and socialistic. It recognizes the necessity of foreign investment capital, but advocates its close regulation. The party also emphasizes the need for industrialization, agrarian reform, and economic diversification to escape present dependence on petroleum revenues for dollar imports. During 1960, Betancourt and the AD broke with Fidel Castro over the latter's attempt to export his revolution to Venezuela.

In mid-1960, a group of young politicians led by Domingo Alberto Rangel was expelled from the AD because of their attack on the party's moderate leadership. The dissidents, including one Senator and 15 Deputies, formed the MIR, and attracted extreme leftists and Marxists from the AD and URD, primarily in the federal district. The MIR claims to represent the exploited classes of Venezuela. It advocates a national-liberation movement to replace the present government with a Castro-type regime. More specifically, it calls for the nationalization of mineral resources, particularly petroleum, diplomatic relations with the Sino-Soviet bloc, and thoroughgoing land reform. Its revolutionary tactics in 1960 and 1961 failed to arouse popular support and damaged the movement's influence and prestige.

The COPEI, the junior partner in the governing coalition, is second only to the AD in size, with an estimated 400,000 members and 25 seats in the Congress. Founded in 1945 by Catholic intellectuals, the COPEI, in its early years, opposed the AD. Disgusted with the repression of the Pérez Jiménez regime, and favorably impressed with the moderation of Betancourt, the Christian Democrats joined with the AD to carry through a moderate reform program. Since 1958, the party has vigorously supported the Betancourt Administration against extremist attacks from right and left. Rafael Caldera, leader of the COPEI, served until 1962 as President of the Chamber of Deputies. The party draws its principal strength from practicing Catholics of the middle class and from rural and urban labor. The COPEI insists that it is not a clerical party, but freely admits that its social program is based on Christian principles, particularly on the social encyclicals of the Popes. On specific issues, its program is in close agreement with that of the AD.

The URD, Venezuela's third largest party, with more than 300,000 members, has moved far to the left since 1958. An original member of the governing coalition in Betancourt's Administration, the URD broke with him in November, 1960, at the time of the antigovernment student and leftist riots. Shortly thereafter, the party joined with the MIR and the Communists in attempts to replace Betancourt with a Castro-type government. Formed in 1945 by upper-class professional men as a conservative counterweight to the AD, the URD was later transformed into a personalist movement with little ideological content, under the leadership of Jóvito Villalba, an independent politician with a popular following. It grew rapidly during the 1950's, and with the popular Admiral Larrazábal as its candidate in 1958, the party polled almost 35 per cent of the Presidential votes, and elected 45 members to Congress. It seeks to attract the independent voter, and relies more heavily than the other parties on unorganized groups of the middle and lower classes, such as small businessmen, artisans, and slum dwellers in Caracas. It has little strength among rural and industrial labor, students, or professional groups. In its program, the URD is opportunistic rather than ideologically committed. It supports a social and economic program similar to that of the AD, but presents it in a more sensational and extreme manner. It opposes Betancourt's anti-Communist, anti-Castro, and pro-U.S. position.

The Partido Comunista Venezolano, or PCV, with a current membership of about 30,000, and 9 seats in the Congress, is one of the largest Communist Parties in Latin America. Although formally outlawed by the dictatorship, the PCV was less harassed than the AD, and several of its leaders and sympathizers even occupied high positions in the Pérez Jiménez regime. The Communists joined the revolt against the dictator, and though not included in Betancourt's government, supported the Administration until mid-1960. The PCV then announced a policy of militant opposition to the regime's moderate program. Party membership consists primarily of labor and students in the federal district and in the oil fields. The Party has also attracted a few intellectuals. The Communists have cooperated with the MIR in attempts to overthrow Betancourt. They hope to secure Venezuela's neutrality in the Cold War, and to increase anti-U.S. sentiment in the country.

The next general elections in Venezuela are scheduled for the end of 1963, and it appears that Betancourt's chances of fulfilling his term, short of assassination, are still very good. Furthermore, should Betancourt continue the current pace of his reform program, his AD Party should have little difficulty in retaining its leading position. Currently, there is no serious threat to the regime from either the right or the left. Revolts by extremists from both sides of the political spectrum have failed to attract mass support, and have been crushed with comparative ease. In addition, with broad segments of the population committed to constitutional order and moderation, the extremists have only damaged their position by resort to violence. This is not to say that Betancourt has no problems. Venezuela is just beginning to emerge from an economic recession. Unemployment and illiteracy are still high, and the housing shortage is a nightmare. Neither has Betancourt implemented all the reforms he has promised, nor has he solved all the social and economic problems that he inherited from Pérez Jiménez. Betancourt has also failed to stamp out terrorist activities that have swept over Venezuela since his inauguration. During 1962, particularly, murders, robberies, and property destruction under the direction of the Communist Armed Forces of National Liberation (Fuerzas Armadas de Liberación Nacional, or FALN) gravely, if only temporarily, disrupted normal economic and social life. In Betancourt's favor, however, is the fact that Venezuela's laboring classes and military forces have continued to support the regime. Venezuela, the richest country in Latin America, has the potential to meet adequately its remaining social and economic difficulties. In sum, then, Betancourt has been willing and able to implement reform programs that are more extensive and effective than any others in Latin America, although less sweeping than Cuba's. His government has vigorously attacked the problems of land reform, housing, education, and medical care. Betancourt has accomplished a great deal during his tenure, and he can be expected to continue the program to the end of his term.

PERU

Peru today is one of several countries in Latin America that has experienced little change from nineteenth-century political and social patterns. A small upper class of landowners and wealthy urbanites dominates political life, while the vast majority of the population—in large part Indian—plays no effective role. The small, fragmented middle class has little consciousness of unity. Many of the more ambitious among the latter strive to emulate the upper class rather than to develop a middle-class political program.

In this premodern setting, pressure groups play a far more vital role than parties (with a single exception) in national political life. Most of these groups promote the interests of the powerful oligarchy of closely interrelated families. In general, members of the elite have preferred not to hold political office, but rather to exercise their influence indirectly. There have been exceptions, of course. The two outstanding recent examples are deposed President Manuel Prado and his ex-Prime Minister, Pedro Beltrán. Various families of the oligarchy control the press and other communications media, as well as employer associations of producers and merchants. Seven of these virtually dominate Peruvian economic and political life. The National Agrarian Society, the National Society of Industries, and the National Mineral and Petroleum Society are the big three. Of lesser, but still considerable, importance, are the National Fishing Society, the Association of Chambers of Commerce of Peru, the Merchants' Corporation of Peru, and the Chamber of Commerce of Lima. These seven frequently form a common front to promote, or to counter, legislation and government policies affecting their interests.

Labor and student organizations can also exert some influence on the government, but to a much smaller degree than the oligarchical groups. Unionized labor, about 400,000 strong, operates largely through the American Revolutionary Popular Alliance (Alianza Popular Revolucionaria Americana, or APRA), a political party of the non-Communist left. During the late 1950's, labor unrest was growing to serious proportions, but it has abated somewhat since 1960, with the government's promotion of programs to ease the land and housing problems. Students, as volatile in Peru as in most other countries of Latin America, engage in political action through their university student federations. Various student

groups at the University of San Marcos, in Lima, with an enroll-
ment of about 12,000, have affiliated with the Apristas, the Christian Democrats, and the Communists. Rural labor is largely unorganized, although a Peruvian Peasants' League has been formed under the leadership of Rafael Avalos, and probably under the auspices of APRA.

Of all the major political parties of Peru, only APRA has demonstrated its power to attract and maintain substantial popular
support over a period of years. The explanation for APRA's en-
durance in Peru for more than three decades, in the face of
political persecution and harassment, lies in the quality of the
party's leadership, and in the relevance of its ideology and program to the needs of the country. At first extremist and Marxist,
APRA has modified its philosophical base to conform with the
moderate reformist thinking that is widely accepted not only in
Peru, but throughout Latin America. Vigorously anti-Communist
and vociferously nationalistic, APRA has securely protected itself
from charges of foreign influence in its leadership, in its goals, or
in its specific program of land, tax, educational, and other reforms.

Conceived originally as an international Latin American revolutionary movement, APRA was founded in Mexico, in 1924, by its
leader-in-exile, Víctor Raúl Haya de la Torre, as a challenge to
the dictatorship of Augusto B. Leguía (1919–30) in his native
Peru. Although the movement never developed on an international
scale, the Peruvian Aprista Party was organized in 1931 to participate in the elections of that year. Haya de la Torre stood for the
Presidency, but was robbed of his victory by the opposition, which
controlled the ballot boxes. Despite the fraud, APRA won twenty-
three seats in the constitutional convention, but a new *caudillo* outlawed the party and jailed or exiled its leaders. Regaining legal
status in 1945, APRA secured 82 of 197 seats in the Congress,
and materially assisted the election of José Luis Bustamante as
President. Following an outbreak of violence and a navy revolt—
both blamed on APRA, despite the lack of any proof—Bustamante
forced the Aprista members to resign from his Cabinet and outlawed the party in 1948, to appease the powerful oligarchy.

Still not satisfied, the oligarchy supported a military coup led by
General Manuel Odría. After two years of provisional rule, Odría
had himself elected President in 1950, hand-picked his Congress,
censored the press, and based his regime on army and upper-class
support. Odría's dictatorship was relatively mild, economically progressive, and administratively efficient. Under pressure from civilian

groups, the dictator permitted free elections, in June, 1956, for the Presidency and both houses of Congress—to serve a constitutional six-year term. Moderate conservative Manuel Prado, supported by APRA and his own personal party, the Peruvian Democratic Movement (Movimiento Democrático Peruano, or MDP), emerged the victor in the Presidential contest over leftist Fernando Belaúnde Terry and conservative Hernando de Lavalle, who had the support of Odría. Since APRA was outlawed and could not run its own Presidential candidate, it supported Prado in return for a promise of legalization, which Prado promptly fulfilled. Aprista candidates for Congress ran as independents. As a result of the congressional elections, Prado's MDP, with 70 seats in the Chamber of Deputies and 21 in the Senate, formed a coalition government with the Aprista Independent Parliamentary Democratic Front, which held 33 seats in the lower house and 5 in the upper, and with de Lavalle's National Unification (Unificación Nacional, or UN), which had 15 Deputies and 5 Senators.

Despite some shifts in party allegiance, the basic alliance between the APRA and Prado's MDP held up for the six-year term. For the June 6, 1962, Presidential and congressional elections, seven parties vied for power, but there were only three serious contenders for the office of chief executive: former President Manuel Odría; the APRA leader, Haya de la Torre; and the Popular Action (formerly National Action) leader, Belaúnde Terry. So deeply had the Aprista doctrine of reform penetrated the fabric of Peruvian society that every major party with expectations of winning the 1962 general elections paid at least lip service to the need for social-welfare legislation, particularly in agrarian, housing, and educational affairs. The more conservative parties offered, at best, palliatives. Belaúnde, Beltrán, and the Christian Democrats presented more realistic programs, but only the APRA, with its middle-class leadership and lower-class support, had the political organization to give solid backing to its program. With minor parties polling about 10 per cent of the vote, no candidate received the one-third majority necessary for election. Under these conditions, the decision should have been made by the newly elected Congress. Aprista candidates ran strongly, and took about 45 per cent of the congressional seats, but no one party won an absolute majority. Negotiations then proceeded among the leaders of the three principal parties: Haya de la Torre of APRA, Manuel Odría of the Odriísta National Union, and Belaúnde of the AP. During the first week of July, Haya de la Torre announced his renunciation, in the face of army opposition, and conferred with Belaúnde on the possibility of a pact. When these talks failed, Belaúnde demanded cancellation of the election or revolution. Haya, in the meantime, met with Odría, but before a pact could be negotiated, the army, on July 18, arrested President Prado, nullified the election on charges of fraud, and set up a military junta. The junta quickly disclaimed any intention of establishing indefinite military rule and promised elections for June, 1963. Civilian protests were few and ineffective. APRA's younger leaders did not give full support to the party's strike call, apparently because they were disgruntled with the older leader's attempted deal with Odría. On the eve of the June 9, 1963, elections, a repetition of the previous year's inconclusive results appeared likely, as the same three major candidates had all campaigned strongly. Speculation was rife as to whether the military would again block APRA should it emerge the winner. With 90 per cent of the slightly over 2 million registered voters participating, Haya de la Torre again received almost exactly one-third of the ballots, but this time trailed Belaúnde by 100,000 votes. Since the fifty-one-year old Belaúnde was generally considered to be the preference of the military, the junta did not hesitate to hand over power to him. What the populist leader will do with it remains to be seen, and the political future of Peru remains uncertain, especially in view of the fact that, while all major political groups admit the need for reform, all (including APRA) fear the consequences of uncontrollable and radical change.

The Peruvian Communist Party (Partido Comunista Peruano, or PCP), outlawed by the Constitution, may not enter candidates in elections, but it labors under few other restrictions. With an estimated 8,000–9,000 members, and perhaps twice as many sympathizers, the PCP has fought with APRA for control of the Confederation of Peruvian Workers. It has succeeded in capturing about one-eighth of the organized Peruvian labor force, primarily in the south. It has also placed some of its members in key positions in the Confederation, and has begun to gain adherents among agricultural laborers. The Communists have been struggling to wrest control of the University Student Federation from APRA. In the December, 1960, student elections in the University Federation of San Marcos, representing about 12,000 students, the PCP, with the assistance of pro-Castro students, elected the President of the students' federation with a plurality that almost equaled the combined votes of the Aprista and Christian Democratic candidates. In the political arena, however, the Communists have been able to elect only a few members to Congress under other party labels. Prospects are slight that the PCP will gain legal status. All major Peruvian parties are anti-Communist, even the socialistic-oriented Apristas.

URUGUAY

Political power in Uruguay is divided between elite and middle-class groups. The former dominate the rural areas, four-fifths of which are devoted to livestock grazing. The latter, with lower-class support, share control with business and commercial interests in Montevideo and its environs. The landed magnates have organized the Rural Federation, a highly effective interest group. Business interests are also well organized in confederations, with each type of business activity controlling its own association. In general, urban business groups have appeared more powerful than the landowners, but when the latter's vital interests are at stake, they have been able to force the government's hand. All interest groups exert continuing pressure on both the executive and legislative branches of the government, and use techniques closely resembling those used by their counterparts in the United States. The Church, the military, and labor do not constitute major interest groups in Uruguay. In the early decades of the twentieth century, middle-class leaders sponsored, and business interests acquiesced in, a broad program of benefits to urban labor through liberal social-welfare legislation. In recent years, however, labor has not had the strength to force through continued wage increases commensurate with steady inflation.

Discounting some minor opposition from socialists, Communists, and Christian Democrats (Civic Union), two parties dominate the political arena, the Colorados and the Blancos. Until the general elections of 1958, some observers had considered Uruguay a modified one-party state, in that the socialistic Colorados (originally a liberal-traditionalist party) had governed the country for about ninety years, despite strong opposition from the landholders, who dominated the rural provinces. With the Blanco (conservative-traditionalist) victories of 1958 and 1962, and the peaceful transfer of power in the former year, Uruguay has laid to rest any doubts about her two-party system.

Uruguay is the only country in Latin America that has experimented with a plural executive as a means of curbing Presidential authority and sharing executive power between major political parties. From 1918 to 1934, the country first tried having a single executive share power with a National Council of Administration, elected by proportional representation. This system was replaced in 1933 with the conventional single executive and a nine-man appointive ministry. The major parties were represented proportionally in the ministry, and a majority could override Presidential decisions. In 1942, minor changes in the executive branch granted the President greater freedom from the dictates of his Cabinet. Finally, in 1952, a nine-man National Council of Government, with a rotating Presidency, replaced the President. In effect, the ministry was retained. The party with the majority vote receives six seats on the Council, and that with the minority vote receives three. This method of distribution of the elective executive offices is carried down to the provincial level. Patronage is shared at all governmental levels, in like manner, by a formal legislative enactment of 1931.

The Blanco victory of 1958 resulted, in large part, from the inability of Colorado leaders to mitigate the deepening economic crisis. Concentrating their attention for many years upon the needs of the urban population of Montevideo (containing about half the total of the entire country), the Colorados pushed industrial development, social welfare, and nationalization. Although the basic economy of Uruguay was, and still is, agricultural and pastoral, the Colorados neglected rural development. Consequently, the economy became seriously unbalanced. The Blancos, representing rural and some urban upper-class interests, are attempting to restore the balance, and are inclined to favor the gradual extension of social welfare into the rural areas.

The legalized Communist Party is small (4,000 members) but articulate. For the November, 1962, elections, the Communists formed the Leftist Liberation Front (Frente Izquierda de Liberación, or FIDEL) with small pro-Castro and nationalist groups. FIDEL won four seats with slightly more than 3½ per cent of the popular vote. Communist strength is concentrated primarily in intellectual and labor circles, but the vast majority of workers, students, and professional people are not Communists. The Communists pose no threat to Uruguay's democracy.

GUATEMALA

Guatemala offers a prime example in Latin America of a country that is suffering politically, economically, and socially from an arrested revolution. Until the coup of March, 1963, the political system had consisted of a number of squabbling parties, few of which are representative of any economic or social sector of the country. Most have their origins in the past decade, and were founded to further the designs of ambitious politicians, rather than to pursue a program of action. Highly centralized, irresponsible, and possessing little rank-and-file membership, these parties have been forced into unstable political coalitions to form either a government majority or the opposition. The closest political alliance thus far has been formed by the opposition Revolutionary and Christian Democratic parties, which together constitute the non-Communist left in Guatemala. They have cooperated well on labor and social-welfare legislation, but have split on questions concerning political office and international affairs.

Guatemala's current political difficulties have their origin in the revolution of 1944 and its aftermath. Until that year, Guatemala had been firmly controlled by the elite within the minority Ladino class, that is, the sector of society that spoke Spanish and in general was Western-oriented culturally. Political organizations consisted of the traditional conservative and liberal parties, which vaguely represented upper-class rural and urban interests, respectively, but served in fact only as instruments for political control by the dictator, who offered protection to the social and economic *status quo*. The Indians, who form the bulk of the population, remained outside effective national life. Those who belonged to neither class (teachers, intellectuals, some professionals and businessmen, and university students) felt frustrated in their political and economic ambitions. Revolting against the dictatorship of Jorge Ubico (1931–44), they set out their goals in the new Constitution of 1945. Combining socialistic and nineteenth-century liberal aspirations, this younger generation postulated state responsibility for economic development and social welfare, guaranteed private property and the free enterprise system, and supported political democracy, limited government, and the neutralization of the armed forces.

Under the first revolutionary Administration, that of Juan José Arévalo, few substantive changes occurred in any phase of Guatemalan life, but radicals and extremists began to occupy vital positions within and outside the government. Under Arévalo's successor, Jacobo Arbenz, the pace of reform stepped up in social and economic affairs, but at the expense of political liberalism. Extremists consolidated their positions, and Communists began to achieve prominence in the new labor unions (both urban and rural), the government and political parties, and influential intellectual circles.

In 1952, the Communist Party was legalized and became part of the government coalition. Political power rested with the President, who was assisted by an inner circle of intellectuals, politicians, and army officers controlling the patronage and all the financial resources of the government. Potential army opposition was bought off, and the elite and the Church were too ill organized and weak to offer effective resistance.

As labor grew in stature under Communist direction, and as ties with the Soviet bloc increased, opposition began to grow, especially in the army. Exiles, gathered in Honduras, invaded the country in June, 1954, with U.S. support and encouragement. When army leaders refused to support Arbenz, his regime collapsed. The leader of the invading forces, Colonel Carlos Castillo Armas, had himself elected President in November, 1954, and, in March, 1956, established a new Constitution and installed a new Congress. Resisting the political pressures of those who wanted to restore pre-1944 conditions, Castillo Armas accepted the principles of the revolution of 1944 and many of its specific reforms. He verbally supported democracy, social reform, economic development, and nationalism, but his program was basically conservative. He permitted labor unions to organize and bargain, but he screened the leaders and discouraged national confederations. He continued agrarian reform, but on a lesser scale. In his educational program, however, he surpassed the combined accomplishments of Arévalo and Arbenz. He suppressed student political demonstrations, however, and on several occasions imposed a temporary censorship on the press. Under Castillo Armas, political democracy progressed no further than it had under his predecessors. A single progovernment party dominated politics, elections were controlled, and power was concentrated in the hands of the President, who was supported by the army. Martial law and exile, particularly of Communists, were used to suppress disorder, but on the whole, civil liberties were respected. Castillo's career was cut short by his assassination, in July, 1957.

The ensuing period was marked by interim governments and political instability. To assure its continuance in power, Castillo's political machine called for elections in October, before rival political parties could properly organize. The elections were nullified, however, by mob action supported by the army, and new balloting was scheduled for January, 1958. In the second election, the most honest and free in Guatemalan history, Miguel Ydígoras Fuentes, a long-time aspirant to the Presidency, won a plurality with his personalist Democratic National Reconciliation (popularly called Redención) Party, and was formally elected by Congress in February. The government was relatively stable under Ydígoras, and some progress was made toward political maturity. The Indians were slowly being drawn into national life, particularly through some of the political parties, and the victory of Ydígoras' Redención Party and its ally, the National Democratic Movement (Movimiento Democrático Nacional, or MDN), in the congressional elections of December, 1961, put him in a very strong position. Conflicting social and economic demands plagued his regime, but his downfall came from military intervention to meet an alleged Communist threat. The Communist Guatemalan Labor Party (Partido Guatemalteco del Trabajo, or PGT) was outlawed by the Constitution of 1956, and most of its leaders have been in exile since then. The Communists have little political effectiveness, except among students and the small organized labor movement, but they looked toward the general elections scheduled for December, 1963, and the candidacy of Juan José Arévalo; as a vehicle for influencing the course of future events. Arévalo, in exile in Mexico until March of 1963, had not overtly sought the support of the Communists, but his known nationalism and anti-U.S. posture, as well as his broad political tolerance, made him their choice. When he returned to Guatemala in March, the military ousted Ydígoras and took control of the government, with Colonel Enrique Peralta heading the new regime.

In general, political power in Guatemala is exercised primarily through the executive branch of the government. Political fragmentation—combined with armed forces support of the regime—permitted the President to govern by decree when he deemed it necessary. Political stability has been seriously threatened in recent years. Until the coup of March, 1963, the President's ability to play off rival political and social factions against each other, and to focus popular attention on international issues—such as Guatemala's claim to British Honduras—had reduced the pressures.

EL SALVADOR

Prior to the *coup d'état* of October, 1960, El Salvador was tightly controlled by a group of families connected by ties of blood, marriage, and economics. For the most part, the leaders of this bloc were content to leave political offices to professional politicians or to the military—whoever could best guarantee the continuance of the social *status quo*. The middle class was small and politically weak; the lower class, except for a few thousand organized urban workers, exercised no influence in political life. Despite a rigid social structure, El Salvador had made some apparent progress in the first three decades of the twentieth century toward stable and constitutional (if not always democratic) government. Beginning in 1931, however, with the rule of General Maximiliano Hernández Martínez, a long period of dictatorship, punctuated by periods of disorder, overtook the country.

Following the ouster of Hernández in 1944, a series of provisional governments and coups culminated, in 1948, in the seizure of power by a group of young army officers. Lieutenant Colonel Oscar Osorio, emerging as the dominant figure, had himself elected President, in 1950, for a six-year term. At the end of his tenure, he sponsored Lieutenant Colonel José María Lemus as the nominee of his political organization, the Revolutionary Party for Democratic Unification (Partido Revolucionario de Unificación Democrática, or PRUD). Elected virtually without opposition, Lemus, after a series of clashes with university students, was overthrown in October, 1960, in a bloodless coup by a leftist junta. A countercoup by the military in January, 1961, installed a more moderate, civilian-military Directorate, which prepared El Salvador for the return to constitutional government by holding elections, in December, for a Constituent Assembly. The Assembly quickly adopted a revised version of the Constitution of 1950, reconstituted itself into a legislative assembly, and named a provisional President in January, 1962. The Directorate was dissolved, and elections for a constitutional President were scheduled for April. Colonel Julio Rivera, an ex-member of the Directorate, was elected. Opposition parties abstained from the election.

Contrary to previous coups and revolutions in El Salvador's history, those of 1960 and 1961 were motivated more by social and economic issues than by political ones, though the latter, of course, were not absent. During the administrations of Osorio and Lemus, some progress had been made toward economic development and social welfare. Roads were built, electric-power output was significantly increased, some health and sanitation measures were begun, and a few starts were made to alleviate critical housing and educational shortages. Lemus, in particular, seemed aware of the acute problems facing the rural lower classes, with their high illiteracy, birth, and infant mortality rates, and their minimal incomes and levels of living. Lemus, however, was limited in his ability to carry out needed reforms because of the political power of the landed families, whom he did not seriously challenge.

The leftist junta that overthrew Lemus had no such qualms. Communists and other extremists who supported the junta moved rapidly to build their strength by carrying out agitation and organization programs among rural workers—activities that had been illegal under the old regime. Before they could consolidate their positions, however, a more moderate reform group of military personnel and civilians overthrew the junta and inaugurated its own program.

The Directorate, as the new government was called, confirmed its adherence to the social-reform recommendations of the Act of Bogotá and the Alliance for Progress. It quickly nationalized the Central Bank, reduced urban slum rentals, and ordered rural wage increases. Despite some grumblings from the upper classes, the Directorate built up wide popular support for its program, and then quietly dissolved itself with the re-establishment of constitutional government early in 1962.

A new political party system emerged from the revolutionary period of 1960–61. The PRUD disappeared; its place was taken by the socialistic National Conciliation Party (Partido de Conciliación Nacional, or PCN), organized by Julio Rivera, a leading member of the Directorate. In what appeared to be a free election on December 17, 1961, the PCN won about two-thirds of the popular vote and all the seats in the Assembly. The political opposition consists of the centrist Authentic Constitutional Party, the Union of Democratic Parties, and the April and May Revolutionary Party (Partido Revolucionario de Abril y Mayo, or PRAM), a Communist-front organization with several thousand members, including Communist and pro-Castro groups. The small Salvadoran Communist Party, with an estimated 500 members, had infiltrated some labor and student groups in the 1950's, but its strength was reduced by the firm anti-Communist position of the revolutionary government, and by the reform program now in progress. It poses no immediate threat, but a breakdown in order, or a failure of the reform program, would see a rapid rise in its strength, as during the period from October, 1960, to January, 1961.

COSTA RICA

Politically, socially, and economically, Costa Rica presents some marked contrasts with her neighbors in Central America. With a predominantly European population, a literacy rate of about 80 per cent, a fairly equitable distribution of land and other wealth, and a tradition of stable and democratic government, Costa Rica is afflicted with fewer of the problems confronting the rest of the area. These favorable factors should not be overstressed, however. The lot of the coastal Negro minority is unenviable, per capita income is low, and revolutions, dictators, and would-be dictators have at times threatened the nation's democratic traditions.

Costa Rica's current political conflicts, parties, and leaders originated in the troubles of 1948. Following the elections of that year, outgoing President Teodoro Picado and ex-President Rafael Angel Calderón Guardia, with the support of local Communists, tried to impose Calderón as the head of government, despite his defeat by Otilio Ulate in the Presidential elections. In a brief but bloody and bitter civil war, the Picado-Calderón forces were defeated by those of Ulate and José Figueres, a plantation owner. Figueres headed a provisional government for eighteen months, after which he turned the government over to his ally, Ulate, the legally elected President. Converting his Army of National Liberation into the National Liberation Party (Partido de Liberación Nacional, or PLN), Figueres stood for the Presidency himself in 1953, winning office with a comfortable 65 per cent of the popular vote. After making campaign promises of economic development and improved living conditions for the lower-income groups, Figueres, in office, promoted a mildly socialistic program. With the end of his term approaching, more conservative groups in Costa Rica presented Mario Echandi Jiménez as the candidate of Ulate's personalist National Union Party (Partido de Unión Nacional, or PUN). Figueres' PLN nominated Francisco Orlich. In an unexpected upset, Echandi narrowly won by a majority of 8,000 votes. The PLN defeat can be attributed to its overconfidence, and the defection of a sizable faction led by Jorge Rossi, who also ran for the Presidency and siphoned off PLN votes from Orlich.

The defeat was a shock to Figueres and his party. Immediately after the elections, the PLN began work to win the elections scheduled for February, 1962. It set up the Institute of Political and Social Studies to train Costa Rican political leaders, and developed a country-wide organization, extending to the grass-roots level, even in rural areas. When the 1962 elections arrived, this smooth-working machine delivered more than 50 per cent of the vote to the PLN Presidential candidate, Francisco Orlich (the loser in 1958), and to the PLN congressional candidates—thus giving the party 30 seats in the legislature, an absolute majority. The extent of the PLN victory in 1962 was as surprising as its defeat in 1958.

On the whole, the campaign was conducted on a relatively high level, despite some biting criticisms leveled at each other by the several opponents. Four parties entered Presidential candidates and congressional slates. In addition to the moderately leftist PLN, there were the centrist Republican Party (Partido Republicano, or PR), led by Calderón Guardia; the conservative National Union Party (PUN), led by Ulate; and the Communist-line Popular Democratic Action Party (Partido de Acción Democrática Popular, or PADP), led by Enrique Obregón. The conduct of President Echandi was admirable throughout the campaign. He maintained a policy of complete neutrality, and enforced peace, quiet, and order on election day. More than 385,000 voters turned out, representing more than three-quarters of the registered electorate—in contrast to 1958, when only 221,500 ballots were cast. The large increase is attributed to the work of the PLN, particularly in the rural districts.

In the past, elections were won and lost in San José, but the rural vote proved decisive in 1962. Ulate and his PUN conducted his campaign on the old personalist style, with little or no organization. Sensing defeat, many of his supporters deserted him for Orlich rather than for Calderón, whom they feared and hated. The PUN, however, won 8 congressional seats. Calderón and his Republican Party were better organized than Ulate, but started late and neglected the rural areas. Calderón based his calculations on the vote in San José, and had the electoral patterns of 1958 been repeated, Calderón would probably have won. As it was, he polled 35 per cent of the Presidential vote, and his party won 19 seats in Congress. The Communist-line PADP Presidential candidate polled only 3,300 votes, and its congressional slate only 9,000 (2 per cent). The small Communist Popular Vanguard Party (Partido Vanguardia Popular, or PVP), with an estimated membership of 300, has been outlawed since 1948. Its primary strength is in labor and front groups, but it poses no threat to Costa Rica's political democracy and stability, which the elections of February, 1962, strengthened further.

THE DOMINICAN REPUBLIC

The long and often bloody military dictatorship of Rafael Trujillo (lasting from 1930 to 1961) preserved the social structure of the rural area, with its system of large landholdings, its plantation economy built upon sugar, and its dependent and illiterate peasantry. In the cities, however, the era of Trujillo brought important social and economic changes. The development of social and educational services and the founding of light industries created thousands of jobs in government and private employment. Urban lower and middle classes grew accordingly, and although deprived of political expression, the latter provided the leaders of an underground political opposition. The assassination of Trujillo destroyed the power structure the dictator had created. Middle-class demands for an open political system attracted labor support, and since May, 1961, the Dominican Republic has been struggling to achieve a new political order based on democratic political procedures, further economic development, and a more equitable distribution of national income.

In the early years of the twentieth century, the Dominican Republic was subject to U.S. intervention, including marine occupation, military rule, the reorganization of its armed forces, and the supervision of its finances. Although certain material benefits accrued to the island republic, no permanent gains toward stable and democratic government resulted from the U.S. occupation. Within six years after the withdrawal of the last U.S. troops in 1924, the country fell under the rule of General Rafael Trujillo Molina. Until his assassination in May, 1961, General Trujillo governed the Dominican Republic, usually as President, but sometimes as President-maker.

No one can deny the many material benefits the Trujillo regime brought to the country. Peace and order prevailed, roads and port facilities were built, light industries were created, and schools and hospitals were constructed. The price, however, for these improvements was the concentration of untold wealth in the hands of the extensive Trujillo family and their allies, and severely repressive measures against all political opposition. In addition, not all segments of society benefited equally. The capital city and the larger towns, with their growing middle classes, were favored over the rural areas, where the lot of the peasantry probably deteriorated. During the last years of the regime, the general economy also declined, with heavy expenditures for military equipment, as well as the disruption of social and economic life by senseless arrests and persecutions. Furthermore, in 1960, the United States and several Latin American countries broke diplomatic relations with the Dominican Republic and imposed economic sanctions against it because of Trujillo's involvement in an assassination attempt against President Rómulo Betancourt, of Venezuela. The increasingly irrational activities of Trujillo provoked the growth of the widespread conspiracy that resulted finally in his assassination.

After the death of Trujillo, his puppet President, Joaquín Balaguer, with the support of Rafael Trujillo, Jr., attempted to take over the reins of power. The younger Trujillo, as commander of the armed forces, undertook a wide search for his father's murderers. After some initial excesses in executions and arrests, they began to dismantle some of the most oppressive features of the old regime, and promised to provide smooth and peaceful transition to more democratic practices in government. Whether these moves stemmed from any real devotion to democracy and constitutionality, or from a desire to make an oppressive regime more palatable, or from some mixture of motives, cannot be stated with any degree of certainty at this time. Whatever the motivations, President Balaguer and the younger Trujillo began to nationalize some of the Trujillo family's vast holdings, restrained the secret police after the initial roundup of assassination suspects, disbanded several private armies, and permitted opposition political parties to operate, with the sole restriction that they should not resort to violence. Several parties quickly organized during the summer and began preparations for the elections scheduled originally for early 1962. Clashes occurred between government supporters and these opposition groups, but the regime took steps to ensure a modicum of civil and political liberty. Except for a general strike in November and December—supported by the leading opposition group, the National Civic Union (Unión Cívica Nacional, or UCN)—all parties observed the truce rather scrupulously. Only the Dominican Popular Movement (Movimiento Popular Dominicano, or MPD—now outlawed) gave evidence of radical revolutionary motivation, with its use of Castrista and Communist slogans and symbols, but it too was contained.

With the failure of the strike, the government announced its own formula for proceeding toward a constitutional regime. Balaguer proposed a seven-man Council of State to act as a provisional government, to call for a Constituent Assembly in August, and to prepare for general elections to be held within a year. The opposition and the government compromised their remaining differences, and the Council, having legislative and executive power, was set up on December 29, with Balaguer as temporary President. The Council of the OAS then recommended the lifting of sanctions. The United States resumed diplomatic relations the first week of January, 1962, and announced its intention to render economic assistance. At this point, the commanding general of the armed forces, Pedro Rodríguez Echevarría, attempted a coup to re-establish military rule, but his fellow officers refused to support him. The Council was reinstated, Balaguer resigned, and under the leadership of Rafael Bonnelly, one of the top leaders of the UCN, measures toward constitutional order were resumed. Presidential and congressional elections were held on December 20. Approximately thirty parties entered candidates for the contests, but well before election day, it became clear that interest centered on the left-of-center Dominican Revolutionary Party (Partido Revolucionario Dominicano, or PRD) of long-exiled Juan Bosch, friend of President Rómulo Betancourt of Venezuela, and on the right-of-center UCN of Viriato Fiallo, who had fought Trujillo within the country. With an excellent turnout of voters in a relatively peaceful election, Bosch and the PRD defeated Fiallo and the UCN by a margin of better than two to one, despite the latter's superior organization. Bosch took office February 27, 1963.

The political party system is still fluid. The Dominican Party, organized originally by General Trujillo as his personal political vehicle —and the only party allowed to operate freely under the dictatorship —was declared dissolved by President Balaguer in November, 1961, and the neo-Trujillista Democratic Front (Frente Democrático, or FD) never got off the ground. The largest anti-Trujillo group, the National Civic Union (UCN), was organized in the late summer of 1961 under the leadership of Dr. Viriato Fiallo, a physician. It is composed largely of middle-class, professional, and student elements. It enjoys some labor support, but does not have control of the labor movement, which is still largely unorganized politically. The UCN did not formally become a political party until February, 1962, in spite of the fact that members of the Council of State, including President Bonnelly, were members of the organization.

With the advent of the UCN to power, the 14th of June Party (Partido 14 de Junio, or PCJ) became for a time the major opposition force, and its Castro-Communist elements have attempted to subvert public order and political stability. In late February, 1962, the Council of State invoked emergency powers to counter extremist agitation and terrorist activities, and deported subversive leftist leaders. The Communist Dominican Popular Socialist Party, with a negligible following in the republic, was outlawed, and its leaders were in exile in Cuba. There has been some Communist influence in the illegal Dominican Popular Movement and in the National Revolutionary Party (Partido Nacionalista Revolucionario, or PNR), founded in October, 1961, with a then pro-Castro and pro-Communist line. By the time of the elections of December, 1962, the extreme left could demonstrate little strength. The PCJ, the strongest of these parties, was split between its moderate and extremist wings, and the others suffered from illegality, poor leadership, or both. Their attempts to disrupt the elections and provoke anarchy and civil war were frustrated by the authorities with little difficulty.

With the decline of the extreme left, particularly the PCJ, during 1962, Juan Bosch's PRD became the prime challenger to the UCN. With its call for social reforms and its appeal to the lower classes, the Party rapidly gained in popularity. Bosch's overwhelming victory continues a trend in Latin America of Presidential victories by men with strong personal appeal, a reform program, but without great organizational support. Whether Bosch can build the organization to carry out his ambitious economic development, social reform, and political democratization plans, only time will tell.

THE NONCOMPETITIVE SYSTEMS

In an effort to avoid the instability of the competitive systems, three countries of Latin America have attempted to establish political institutions and practices that prevent serious challenges for power and political offices. Mexico has concentrated power in a single political party; major differences are settled within the organization by a handful of leaders responsive to the primary interest groups in the country. Organized on a functional as well as geographic base, the party has monopolized power since its founding in 1929. Opposition parties to the right and the left have been permitted to organize and operate, but only within limits. Illegal methods have been used to stunt the growth of these parties, and ballots have been fraudulently counted. Nonetheless, the official party, symbolizing the ideals of the Mexican revolution, still commands the loyalty of the majority of the politically active elements in the nation.

Bolivia has attempted to imitate the Mexican experience, but without the same degree of success. The official revolutionary party succeeded in incorporating large segments of the population into the organization, but its moderate middle-class leaders have not been able to retain the loyalty of, and exercise control over, agrarian and urban lower-class followers. The right wing of the revolutionary movement formed its own party in 1960, and the left threatens to withdraw if it cannot gain its ends. As a result of these pressures for disintegration, the leadership of the official party has been forced to resort to more drastic methods than those of its Mexican counterpart to maintain control of the government. Political restraints on the opposition parties are more crude, and electoral fraud more obvious, than in Mexico.

The third country in this category, Colombia, has utilized a significantly different approach. In an effort to end bloody party strife of many years' duration, the two major parties agreed in 1958, after the overthrow of dictator Gustavo Rojas Pinilla, to establish a National Front, in which political offices were to be divided equally between them for a set number of years. Both parties continue to exist, to maintain their identity apart from the government, and to quarrel within and between themselves on issues, but not over offices. The pact, however, has been threatened since late 1960 by disgruntled forces in both parties. The Liberal dissidents insist that in an open election, a Conservative could not win the Presidency, and they advocate breaking the pact and returning to the competitive system. For their part, the major Conservative factions had extreme difficulty in agreeing among themselves on a Presidential candidate for the 1962 elections. Adherents to the National Front within both parties, however, scored large enough victories in the 1962 congressional and Presidential elections to assure continuation of the system for the next four years.

MEXICO

Following the destruction wrought by ten years of revolutionary warfare, and the uncertain quest for stability of the 1920's, strong man Plutarco Elías Calles forged a political party for the revolution in 1929. Initially, this official party's strength rested almost entirely on military commanders who governed various geographical sectors of the country. For six years, Calles governed Mexico from behind the scenes, through the mechanism of this party, but in 1935, his protégé, President Lázaro Cárdenas, forced him into exile. Cárdenas reformed the party by giving it a functional as well as geographic base. He instituted formal representation within the party of farmers, laborers, the armed forces, and the "popular" groups, which included everyone else except the clergy, large business, and industrial managers and owners. Through this party and its allied groups, Cárdenas transformed Mexican society by carrying out vast agrarian reform, implementing a far-reaching program of social and economic benefits for urban labor, and by nationalizing Mexico's most prosperous enterprise, oil. He brought peace, for

the first time in years, in Church-state relations, encouraged education and health measures, urged the expansion of the Mexican
economy, and named a moderately conservative successor to consolidate the social gains. Since 1940, emphasis has been placed
upon increasing production, both industrial and agricultural, rather
than upon further division of wealth. The social program has not
been abandoned, but the hectic pace of the early years has been
slowed.

The founding of the official party, in 1929, started Mexico on the
road to the institutionalization of power. Nothing indicates this
more clearly than the consequent adjustments that occurred in the
role of the army and in the position of the President. The army,
persuaded by Calles to form the party in 1929, was forced by
Cárdenas to share power with other groups, particularly labor, in
1938. It was then dropped from the party, and disbanded as a
congressional bloc in the 1940's. At the same time, the *caudillo*-
type leader began to disappear. Calles was forced out, Cárdenas
and his successors have limited themselves to one term, and the last
three Presidents have been civilians, lacking the color and powerful
personalities of the early revolutionaries. Today, the President is
still the single, most powerful political figure in Mexico, but he retains this position only during his term of office, and his power is
by no means absolute. The President must respect power groups
within the official party, now known as the Institutional Revolutionary Party (Partido Revolucionario Institucional, or PRI), and
the major interests of the country, which are organized into large
and influential pressure groups. To retain the loyalty of these
groups, and therefore to maintain the political stability of the country, the President must be responsive to their demands, he must
justify his actions in terms of the revolution's mystique, and
he must consider at all times the hard realities of Mexican economic
development.

Within the party, the two most powerful groups are the bureaucracy and the labor unions. In the last twenty-five to thirty years,
as government activities have expanded into many and varied fields,
government workers not only have increased rapidly in numbers
but have improved considerably in technical skills. Now number-
ing over 300,000—including some 80,000 public-school teachers—
the bureaucracy is well led, tightly organized politically, and unquestionably loyal to the regime. Although under party discipline,
which exacts acceptance of final decisions on matters affecting its
welfare and ideology, the bureaucracy can exert tremendous pres-

sure on government leaders. Urban labor, the most powerful interest group in the late 1930's, has declined in relative strength, and has moderated its demands since 1940. It still plays an important role in the party and government; no political leader can hope to advance far in Mexico today on the basis of an antilabor position, and labor leaders are powerful political figures. Through their formal association with the official party, labor unions are so closely intertwined in the political system that government and labor leaders must maintain a smooth-working relationship. It is the duty of the labor leaders to report realistically on labor's desires, needs, and discontents, to counsel and advise the government on labor policies, and then to justify to the membership and carry out the policy adopted by the government.

Rural labor, also formally within the party, was never politically powerful, and is now the weakest sector of the party. Rural needs, however, have not been ignored. Rural leaders hold sinecures in the government, as do other groups, and the rank and file have been assisted with roads, irrigation, and financial benefits—to meet their minimum demands. Intellectuals, at one time a powerful force in developing the ideology and direction of the revolution, have been shunted aside in favor of the technicians and administrators of the bureaucracy, as interest has shifted from reform to economic development. Today, intellectuals are respected but occupy at best a secondary position in the power structure.

The business community has not yet been incorporated into the formal structure of the official party, but business has occupied key posts, particularly in financial agencies, in the government. As a result, they are as deeply involved in the political system as is labor. Penalized in the 1930's, they have risen to the heights of power, which they have shared with the bureaucracy since 1940, when the party and government began to stress the necessity of economic development and to encourage industrialization and increased production. Businessmen, bankers, and industrialists are organized into chambers of commerce and industry, which in turn are federated in a national body. These federations are semipublic organs under a degree of government control, but they also serve as vital contacts between business and government.

Despite the concentration of power, the Mexican political system is not dictatorial, much less totalitarian. Mexican citizens enjoy a high degree of civil and political rights. Freedom of dissent is well protected, property rights are respected, and religious practices of all types are permitted. Within the party and the government, rival interest groups fight out their battles for favor or preferment, and thus far have preserved something of a balance of power. Policies in recent years have favored the propertied groups over the labor force, urban and rural; but the latter have not been neglected. The basic political pattern in Mexico today is stability and moderation, and with the present economic growth rate, combined with current political policies, this trend is not likely to be upset. Only serious dislocations in the economy, or the failure of leadership to provide minimum needs of major pressure groups, will evoke widespread violence and a renewal of revolutionary measures.

The principal opposition parties are the National Action Party (Partido de Acción Nacional, or PAN), on the right, with five seats in the Chamber of Deputies, and the Socialist People's Party (Partido Popular Socialista, or PPS), on the left, with one seat. PAN was organized in 1939, as the representative of Catholic and conservative interests in opposition to Cárdenas and the official party. In recent years, it has attempted to transform itself into a Christian democratic movement by basing its principles upon the papal social encyclicals. As a result, it has come to accept many of the basic reforms of the revolution, but wishes to instill Christian principles into revolutionary institutions, particularly the schools. Beyond this, however, PAN is a party of "me-too-ism." Without adequate funds, with little grass-roots organization and little hope of electoral success at any level, it has been largely ineffective, in a positive sense, as a political opposition. The PPS, in reality a Communist-front party, is smaller and even less effective. Led by Vicente Lombardo Toledano, it enjoys some prestige as a result of its chief's close association with Cárdenas in the 1930's. The Communist Party is currently split internally and harassed externally; several of its top leaders have been jailed since 1959. Until the missile crisis of October-November, 1962, Mexican sympathies for the Cuban revolution (combined with long-standing hostility to intervention and suspicion of the United States) created a favorable atmosphere for Communist, pro-Castro, and anti-U.S. propaganda; the Party, however, was not able to increase its strength appreciably, and its prestige further declined when it supported the Cuban-Soviet defense of missile bases in Cuba.

BOLIVIA

Bolivia testifies to the fact that social revolution, of and by itself, does not provide the answer to poverty and political instability. Bolivia's social and economic problems are of long standing: illiteracy, subsistence agriculture, low worker productivity in all fields, and dependence on one product (tin) for government revenues and foreign exchange. The country's immediate political difficulties are of more recent origin, and are directly traceable to the revolution of 1952, which overturned the traditional order of society. The revolution destroyed the old army and the upper class (the Catholic Church in Bolivia has never been an important political force), and brought to power lower- and middle-income groups. The latter however, have been weakened in recent years by the growing power of *campesino* and labor organizations, supported by militia and *carabinero* units representing lower-class interests. The revolution has also produced a political party that has attempted, like the Mexican PRI, to symbolize the revolution, but unlike its Mexican counterpart, the Bolivian party is battered and torn by factionalism. In addition to competing ideological groups advocating moderate, as opposed to radical, solutions of social and economic problems, there are competing politicians within each group who represent, largely, their own personal ambitions. One moderately conservative faction has already left the party, and a stronger leftist coalition may well break away if it does not gain control of the party.

Prior to 1952, political control rested in a small upper class, whose wealth and power were based upon a near-monopoly in mining and land ownership, and upon the army support they purchased. The Indian majority of the population existed outside the stream of national political and economic life. The traditional order was first challenged in the mid-to-late 1930's, following the defeat suffered in the Chaco War (1932–35) with Paraguay. The severe losses in men and territory had eroded the prestige of the army and the oligarchy. Widespread discontent was openly voiced by the lower classes, who during the war had for the first time experienced broad social contacts, new values and aspirations, and a consciousness of nationality. Out of the ferment grew several reform-minded political organizations. The strongest of these was the Nationalist Revolutionary Movement (Movimiento Nacionalista Revolucionario, or MNR), led by middle-class intellectuals whose chief spokesman was Víctor Paz Estenssoro, a professor of economics. These men were imbued with radical economic doctrines and anti-foreign nationalism focused primarily against U.S. investments in Bolivian tin-mining operations. From 1943 to 1946, the MNR briefly shared power with the military and carried out some limited reforms, but it was restrained by the army faction, whose allegiance with the elite was still intact. In free elections in 1951, the MNR

Presidential candidate, Paz Estenssoro, was voted into office. He was denied his victory by the army, which was subsequently defeated and destroyed when the MNR revolted in April, 1952. The leaders of the revolt recalled Paz from his exile in Buenos Aires to assume the Presidency.

For the first time, the MNR enjoyed the full power necessary to carry out its revolutionary program of incorporating the lower classes into the nation and depriving the privileged orders of their special benefits. In the early months of his Administration, Paz moved rapidly to change much of the social and economic structure of the country. The new President named Juan Lechín, a radical leftist labor leader of the tin miners, as his Minister of Mines, and in October, with great ceremony, nationalized the mines. Paz also proceeded with plans to expand educational, wage, and other security benefits to the lower classes. He proceeded so slowly and cautiously with agrarian reform, however, that the government and the MNR almost lost control of the situation when locally organized peasant groups began to seize land forcibly. MNR organizers moved quickly into the areas of disturbance, successfully imposed their authority over the local leaders, and took credit for the tremendous land expropriation movement that provided farms for thousands of small holders. At the same time, the party, as it rapidly expanded, developed some skill in handling organizational problems. The MNR reached into every social and economic corner of Bolivia, incorporating lower-class urban and rural groups and the bulk of the rural Indian population into the party. These groups at first reinforced, but eventually weakened, the original middle-class elements that directed the party. Party leaders also enlarged the party machinery, and meshed it with the government at all levels.

Initially, Paz and other MNR leaders exhibited a strong anti-U.S. bias. However, after the United States had recognized the regime, and had expressed sympathy for the goals of the revolution, the party adopted a more friendly attitude and sought U.S. financial and technical assistance. The United States, for its part, continued to purchase tin from the nationalized mines, extended large-scale Point Four aid, and encouraged private capital to invest in various minor industries.

For the four years of his first Administration, Paz ruled by executive decree, without a legislature. In June, 1956, however, he held elections for the Presidency and both houses of Congress. The MNR made a sweep of the Presidency and the Senate, and won 60 of the 68 seats of the Chamber of Deputies. Paz's protégé, Hernán Siles Zuazo, took office as President on August 6, 1956. During his four-year term, Siles represented a continuation of moderate control within the MNR. In his attempts to halt inflation, encourage economic development, and diversify national production, he met determined opposition from Juan Lechín, whom he eventually forced out of the government. Faced with radical opposition to his program, Siles threatened on several occasions to resign, but his gesture, each time, provoked widespread popular support for his Administration. With these maneuvers, and the help of continuing U.S. economic assistance, Siles peacefully completed his term of office.

In the general elections of June, 1960, Paz once more returned to the Presidency, with Lechín as Vice-President. The MNR again won a sweep of the Senate, and all but 2 of the contested seats in the Chamber of Deputies, giving it a total of 51. Its previous impressive majority had been reduced by the defection of a more conservative wing of the party styling itself the Authentic Nationalist Revolutionary Movement (Movimiento Nacionalista Revolucionario Auténtico, or MNRA) and led by Presidential aspirant Walter Guevara Arce, Former Foreign Minister and Minister of Government under Siles. Guevara Arce officially polled only about 140,000, to Paz's 735,000 votes; but his party, now called the Authentic Revolutionary Party (Partido Revolucionario Auténtico, or PRA), won 14 seats in the Chamber. The June, 1962, congressional elections further consolidated MNR strength. With a record turnout of over one million voters, the government party captured over 83 per cent of the votes counted. The opposition parties split the remainder, with the Bolivian Socialist Falange (Falange Socialista Boliviana, or FSB) getting 7 per cent, the PRA 4.2 per cent, and the Communists and Christian Democrats each less than 2 per cent.

Opposition parties are permitted to organize and to propagandize, but their activities are severely restricted, and elections are frequently fraudulent. Further to the right of the PRA stands the FSB, anti-Communist and opportunistic. Founded after the Chaco War, the FSB was ideologically close to the MNR prior to 1952. Following the revolution, it attempted to serve as an opposition party by attracting upper-class support. As its conspiratorial activities failed, the upper class deserted it, and the party was reduced to its original middle-class composition. The FSB continues to advocate conservative policies, including government restrictions on labor demands. The party officially polled only 79,000 votes in the Presidential elections of 1960, and won only 3 seats in the Chamber of Deputies; but in free elections, it might well combine with moderates, inside and outside the MNR, to produce an electoral victory. Several other small parties on the right did not participate in the 1960 elections.

On the left are three Communist parties: the orthodox Bolivian Communist Party (Partido Comunista Boliviano, or PCB), the (Trotskyite) Revolutionary Workers' Party (Partido Obrero Revolucionario, or POR), and the Party of the Revolutionary Left (Partido Izquierdista Revolucionario, or PIR). All three parties are small, each with fewer than 5,000 members, and all are divided internally. The PCB, however, exerts influence far out of proportion to its numbers, because of its success in infiltrating the MNR-affiliated Bolivian Workers' Central (Central Obrero Boliviano, or COB), which includes intellectuals, writers, and artists as well as manual laborers. The Communists have been particularly successful in placing some of their members in strategic positions within the mineworkers' union. The Trotskyites exert some influence among the mineworkers, white-collar employees, and Indian peasants.

The greatest threat to the moderate orientation of the Bolivian Government comes from radical elements within the MNR, led by Vice-President Juan Lechín—a leftist, an extremist, and a disruptive force within the party. The left sector of the MNR under Lechín did not participate as a separate party in the 1960 or 1962 elections. It has, however, from time to time threatened to leave the MNR. The mining unions, strongly influenced by Lechín and the Communists, have become gravely dissatisfied with their deteriorating economic conditions. The Bolivian Workers' Central, which, as an associate of the MNR, enjoys virtual cogovernment with the party, has come under radical influence, and though it thus far has been restrained by the moderates under Paz, there is no certainty that it can be kept in line. Furthermore, dissatisfaction with economic developments in the rural areas has now reached dangerous proportions. The peasant organizations, once the main prop of the moderate Siles Administration, are now perennially quarreling among themselves. Paz has been trying to act as peacemaker among the squabbling factions and wings of the party, attempting desperately to hold it together under moderate leadership. The moderates appear, at least over the long haul, to be losing strength to the leftist extremists, although there were some important moderate gains in the aftermath of the 1962 Cuban crisis. With Presidential elections scheduled for 1964, Bolivia is approaching a crossroads in its revolutionary development, and even Paz Estenssoro may prove unable to prevent a breakdown of the delicate political balance.

COLOMBIA

Colombian political life and economic power are controlled by a small and homogeneous upper class of landowners, urban industrialists, and businessmen. The entrepreneurial class is able and intelligent, and the elite, as a whole, is comparatively enlightened and aware of the social and economic problems of the country. A gap exists, however, between awareness and effective action. Political conflicts have not materialized along class lines, as in many other parts of Latin America, but along party and regional lines. The two traditional parties, the Liberals and the Conservatives, both represent cross sections of Colombian society. Party programs vary only slightly, neither offering a true reform program. Regionalism results from the nature of Colombia's rugged geography. Long isolated from each other during the nineteenth and early twentieth centuries, the various parts of the country have established regular contacts only since the coming of air transportation. Even today, however, regional rivalry and antagonisms persist. Religious unity and the firm attachment by family to a given political party have contributed to the absence of class struggle. Furthermore, in local areas, power is wielded by the cacique and the parish priest allied to one of the two traditional parties.

Colombian politics during the nineteenth century revolved primarily around the quarrels between the Liberals and the Conservatives over the questions of Church-state relations and the powers of the central and provincial governments. Although the Conservatives controlled the country from 1884 to 1930, Colombia experienced its first real gains toward political democracy during the last twenty years of this period. Press censorship declined, political issues were freely argued, elections were conducted with a degree of fairness and honesty seldom existing before, and the opposition Liberals not only won seats in Congress, but were frequently invited to occupy Cabinet posts. The world depression, beginning in 1929, with its attendant economic crisis in Colombia, damaged the Conservative government of President Miguel Abadía Méndez, and split the party. Contrary to much of the rest of Latin America,

Colombia transferred power, in an orderly and peaceful election, from the incumbent Conservatives to the opposition Liberals. Although the Liberals modified the Constitution to permit the expropriation of oil properties, and to extend state protection to labor, the government enacted only mild social legislation, such as the forty-eight-hour week, and some provisions for unemployment compensation.

The Liberals' failure to enact further needed welfare legislation, combined with their lack of unity on wartime policy and Church-state relations, split the party during the scandal-ridden second Administration of Alfonso López (1942–45). López resigned under pressure in 1945, and although his term was completed by the able and popular Alberto Lleras Camargo, the Liberals were not able to resolve their internal differences. The continuing dissension within Liberal ranks permitted the Conservative candidate, Mariano Ospina Pérez, to win the Presidency in 1946. Ospina's attempts to calm political passions and conciliate political opponents were blocked by extremists in both parties. Legislative deadlock, frequent Cabinet crises, and inflationary speeches eventually took their toll. Minor violence led to police and military action and, by 1947, to the imposition of a state of siege in several areas. Finally, the assassination of Liberal extremist Jorge Eliécer Gaitán, on April 9, 1948, touched off riotings, arson, and looting in Bogotá. Violence spread to the provinces, with sporadic but bitter fighting between Conservatives and Liberals. In the elections of 1949, the Liberals, still divided, refused to enter a Presidential candidate, thus leaving an extremist Conservative, Laureano Gómez, the sole candidate. Upon taking office in 1950, Gómez dissolved Congress, clamped on a tight press censorship, and ruled by decree.

Unable to bring the bloody civil war to an end, despite his harsh measures, Gómez was overthrown by a military coup in 1953. A Constituent Assembly, called by the military government, proclaimed General Gustavo Rojas Pinilla, the leader of the coup, President in July, 1954. Despite his initial wide popular support, his early liberalizing tendencies, and some success in lessening the fratricidal strife, Rojas Pinilla failed to end the fighting. After the violence and bloodshed continued for some time, he reimposed the restrictions of his predecessor and eventually converted his regime into an open dictatorship. With the military government growing more oppressive, the national leaders of the quarreling parties united to force the resignation of the army strong man in May, 1957. A military junta temporarily assumed power, and the Liberal and Conservative parties discussed means of compromising their political differences.

The result of the party talks was the creation of a National Front government, in which both parties participate but are left free to criticize and oppose the Administration. According to the agreement, which is to last until 1974, the Presidency alternates between the parties, offices are equally divided at all levels and branches of government, and certain types of legislation must be approved by a two-thirds majority. The outcome of the pact has been mixed. It performed most satisfactorily the initial task of returning the country to constitutional government with a modicum of party cooperation, the re-establishment of civil liberties and democratic processes, and the stabilization of the financial and economic situation. However, as a means of progress in economic and social reform, and as a political mechanism, it has not been notably successful. The pact brought peace between the leaders of the two parties, who for the most part represent upper- and middle-class interests, but it provided no sure means to carry out reform—even though rapid and deep-seated change must take place if more devastating and violent social revolution is to be avoided.

Since 1960, Colombian politicians have begun to squabble again over political office—not, as before, on an interparty basis, but rather on intraparty terms. In the elections of 1958, Laureano Gómez gained control of the Conservatives when Alberto Lleras was nominated by the Liberals for President. As a result, the Lleras Administration worked with the Laureanistas. In the 1960 elections, however, the Conservatives split evenly, while a minority Liberal faction under Alfonso López Michelsen began to attack the interparty pact on the grounds that, since the Liberals have a clear nationwide majority (they received 58 per cent of the total vote in 1960 and about 55 per cent in 1962), the Conservatives had no right to the Presidency during the next term. López Michelsen himself has ambitions to become President, and ran against the National Front candidate in 1962. Currently, there are, in fact, four political forces in a system that was designed for only two. The Liberals under ex-President Lleras and Carlos Lleras Restrepo have been cooperating with the moderate Conservatives under President León Valencia and Mariano Ospina, while the ultra-Conservatives under Gómez, and the minority leftist Liberals under López Michelsen, form an opposition—albeit disunited.

Other problems have also defied solution. In the beginning, important legislation received the necessary majority vote, but as political strife has increased, each issue has become a test of strength among the factions. Although a mild agrarian-reform bill was passed in 1961, social and economic legislation has tended to bog down. Some progress was made in increasing agricultural and industrial production during Lleras Camargo's four years, but price declines in exports, particularly in coffee, virtually wiped out the gains. The foreign debt increased, the cost of living rose steadily, and the balance of payments continued adverse. None of these problems proved disastrous to the economy, but they have produced stagnation in the real income of the lower classes, with resulting political and social unrest. Nor has party peace been entirely achieved. National leaders reach agreements on important matters, but at the department level, party competition is still often highly personal, and at the village level, very little harmony has been achieved. Further complicating the problem of national unification is the persistence of strong regional attachments. Within Colombia, various opinions are expressed concerning the party peace pact and its accompanying difficulties. Some blame the leaders for not pulling together to make it work, some blame the Administration for *"desgobierno"* (the lack of strength to exert authority), and others insist that the system no longer meets the political needs of the country. The latter point out that the pact provides no machinery for settling disputes, that it freezes the *status quo,* and that it prohibits the emergence of new leaders and new ideas.

Throughout the period of civil strife, the Communists have attempted to take advantage of the disorders to strengthen their own position. The Communist Party of Colombia (Partido Comunista Colombiano, or PCC), however, has had only minimal success in penetrating legitimate political and social groups in the country. Communist influence has been increasing among the guerrilla bands (many little more than bandits) that still exist, but they have had little success in unifying their organization and activities. The nature of Colombian society—in which family political attachments are practically hereditary, and in which clerical political influence at the grass-roots level is still strong—makes Communist inroads particularly difficult. Consequently, the PCC currently presents little danger to the country.

The major threat to Colombia's efforts to re-establish democratic government lies not in Castro-Communist subversion, but in the breakdown of public order following a disintegration of the accords between the country's two major political parties. Despite the weaknesses of the peace pact and the quarreling of politicians, there appears to be no alternative to the continuance of Liberal-Conservative coexistence other than the renewal of general violence. Such an outbreak might well lead to social conflict across party lines, in view of the increasing insistence among the lower classes on improved standards of living.

The results of the congressional and Presidential balloting in March and May, 1962, respectively, have purchased additional time for Colombia to proceed with the tasks of quieting political conflict and pushing needed reform legislation through Congress. The congressional elections were critical, for they forecast the outcome of the Presidential race. In addition to the four major factions, two minor political groups—the pro-Castro Left Liberal Revolutionary Movement, on the far left, and Rojas Pinilla's National Popular Alliance, on the far right—ran candidates for the Senate and the Chamber of Deputies. The election produced the following line-up in the Senate and Chamber, respectively: Liberal (National Front) —37, 59; Conservative (National Front)—31, 50; Conservative (Laureanista)—16, 36; Liberal Revolutionary Movement (Movimiento Revolucionario Liberal, or MRL)—12, 33; National Popular Alliance—2, 6.

The implications of the election are obvious enough. The National Front was given a solid endorsement by majorities in both leading parties. The extremists of right and left were firmly repudiated, but the major opposition factions within the Liberal and Conservative parties have demonstrated sufficient strength to continue their threat to the Front.

The Presidential election was anticlimactic. The candidate of the Front, moderate conservative Guillermo León Valencia, won handily over his opponents: Alfonso López Michelsen, of the MRL; Jorge Leyva, of the opposition Conservatives; and former dictator Gustavo Rojas Pinilla. The result of the voting, in round numbers, was: Guillermo León Valencia, 1,650,000; Alfonso López Michelsen, 625,000; Jorge Leyva, 310,000; Gustavo Rojas Pinilla, 55,000.

Although Valencia inherits grave social and economic dislocations from the preceding Administration, his political position is rather good. The National Front has the two-thirds majority in the Senate necessary to pass major legislation, but it does not have the same advantage in the Chamber of Deputies. However, the defeats suffered by the dissident Conservatives, particularly in the Presidential contests, may well swing some of the Deputies of these factions to support Valencia in return for political favors. Control of both houses of the Congress will not, however, guarantee that the National Front will, or can, enact needed reform legislation, and a Conservative President is less likely to advocate rapid change than a Liberal one. All things considered, Colombia is perhaps at the crossroads. Will her traditional vertical parties prove adequate for political, economic, and social development needs, or must she resort to ideological alignments, class conflict, and the renewal of bloodshed before she can consider the luxury of a fully competitive system?

MASS-BASED TOTALITARIAN REGIME: CUBA

The example of Cuba illustrates how surprisingly weak and ineffective the institutional props of a regime may prove in the face of a major challenge, and how rapid and radical the change in domestic policies and international orientation can be. The advent of Castro laid bare the absence of strong social and political institutions. He quickly silenced or destroyed the institutions that traditionally served as a stabilizing force—political parties, the military, the Church, and private capital allied with the U.S. economy; he then derived his power from the masses through appeals to their hatred of established institutions, including those that had tied Cuba to the United States. This lower- and lower-middle-class support has been increasingly organized and institutionalized. As a conservative estimate, about 25 per cent of Cuba's total population of 7 million has been regimented into mass organizations for youth, women, "revolutionary defense," and others—all of which are subordinate to the Integrated Revolutionary Organizations (Organizaciones Revolucionarias Integradas, or ORI), a protoparty of the Soviet type.

Much of Castro's early mass support resulted from the redistribution of wealth during 1959 and 1960, the expectation of further social benefits, and an idealistic sense of identity with the revolutionary government. Loyalty to Castro is strongest among the youth, whatever their class origin, and among the landless peasants. Support for Castro among small landowners and organized urban labor, never completely proregime, appears to have decreased substantially. Many lower-middle-class urbanites, especially those holding government jobs, have identified their future with that of the regime, but middle-class professional and managerial groups either have gone into exile or offer a sullen and silent opposition. Special efforts were made during 1961 to prevent the flight of professional people and small businessmen through economic incentives and travel controls. The government, however, has made it clear that the role of the middle class is restricted and temporary, and conditioned to the needs of the revolution. The regime has a forced-draft program to develop managerial and technical skills among the politically more reliable workers and peasants. The wealthy upper class has been systematically destroyed.

Between the time of her independence and Castro's seizure of power, in January, 1959, Cuba had experienced a troubled history. Political freedom from Spain was exchanged for political semi-dependence upon the United States until 1934, and economic dependence until Castro broke the ties during 1959 and 1960. In its brief republican history, Cuba has never known equitable economic distribution or enjoyed more than a brief period of political democracy. In the late colonial and early independence years, the once-large group of small landowners was slowly forced out of operation as the national agriculture shifted to large-scale sugar production, more than half of which was controlled by U.S. interests. Although Cuba had the third- or fourth-highest per capita income in Latin America by the 1950's, the benefits accrued primarily to the upper and middle classes, and to a lesser extent to organized urban labor. The half-million workers in the sugar fields and unorganized urban workers lived with their families in bitter poverty, with little or no sense of participation in national affairs. The upper and middle classes controlled government policy, with the result that freedom, democracy, and liberty were meaningless terms to most of the lower classes. It should not be surprising, then, that it is this latter group that supports Castro.

Except for the government of Cuba's first President, the honest and conscientious Tomás Estrada Palma, every Cuban Administration has been corruption-ridden, differing only in degree. On several occasions before the abrogation of the Platt Amendment in 1934, the United States "legally" and openly intervened in Cuban affairs to restore order; and only one or two Cuban Governments between 1898 and 1959 could be called truly representative of the Cuban people. After years of venality, violence, electoral fraud, and betrayal of trusts, a strong man appeared in the late 1920's—Gerardo Machado. Popular opposition to Machado, however, finally led to a reign of terror and violence, culminating in his overthrow, in 1933. In the ensuing disorders, Sergeant Fulgencio Batista rose to power as President-maker. He dominated Cuban politics during the remainder of the 1930's and, in 1940, had himself elected President. Following his four-year term, Cuba had two free elections, in 1944 and again in 1948. Those eight years following Batista's Administration marked a partial return to the old pre-Machado era, with open and uncontrolled graft and corruption, a breakdown in law and public administration, and a failure of the politicians to live up to promises for economic development and social welfare. With mounting popular criticism of the Administration, Batista executed a *coup d'état* in March, 1952, just prior to scheduled national elections. He justified his illegal seizure of power on the grounds that President Carlos Prío Socarrás was about to conduct a fraudulent election. Within a few months, Batista established a thoroughgoing dictatorship, dismissing Congress, muzzling the press, and jailing his opponents. Although he later eased the restrictions on civil liberties, and tried to regularize political conditions, the invasion of Fidel Castro with a small band in the Sierra Maestra, late in 1956, disrupted Batista's efforts. His inability to defeat, or even to contain, the rebellion led him to adopt ever harsher measures of repression, until both his civilian and military support eroded away. Without ever winning a pitched battle of any magnitude, Castro forced Batista to yield power and flee the country on January 1, 1959.

Prior to Batista's coup of 1952, nine political parties registered 50,000 members or more, but only two were serious contenders for power. Both of these had their ideological origins in the revolution against Machado. The Cuban Revolutionary Party, or Auténtico, as it was popularly called, was founded in 1934, with a program calling for political democracy, economic development, and social reform, including mass education and agrarian reform. The party finally came to power in 1944 and retained control until Batista's coup. The Auténticos adhered to their political platform of civil liberties and free elections, but moved slowly on their economic and social promises. The party's caution with reform, and its failure to enforce honesty within its own ranks, led to the withdrawal, in 1946, of a faction led by Eddy Chibás, who formed the Party of the Cuban People, commonly called the Ortodoxo. After his assumption of power, Castro did not permit political parties, except for the Communist Popular Socialist Party (Partido Socialista Popular, or PSP), to reorganize or engage in political activities, despite his earlier promises to re-establish the Constitution of 1940 and Cuba's traditional political institutions. Nor did he permit his lieutenants in his own military movement—the 26th of July Movement—to transform the organization into a political party.

In place of parties, Castro used, first, his own personal magnetism to assemble huge crowds to shout support for his proposed policies. It was an easy step from this informal arrangement to the establishment of mass organizations for the rapid and more efficient mobilization of the mobs, for whatever purpose the government desired. Committees for the Defense of the Revolution, the Federation of Cuban Women, and the Association of Young Rebels have each enrolled several hundred thousand members.

The third stage in the organization of the masses for political action was carried out in July, 1961, when Castro announced the formation of the ORI, which included the PSP as well as the now moribund Twenty-sixth of July Movement and the Revolutionary Directorate. The ORI was described as a transitional stage toward the final establishment of a Marxist-Leninist party to be called the United Party of the Socialist Revolution (Partido Unido de la Revolución Socialista, or PURS). All mass organizations are subordinate to the ORI, as they will be to the PURS, but the party itself is to be a limited-membership elitist organization of dedicated revolutionaries. On March 9, 1962, the leadership of the ORI announced the formation of a new twenty-five-man Directorate, without officers; but within two weeks, Fidel named himself as First Secretary and his brother Raúl as Second Secretary, with "Ché" Guevara, President Osvaldo Dorticós, Blas Roca, and Emilio Aragonés as other members of the Secretariat. On March 25, Raúl was named Vice-Premier. Blas Roca was the only Communist in the Secretariat, and the Directorate itself contained, at most, ten PSP members. These moves presaged Fidel's dramatic speech of March 26, 1962, in which he struck out bitterly at what he labeled the sectarianism of certain old-line Communists, particularly Aníbal Escalante, a member of the Directorate and the Secretary of the ORI. Castro accused Escalante of packing the ORI with Communists, to the exclusion of other revolutionaries, and of interfering with the government ministries. Sensing the possibility that the ORI and its successor party, if dominated by the Communists, would wrest control of government agencies and mass organizations from his personal followers, Fidel moved to restore a balance of power, as well as unity between PSP members and other revolutionaries.

The role of the Communists in the Cuban revolution has been a curious one. Outlawed by Batista, and reduced to a hard core of perhaps 12,000 when Castro took over, the Communist PSP claimed a membership of almost 100,000 by 1962. Few Communists fought with Fidel in the Sierra Maestra, and the Party itself did not support him until the downfall of Batista became obvious. Because of their reluctance to commit themselves to his cause, Fidel at first demonstrated caution and mistrust in his relations with the Communists. Once he came to power, the Communists alone, however, gave Castro the unquestioned loyalty that he demanded of all his followers. And this perhaps explains why he permitted the PSP to maintain its identity. In addition, the discipline, the training in organizational matters, and the dedication of the Communists soon convinced Fidel that in them he had found the kind of support he needed for the success of his revolution. More and more, he began to rely upon their administrative abilities and their advice. In the fall of 1959, PSP members could be found in some lower- and middle-level positions of power. First they moved into labor, then into education, and lastly into the military. By March of 1962, Communists occupied posts at all levels throughout the government, and appeared to dominate the ORI.

During 1961, Castro more and more began to use Communist terminology to describe the course and progress of his revolution. At first, his Marxist utterances were not taken very seriously, because a vague kind of Marxism has long permeated the thinking of many Latin American students and intellectuals. Finally, in December, Castro publicly announced that he was a Marxist-Leninist. It is unlikely, however, that Castro is a disciplined Communist, such as the directors of the PSP or of Communist Parties elsewhere. His personality, his methods of operation, and his political position argue against it. In fact, his December speech can be interpreted as an attempt to gain a commitment of continued Soviet aid to a revolution that must have outside assistance to survive.

As a result of the creation of the new organizations, Fidel Castro is no longer the sole arbiter of power in Cuba, as he was when he assumed control in 1959. He is still the most powerful individual in the government, and he reaffirmed this position by his establishment of the Secretariat of the ORI, and his condemnation of Escalante in March, 1962. However, his regime still depends heavily on the Communists to sustain it. On the other hand, the Communists cannot operate without Castro. Raúl, Fidel's brother and Minister of Defense, is still the heir apparent, but old Communist Carlos Rafael Rodríguez is competing with "Ché" Guevara, Fidel's close adviser during the revolution and after, for the Number 3 position in the hierarchy. The power structure of revolutionary Cuba has not yet been stabilized, and the possibility of an eventual power struggle between Fidel and the Communists cannot be entirely dismissed. The missile crisis in October, 1962, did not affect Castro's control within Cuba, though top officials were disillusioned with the Soviets. An accommodation was reached during Castro's visit to the U.S.S.R. in 1963, however, and the Cuban regime paid lip service to the possibility of a peaceful road to power in such countries as Chile and Brazil. The more important effect of the October crisis, however, was upon future Cuban-Soviet relations, which were thrown into a degree of uncertainty, although Soviet commitment to continued support for Castro was never in doubt. The existing Cuban-Russian dispute over the appropriate Communist strategy in the hemisphere was widened, as Castro openly advocated the violent road of guerrilla warfare and terror in the cities.

CONCLUSIONS

Almost no two countries in Latin America exhibit parallel political-party and interest-group relationships and relative strengths, and any discussion of the political development of the area must proceed on a country-by-country basis. Of course, certain basic general problems, such as underdeveloped and unbalanced economies, maldistribution of wealth, and overconcentration of political power, are common to all. These difficulties are now accompanied by rising hopes and demands on the part of those who have been denied, and by resistance to change and lack of social consciousness on the part of those in power. But when and how any particular out group reacts politically depends largely upon the severity of their problems, the awareness of their potential strength, and the degree of confidence in the intentions of their national leaders to ameliorate their conditions.

Political trends in Latin America for several decades have indicated that the middle classes have begun to move into positions of power, and that the lower classes have begun to organize and operate as pressure groups. The latter, however, have not yet become primary power factors, except in Bolivia. In some countries, the movement has advanced rather far; in others, it has barely begun. In this process, urban groups, with a few exceptions, appear more powerful than rural organizations, and the new political parties with social democratic tendencies speak more strongly for urban than for rural interests, although they have not neglected the latter. The elite have begun to give way in most countries, but everywhere reluctantly. The military, at one time the principal prop of the elite, is now split over the degree and rate of change acceptable, but few military leaders are willing to assume power in their own right. The Catholic Church hierarchy—like the military, a former prop of the elite—is also split on social and economic questions, and Catholic lay leaders have begun to form political parties akin to the social democratic parties, but based in principle on the social teachings of recent popes. They deny any kinship with the old clerical, conservative parties of the past.

Because of the growing awareness of social questions, successful candidates for the Presidency in most countries of Latin America must have not only an appealing personality, as was required in the past, but also a socio-economic reform program to attract the vital urban lower-class vote. In some instances, such candidates can be elected to the highest office in the land without much organized support in the form of political parties or interest groups. Quadros, in Brazil, offers a case in point. Once the candidate achieves power, however, the majority that elected him becomes politically passive, or is unable to find an effective means to support him. The reform-minded President frequently finds himself isolated or buffeted between small, but well-organized and powerful, interests—which tend to polarize to the right and left. The former demand the maintenance of the *status quo,* and the latter insist on radical change. Evolutionary reform is too fast for the one and too slow for the other, and too often the moderate executive finds that he has lost the organized support of both extremes. Quadros resigned in the face of such pressures, and Velasco Ibarra, of Ecuador, was toppled by blows from the right and from the left. Frondizi, of Argentina, with skill (and perhaps luck), managed to hang on the longest, but he too was finally overthrown. Betancourt, of Venezuela, is an exception in that he has well-organized political support behind him, and the Venezuelan right recognizes that it has no political future by itself.

A radical revolutionary reform program with strong anti-U.S. and pro-Soviet features has been instituted in only one country in the Western Hemisphere—Cuba. It threatens, however, in the words of its leader, Fidel Castro, to convert the Andes into "one vast Sierra Maestra of revolt." Castro supporters are in evidence in every country of Latin America, but their effectiveness and political potential vary enormously from one area to another.

7. Conclusions and Outlook

Our central argument in this work has been the need for change in Latin America; our primary theme has been the variety and complexity of the area; and our major task has been to describe objectively—country by country, and at times region by region—the conditions that emphasize the urgency of reform.

We have used some statistics to make our points, but we have purposely avoided weighing our work with masses of facts and figures that can readily be obtained in several excellent studies on Latin American economics and geography. Rather, we have chosen to concentrate our attention on the consequences of these statistics in human terms, to examine the aspirations of the people (both the haves and the have-nots), and to review the political and social repercussions and conflicts that are nurtured by the great disparity in wealth, as well as the growing awareness of this disparity among the lower classes.

THE CHALLENGE OF THE SIXTIES

Only Mexico, Bolivia, and Cuba have carried out violent economic and social, as well as political, reforms in the twentieth century. In Cuba, the phase of violence has not yet passed, and the regime has continued to resort to terror in suppressing its opposition. Although the results of the revolution within Cuba cannot be judged accurately, the Castro experiment has had a profound impact on the rest of Latin America. In Mexico and Bolivia, elements of the political left have identified their own revolutions with Cuba's. Taking the more optimistic of Castro's claims and promises as reality, the Mexican and Bolivian leaders who have not been satisfied with their own national achievements have advocated emulation of the Cuban revolutionary program. In other parts of

240

Latin America where social change has proceeded more slowly, or where it is virtually at a standstill, a variety of leaders have clamored for the implementation of similar "reforms." Since 1959, several governments in the Caribbean area have uncovered subversive movements linked with the Cuban revolution. Brazil is troubled in its huge but depressed Northeast with Peasant Leagues under a leader who proclaims Castro as his inspiration and model. No country of Latin America is free of Castro-type movements, but some are more immediately endangered than others.

Whence the unrest? The ready answer is economic underdevelopment, uneven distribution of wealth and power, and social and cultural inequities. Although no one denies the existence of these conditions, it must be emphasized that these problems have always plagued Latin America. In fact, the distortions were far more severe in the nineteenth century than they are today. Why, then, the unrest now? The real answer lies in the fact that many members of the lower classes are far more conscious of the inequities today than a century ago. Furthermore, they believe in the possibility of improving their lot, and in political action as the road to success. But this kind of awareness indicates that some change has already taken place in Latin America. The intrusion of the lower classes into politics further implies organization of a political or occupational nature. The realization that their standard of living can and ought to be raised implies a certain degree of "education" and exposure to ideas from outside the area. In reality, new ideas and activities are already flowing throughout the length and breadth of the hemisphere, in some countries penetrating deep into society, in others lapping at the edges.

Of all the so-called underdeveloped areas of the world, Latin America approaches most closely the U.S. and West European types of societies. The area is culturally an integral part of Western civilization, as Asia and Africa are not. Its middle and upper classes are thoroughly Western-oriented, and most members of its lower classes view their problems in Western terms. Only the Indian populations exist outside this framework, but they are confined to a relatively few countries. In Mexico, Guatemala, and Bolivia, the Indians are steadily being absorbed into national life, i.e., into a Western-oriented value system. Economically, too, Latin America presents a sharp contrast with Asia and Africa. Although per capita income is sharply below that of the United States, West Germany, France, or England, and the distribution of wealth and income is not comparable, the major countries of Latin

America are well ahead of those of other underdeveloped regions. Industrialization and urbanization are well advanced, occupational pressure groups have been forced to improve the standard of living of their members, and the larger countries are becoming more and more self-sufficient. Economics are not yet balanced in their development, agriculture still lags far behind other sectors in efficiency and modernization, and productivity per worker does not compare with that of the United States and Western Europe. But great strides have been made. The traditional pattern of rural haciendas and urban administrative and commercial centers, of absentee landlords and depressed peasants, and of raw material exports and consumer goods imports not only has been challenged, but has been partly disrupted. The transition, however, to an industrialized society, to satisfactory economic and social diversification, and to a viable balance among the classes in power and wealth has not yet been completed.

It is the process of transition that lies at the roots of the unrest. The transplanting of families from their tradition-bound and integrated rural communities to the seemingly chaotic and individual-oriented urban setting has resulted in thousands of cases of family disorganization and individual frustration. The promise of the city remains unfulfilled for all too many. A minority have found their way into new forms of social organizations, such as labor unions and political parties. The majority are not yet organized on a permanent basis, but they can be mobilized for mob agitation and violence, or for election campaigns, by hero-leaders who promise an amelioration of their lot. Their successes, limited though they may be, have impressed upon the urban masses the efficacy of political action.

One needs no extraordinary insight to predict that the 1960's and 1970's will be years of turbulence and turmoil in Latin America. Although variations will appear in each country, social, economic, and political changes will continue; in fact, the rate of change is almost certain to increase. Even the more traditional societies will be shaken to their foundations by social forces stimulated in part by the example of Castro. To complicate the situation further, an extracontinental power, hostile to the United States and to the Inter-American System, is willing and able to finance and guide these changes. If Castro, with Soviet assistance, attains his long-term economic objectives in Cuba, his success will not be lost upon Latin American reform leaders. Unfortunately, some of the more radical proponents of change are already distrustful of democratic government, with its interplay of divergent interests, and are placing their hopes in mob-based authoritarian regimes. These extremists argue that the latter alone can enact an integrated social-reform and economic-development program, and that democratic administrations, responding to organized pressure groups, can at best institute limited and patchwork affairs. Democratic government is therefore on trial in Latin America and, to survive, must prove that it can satisfy the needs of the majority of the citizens.

Basically, then, the question is not of change in itself, but of the direction, speed, and methods of change. Two alternatives present themselves in most of Latin America: moderate, evolutionary reform, controlled at least in part by the current governing groups; or sweeping social revolution, of the type under way in Cuba. A third course—not really an alternative—appears likely to be followed in several of the smaller countries in which political and economic conditions are still primitive: the traditional shift from dictatorship to anarchy and return. The first two alternatives, however, are the vital ones; they affect most of the area. If social change is to come peacefully, the governing classes, especially in the larger countries, must modify their traditional social values and political views. None of the elite today deny the desirability of economic development, but few are willing to accept the necessary political and social changes that must accompany economic growth. On the other hand, cracks are beginning to appear in the solid wall of traditionalist opposition to change. In the past five years, some members of the governing elite have at least voiced the need for reform. As yet, they constitute a minority of their class. Because of divergent views as to methods and scope, as well as because of numerical weakness, they have undertaken few satisfactory reform programs.

Granting that the requisite changes occur in the thinking of current leadership groups, can we safely predict that the reform will be carried out smoothly and peacefully? It is doubtful. The changes may be implemented peacefully, but we cannot be sure that the elite will be able to control them. Once the movement gets under way, the upper classes will not be able to plot the lines of change alone. Other classes of society will be impelled into action, following the introduction of important matters that upset traditional ways of thinking and acting. Discontented middle-class intellectuals, already calling loudly for reform, will be encouraged and emboldened to press harder for their goals; and their lower-class following will, in all probability, be led to believe that the changes will be more beneficial and far-reaching than the leaders plan or expect. What begins as evolutionary change could well turn into revolution, if not properly planned, guided, and controlled.

In the more traditional countries, such a movement will present far greater difficulties than in others, where some sense of change, progress, and reform is already felt. Furthermore, it is questionable whether, in countries whose traditional order has been preserved almost intact from colonial days, evolutionary change is really possible. Once the upper classes admit that basic reforms are necessary, will the discontented middle-class intellectuals not ask why the reforms have been delayed so long? Will they not accuse the elite of treason to the fatherland in impeding national growth, prosperity, and prestige? Will they not seek to catapult themselves to power by the elite's very admission of failure, tacit though it may be? And will the pent-up bitterness and frustration of middle-class leaders and lower-class followers not seize upon the weakening of the traditional order to bring it crashing down rather than to cooperate peacefully with their "oppressors" in slowly changing society and cultural patterns? None of these questions can be answered with any degree of certainty, but optimistic responses are unrealistic for several countries.

We do not wish to propagate a deterministic philosophy with respect to developments in Latin America, but the evidence of past intransigence, and the unwillingness of hostile forces to compromise political, social, and economic differences, do not lead to optimism for peaceful evolutionary settlements everywhere. Complicating the picture is the fact that in some of the smaller countries, alleviation of distress could not even be procured by the most equitable distribution possible of all available wealth. Several countries are grossly overpopulated in respect to their land, mineral, and industrial resources, and no amount of agrarian reform, welfare service, or education can greatly ameliorate the wretched living conditions of the masses. Massive capital outlays far beyond local capacities, and long-term foreign aid, appear to be the only answer, but whether all the recipient governments would be willing, or able, to meet the conditions required for such aid by the United States under the terms of the Alliance for Progress is problematical. Frequently, the governments and lands most in need of aid are the most traditional, but even those that have begun reform must be cautious not to leave themselves open to attack as subservient to the "Colossus of the North."

PROSPECTS FOR THE FUTURE

It is obvious that economic distortions, social imbalance, and political immaturity are sufficiently grave to constitute a threat of violent social upheaval in every country of Latin America. In some countries, this possibility has more likelihood of becoming a reality than in others. On the other hand, no country has reached the point at which social revolution and bloodshed has become unavoidable. Despite all the weaknesses of Latin American societies, at least half the countries of the region, comprising over 75 per cent of the total population and area, have a better than even chance of successfully pursuing moderate evolutionary reform programs. Countries of this type have access to material and human resources to correct the more serious inadequacies of their systems, and reasonable development and welfare plans to attain their goals. Most of them, however, are deficient in the type of national leaders needed to make the difficult political decisions essential to implement their programs. It is possible, in most cases at least, that cooperation and prodding from the United States, under the terms of the Alliance for Progress, will serve to bring forward the requisite leadership. Among these countries are Argentina, Brazil, Chile, Colombia, Costa Rica, Mexico, Uruguay, Venezuela, Guatemala, Panama, and El Salvador. Not all of these have equally good chances of avoiding Castro-Communist revolutions, and the last three must be grouped here with some misgivings.

Five other countries—Bolivia, the Dominican Republic, Ecuador, Honduras, and Peru—seem to have less than an even chance of avoiding radicalism and violence because of the weakness of their political institutions, the myopia of their governing classes, or the massive discontent of their middle-class intellectuals and lower-class workers. Peaceful solutions are, of course, far from impossible, but all factors considered, the possibility of their avoiding radical solutions to current problems is considerably less than that of the median of the first group.

The remaining three Latin countries of the Inter-American System—Haiti, Nicaragua, and Paraguay—are so primitive and underdeveloped that neither Cuban-type revolution nor Alliance for Progress reform appears probable. Instead, the chances are high that the old pattern of violence and dictatorship will continue to harass their people. This is not to say that these countries will avoid revolution and demagoguery, but it seems unlikely that a Castro-inspired leader could successfully destroy the old order, marshal the masses, accelerate economic development, and attract Communist-bloc support for his program on the scale necessary to maintain a viable regime. Given the undeveloped nature of the institutions of these countries, a leader of this type has almost no organization from which to build up mass support, no substantial amounts of national and foreign wealth to confiscate, and few products to trade with the Sino-Soviet bloc in return for the massive outlays necessary to keep the would-be Castro in power. This does not rule out the possibility of the emergence in these countries of a different type of Communist-inspired regime or "popular dictatorship." We believe, however, that Paraguay will continue to be influenced by Argentina and Brazil, while the others will continue to depend heavily on U.S. assistance and support. For many years, all three will pose difficult political and economic problems for their more powerful neighbors.

Cuba stands alone in the radicalism of its social reform, its dependence upon the Sino-Soviet bloc, its avowed determination to export revolution to the rest of Latin America, and its hostility to the United States and the Inter-American System. The revolutionary period is still too fluid to permit us to foresee the final outcome of Castro's experiment. For the present, given its effective police-state apparatus, the current regime probably still has sufficient support and adequate resources (including Soviet trade and aid) to maintain itself in power for the next few years, short of foreign invasion. Whether in the longer run Castro can maintain his position, or whether he will be swallowed up by an emerging collective leadership, or whether he will eventually be ousted—one can only speculate on these matters. Some of the changes will remain in effect no matter what happens. Much of the land confiscated by the government will never revert to its former owners. The old political parties will never again reorganize in their former image, and the day is long past when the peasantry and its needs can be ignored by those who govern the island. As Argentina could never revert to its pre-Perón mold, or Brazil to its pre-Vargas establishment, so Cuba will never be the same after Castro. In fact, Castro is transforming Cuba far more thoroughly than Perón or Vargas changed their countries. The Cuban revolution, in contrast to the more superficial Argentine and Brazilian experiments under their reform-minded dictators, has struck deep into the very core of society. Castro is not tampering with the system, he is revolutionizing it.

A few miles to the east, in stark contrast to wealthy Cuba—with its rich sugar and cattle lands and its pre-Castro $1.5 billion of foreign investments—lies poverty-stricken Haiti. Plagued since independence with violence, corruption, and poverty, Haiti has not experienced a reform movement since the early nineteenth century, when the French were expelled, the slaves freed, and the land divided. This overpopulated country is woefully short of both human and material resources. Illiteracy approaches 90 per cent, few persons have technical or professional skills, and the majority of the population live by subsistence agriculture. There is virtually no industry. Water and water power are in short supply, and only coffee is important as a marketable export. Political parties are non-existent; pressure groups, including the Church and the military, are poorly organized for political action; and the vast mass of the population is inert and apathetic. The only resource is land, and through wasteful farming methods, its productivity has declined disastrously. As the result of a rapid population increase, brought about in part by the introduction of a few health and sanitation measures, the plight of the masses (numbering more than 300 people per square mile) is truly desperate. U.S. economic assistance has not been geared toward any basic improvements of the socio-economic problems of the country, but rather toward the alleviation of immediate needs. Some longer-range projects had been undertaken, but these have not been completed. Because of the rising tide of nationalism among the politically active minority, the United States was not able to direct the operations of the Artibonite Valley development project to gain optimum use of its resources, or to eliminate corruption among the Haitian officials in charge of the project. During the past several years, work in the valley has been interrupted over disagreements between the countries on these issues. Prior to the 1962 suspension, aid had always been resumed to Haiti, despite the fact that the necessary reforms were not introduced, because the United States feared worsening of the political, social, and economic conditions in the country, with attendant instability, and perhaps violence. By the spring of 1963, the U.S. Government had abandoned all hope of ameliorating the terror, corruption, and suppression perpetrated by the Duvalier regime. The overthrow of the dictator appeared to be a matter of time.

Nicaragua's political future centers upon the problems of the transition of power from the hands of the Somozas to a responsible, and at least nominally representative, successor government. The prospects for this to take place, in view of the elections of February 3, 1963, can best be classed as fair, since the major opposition party did not participate. The same cannot be said for Paraguay, where no start in the direction of democratization is even on the horizon. Stroessner may well be able to remain in power for some time, but unless efforts are made soon to give the opposition some participation in the government, and some hope of eventually coming to power through constitutional processes, future political developments will almost certainly entail violence and chaos. The February, 1963, elections, which conferred upon Stroessner a third term, cannot be considered much of a step in this direction.

Peru and Ecuador, especially the former, have made notable gains in their GNP during the past decade. But profits from new projects have not been equitably distributed, social services have not improved, and the political reins are still tightly held by the traditional ruling elite. Lower-class discontent is rising to dangerous proportions in the cities, and is beginning to manifest itself in the rural areas even among the Indians. Reform-minded leaders and organizations have made little headway in achieving power and solving national problems. Discussion and proposed legislation to remedy some of the worst ills of these countries has been first of all inadequate, and then frustrated, because of the reluctance of the upper class to assent to the implementation of necessary land, tax, and other reform programs. In Peru, the APRA, under Víctor Raúl Haya de la Torre, has moderated its earlier radical program, but the military leaders still will not permit the party to govern the country. At this point, it appears that Peru's leading families may be destroyed unless the Belaúnde government, which took over power from the year-old military junta on July 28, 1963, has both the will and the ability to carry out the painful reorganization of Peruvian society. Whether Peru escapes a Cuban-type revolt may well depend upon how quickly the elite can see the light of Cuban fires—already reflected in the faces of the *campesinos* near Cuzco and the miners of Cerro de Pasco.

Ecuador, like Peru, has one of the most traditional societies in Latin America. Economic development has not proceeded as far and as rapidly as it has in her southern neighbor. Ecuador may have a little more time than Peru, but unrest among the lower classes of Quito and Guayaquil has been troubling the country since the end of World War II. The social structure and upper-class attitudes are similar to those in Peru, but there are no equivalents to APRA, or to reform leaders with the stature of Haya de la Torre. Former President José María Velasco Ibarra, a personalist-type leader with demogogic appeal and a record of moderate reforms, attempted to introduce some changes in the tax and land structures, but he was forced from office as a result of attacks from both right and left, ending with military intervention in the political arena. His successor, President Carlos Arosemena, won left-wing support by his initial refusal to break diplomatic relations with Castro or to vote for the expulsion of Cuba from the OAS at the Punta del Este Conference, in January, 1962. Arosemena's alcoholism proved an intolerable problem, and after a series of public scandals, he was removed by the military chiefs in July, 1963. A junta now governs. On balance, there appears no better chance for immediate reform in Ecuador than in Peru. But before an explosion takes place, Ecuador's elite may have more time than Peru's to consider their position.

Bolivia was placed, with a few misgivings, in the second group of countries, i.e., those having a less-than-even chance of successfully pursuing a moderate reform program and avoiding violent social upheavals and political absolutism of the Castro type. Although the country has experienced a thoroughgoing social and political revolution (which has resulted in land division, abolition of the old army, and the disruption of the political power of the old elite), its reform government has thus far been unable—to any degree adequate to satisfy popular aspirations—to accumulate the capital, and train the personnel, needed to implement its plans for economic development. The political balance is shifting toward the extreme left. Some optimism in the Bolivian situation is aroused by the following considerations: the fact that the moderates have so far maintained control; the commitment of the United States to provide assistance on a continuing basis; and the potential of the country for development, particularly in opening new lands, and in the discovery of new mineral deposits (especially oil). For Bolivia, diversified agriculture, recolonization, and a market economy require a vast program of cultural reorientation of the bulk of the population, which adheres strongly to many facets of its aboriginal Indian culture. This may be accomplished with massive aid, patient and expert technical teams, and time—perhaps several generations. With U.S. help, Bolivia has bought itself time, but little else. Without continued large-scale aid, she cannot begin to close the gap between popular demands and the economically attainable goals. Foreign assistance is an absolute necessity for national survival—to say nothing of progress.

Because of the many pitfalls involved in the transitional road from dictatorship to responsible, representative government, the Dominican Republic has also, with reluctance, been placed among those countries having less than an even chance of avoiding violent upheavals and the possible emergence of a Castro-Communist-type regime. The Dominican Republic suffers under the handicap of an almost total lack of meaningful political experience, the fruit of thirty years of dictatorship. On the plus side, fundamentally the Dominican Republic is economically sound. Much of the land is arable, the communications system is adequate, ports are good, small industry is flourishing, and the population is not excessive in terms of available resources. But the distribution of the national wealth requires reallocation, and the ability of the new leaders to carry through such economic reorganization, to maintain control of the social forces unleashed, and to guide the nation politically through the present crisis constitutes the great unknown quantity. These leaders are well meaning, but inexperienced and untried; some are naïve. It remains an open question whether or not they can beat off the attack of more ruthless and single-minded revolutionaries from the left—who in order to seize power do not hesitate to promise more than they can deliver. In addition, there is the rightist threat posed by the political heirs of Trujillo, who may be seeking to regain power. The new Administration under Juan Bosch certainly has a difficult row to hoe.

Honduras, which may, with justice, be called the forgotten country of Central America, if not all Latin America, is hemmed in by Guatemala, El Salvador, and Nicaragua. For differing reasons, each of its neighbors has been the object of much greater interest and attention. Indeed, Honduras most closely fits the stereotype of a "banana republic." Neither a dictatorship nor a true democracy, in recent decades this rural country, with its 2 million inhabitants, has enjoyed relative political stability and increasingly representative government. Its political difficulties of 1954 were lost in the attention focused on neighboring Guatemala. In the three-way Presidential balloting on October 10 of that year, no candidate received a majority of the vote, although Liberal Ramón Villeda Morales came very close. In this situation, the Vice-President seized power; two years later, he was replaced by a military junta that soon followed through on its pledge of free elections and a return to constitutional government. At the end of 1957, Villeda Morales, with the help of Congress, began a six-year term. His Liberal Party—which represents a broad segment of the political spectrum, running from center to left—holds thirty-six of fifty-eight seats in Congress. In view of the very limited economic potential of the country (bananas are its chief export), and the weakness of its political institutions, we are reluctantly forced to conclude that it has a no better than even chance of getting firmly on the road to economic, social, and political development during the coming decade.

El Salvador's problems are complex. Until 1960, the country was governed by the modified military dictatorship of Colonel José María Lemus. During his term, Lemus attempted to alleviate some of the worst features of rural peasant life, but he was restrained by the political power of the landed families. In October, 1960, Lemus was replaced by a leftist civil-military junta supported by the Communists. The junta permitted peasant organizations to form for the first time, but before the extreme left could consolidate its gains, the junta was overthrown, in January, 1961, by a more moderate Directorate, which drew up its own plans for economic and social reform, and for a return to constitutional government. Urban slum rentals were reduced, and increased benefits provided for rural workers. Longer-range financial and development projects have been undertaken, but there is little hope of raising living levels substantially without heavy foreign assistance. El Salvador's only national resource is land. Fortunately, most of it is arable, but it is overcrowded, with over 300 persons per square mile, and there are few cities and little manufacturing. Ownership of land is concentrated, and productivity is geared largely to exportable coffee, a crop that can sustain only a few at the cost of many.

El Salvador needs a complete reorientation of its economy, as well as of its social structure. The present Rivera Administration, elected in April, 1962, is attempting to carry out some reforms, but the basic problems cannot be tackled without substantial outside aid. Rural reform is essential within the near future if the mounting social and economic pressures are to be channeled into evolutionary change—which would foreclose the possibility of a destructive wave of violence designed to destroy the existing system. Here is a country that seems to be meeting the stipulations of the Alliance for Progress: a government enjoying the support of strong political groups and attempting to transform the country from a traditional elitist order to a more modern democratic political regime, with accompanying social and economic change. It remains a question to what extent the United States is willing and able to underwrite, encourage, and prod the experiment, in view of El Salvador's lack of resources—material and human. El Salvador could well be a testing ground for the Alliance for Progress and all its implications, including the improved well-being of the people, the resistance to Castro-Communist infiltration and subversion, and improved inter-American relations.

Guatemala is not immediately threatened by violent social revolution; nor is it firmly on the evolutionary road. The reforms of the 1944–54 period broke the traditionalist elite's monopoly of power and eased the political, social, and economic pressures for change in both rural and urban areas. Great quantities of U.S. economic assistance have also contributed importantly to the economic development of the country. Following the coup of 1954, however, the pace of reform slowed measurably. Since 1958, elections have been conducted rather honestly (but there was still enough unrest to spark a student revolt in March, 1962). The moderate left is not revolutionary minded; nor is it likely to ally itself with the Communists. Although it has not been spectacularly successful at the polls, the reformist left has won some significant contests, particularly in the capital, and places its trust in the electoral process rather than in force. The same cannot be said of the old Arbencista forces, but their repeated efforts at revolution have not yet come close to success. Nevertheless, in March, 1963, the military decided that the Arbencistas, and their Presidential candidate, Arévalo, represented a threat that warranted suspension of Ydígoras' rule. Under these circumstances, Guatemala will continue to need substantial aid and encouragement from the United States, through the Alliance for Progress, and even then, failure is a real possibility.

Panama is unique in Latin America. More than any other country in the area, it is influenced by the United States. The interoceanic Canal and surrounding territory, under U.S. control, cuts the country in half, but is the country's major source of revenue. Panama is firmly controlled by a few wealthy families with investments in business and land. The left, part of it radical, has been attempting to capitalize on the growing nationalist sentiment, especially among the students, to increase its voice in national politics. Temporarily successful, its position was undercut by U.S. concessions to Panamanian interests, such as the right to fly the Panamanian flag in the Canal Zone. Moderate U.S. economic assistance and technical aid has been contributing to diversification of the economy, particularly in foodstuffs, but Panama's primary problem consists of the great financial disparity between rich and poor. Greater economic development and better distribution are the chief needs of its people. These are slowly being met. Panama, like Guatemala, is not immediately under pressure for sweeping reforms, but improvements must continue. In the not too distant future, the elite must also grant political concessions to the emerging middle and lower classes. The greatest factor for moderate change, as against either freezing the *status quo* or revolutionizing the country, is the presence of the United States in the Canal Zone; but this may not, in the long run, prove sufficient.

The Colombian scene overwhelms the viewer with a mass of contradictions. For several decades prior to 1948, Colombia, by all outward appearances, was steadily building a firm and stable political system. Beneath the surface, however, the two traditional parties, the Liberal and the Conservative, were becoming more and more embittered. The murder of a Liberal leader in 1948 touched off riots that destroyed much of Bogotá's business district, plunged the country into civil war, and eventually brought military dictatorship. Since the overthrow of the dictator in 1957, the two parties have attempted to share power under the terms of a pact that divides offices equally and alternates the Presidency between the parties. Appearances are again deceiving, because beneath the surface, there are in reality four parties, since each of the major parties has sustained serious splits. The pact is thereby endangered: The Conservatives had great difficulty in agreeing on a Presidential candidate to succeed Liberal Alberto Lleras Camargo, and Liberal dissidents insisted that the Conservatives, as a minority party, had no right to the Presidency. Next time around, in 1966, the pact may well shatter on these rocks, and if it does, Colombia may be plunged once more into fratricidal civil war. For the 1962 elections, a majority of the Conservatives supported a candidate acceptable to the moderate Liberals, and Alberto Lleras was able to hold the bulk of the Liberals to the pact, thus giving the political compromise a new lease on life under President León Valencia.

Adding to Colombia's woes is the basic conservatism of the governing families, whether they call themselves Liberals or Conservatives. Colombia, like Peru, has experienced comfortable economic growth in the past decade, but has not divided the fruits equitably among the classes. Unlike the elite of Peru, however, Colombia's upper classes are more flexible. Not only do they talk of reform, but they have begun to implement moderate programs.

If the country moves forward with its agrarian-reform program, enacted in 1961, and carries through on its offer of relief to the urban lower classes, it may continue to stave off Castro- or Communist-type movements. Should the country be driven into civil war over the political issue again, it is quite possible that the fighting might take on, more and more, the aspects of a social revolution. The Communists tried to take advantage of the civil war earlier, but succeeded only in more remote parts of the country. Guerrilla bands, including some Communists, still control isolated villages and farming areas, and could well use these bases to expand their activities in the event of widespread renewal of fighting and the breakdown of central authority. Mixed as the picture is, one may feel justified in placing Colombia in the first category of countries.

Like Colombia, Chile is deeply troubled by popular unrest, but its manifestations are vastly different. Social legislation was enacted in the 1930's for the country's growing industrial and urban population, although much of it has been nullified by inflation and lack of implementation. Chilean land tenure and rural work patterns have changed little since the nineteenth century, and no meaningful agrarian reform has been enacted. Wealth and power remain concentrated in a few hands. The traditional liberal and conservative parties, both representing upper-class families, can only be compared roughly with those of Colombia. The middle-class Radical Party, at one time similar to the Argentine Radical Party, has lost part of its earlier reform drive, and is now in uneasy alliance with the two traditional parties supporting conservative, business-minded President Alessandri. The opposition consists of the Christian Democrats and a coalition of leftist parties, including both the Socialists and Communists, called the Popular Action Front (Frente de Acción Popular, or FRAP). The FRAP has some possibility of winning the next Presidential elections, in 1964, and thus bringing the Communists into a coalition government. Despite these difficulties, political and social, Chile has a better than even chance of avoiding violence and/or a Castro-type government.

Several factors militate in favor of a peaceful and moderate approach to Chile's problems. First and foremost is Chile's long and well-established tradition of peaceful transition of power from one party to another: the reformers can come to power through the electoral process, and will not be subject to armed overthrow by the army or the governing elite. Secondly, part of the elite themselves recognize Chile's social and economic problems and—unlike their counterparts in Peru, but more slowly than in Colombia—are beginning to support measures such as agrarian reform and increased wages, to alleviate some of the worst conditions. They are not yet moving fast enough to satisfy needs, but their flexibility is encouraging. Thirdly, even if the FRAP comes to power, there is a good possibility that the Communists may be contained, as they were in the Popular Front governments of the 1930's and in the postwar González Videla Administration. Some Socialists in the coalition are uneasy in their alliance with the Communists, and present political maneuvers point to the possibility of a future Christian Democrat-Socialist coalition. A government based on this alliance would be certain to move forcefully with reform programs, but would allay the conservative and business fears of a Castro or Communist revolution. Either this or a Christian Democrat-Radical coalition appears to offer Chile the best alternative for avoiding violence, modifying a traditionalist society, and setting the country on the road toward modern political, social, and economic organization. Chile will need some outside economic assistance in her quest for modernity, but above all, her elite will need encouragement, and perhaps prodding, to cooperate in the endeavor.

Despite pro-Castro riots and attempted revolts, which have occurred periodically from 1960 onward, Venezuela appears basically more sound than Chile. Stable political parties, reform governments, and democratic elections are of more recent origin in Venezuela than in Chile, but Venezuela has greater national wealth in both land and minerals. It has the highest per capita income in Latin America. The primary problem is distribution. Oil profits accrue largely to a few workers and enterprises, and to the government. Land ownership is still concentrated in a few hands, in spite of an agrarian-reform program that has already given land to well over 50,000 families. The present reform government of President Betancourt has introduced programs to overcome disparities by using the oil wealth to increase social services, to diversify the economy to provide jobs, and to open new land for settlement. The programs are moving slowly but steadily. Thus far, with excellent grass-roots political organization, President Betancourt's Democratic Action Party, and its ally, the Christian democratic COPEI, have been able to hold the majority of their lower-class following against extreme leftist agitation. Given time—and Betancourt appears to have bought at least some of this vital commodity—the moderate reformers who today control Venezuela may totally undercut the Communist and extreme left by the benefits that the lower classes will reap from their programs. However, improvements must not only continue but also gain momentum. With moderate foreign aid and continued encouragement, Betancourt and his allies have a good chance to succeed, in spite of being the priority target for Castro's subversive efforts. The Presidential elections of late 1963 will be an important test of the political viability of moderate reforms.

Of all the countries of Latin America, Brazil presents the greatest difficulties for assessment, because of its size in terms of area and population, its tremendous regional variation on economic and social questions, and its complexity in political organization. In reality, there are several Brazils: that of the sugar and coffee planters, that of the new industrialists and commercial people of São Paulo, that of the urban lower classes, that of the depressed rural peasantry, and that of the newly rising middle class. Basically, however, Brazil is divided, like most of Latin America, into the traditionalists, who posit a social elite to control political and economic life, and the reformers, or moderns, who advocate greater participation and sharing, by all classes, in the power structure and in the economic benefits of an industrialized and modernized economy. Unlike similar groups in much of Latin America, however, the Brazilian traditionalists and reformers are not polarized into opposing political organizations. In some respects, Brazilian political parties resemble those of the United States, with weak ideological commitments and a membership encompassing great cross sections of various political and social views. Unlike the United States, however, Brazil is plagued by a multiplicity of parties, many of which are oriented toward some particular region or personality.

Although the *favelas* are running sores in every major Brazilian city, the urban lower classes have fared better than the rural groups. Therefore, heavy migration to the numerous cities continues. The social reforms of the Vargas period, in the 1930's, were applied solely to the urban workers, and implementation has not kept pace with need. Leftist agitation for radical solutions to Brazil's inequities resounds through the cities. Nevertheless, the most depressed area of the country is the chiefly rural Northeast. Since the late 1950's, the greatest potential threat of revolution has come from the Peasant Leagues of Francisco Julião in that area.

Brazil, however, can probably avoid extremist solutions. Although the upper classes are reluctant to move rapidly, they do recognize the need for reform. In 1961, the government proposed an excellent plan for development of the Northeast, and prospects for its implementation appear good, despite some planter opposition. Moreover, the majority of the Catholic bishops have spoken for land reform, and are encouraging the government to push ahead in this field. As elsewhere, the upper class may need to be goaded to cooperate with, or at least not to impede, the various projects proposed. Foreign assistance will be necessary, and the United States has already pledged substantial loans to Brazil to help finance needed reforms. Political organization appears the primary weakness of moderate reformists at the present time. Although they can elect a man like Jânio Quadros to the Presidency, they cannot offer him the sustained support he requires to carry out his reform program. Organization will come in time; the question remains: Is there sufficient time left? Considering the long-established tradition of compromise and concession characteristic of Brazilian culture, the answer is likely to be affirmative. Brazil's primary problem appears to be the avoidance of a rural explosion until some remedies can begin to take effect. The urban lower classes also have pressing needs. However, with the higher literacy rate (the vote is restricted to literates) and greater participation in politics, they can eventually win concessions.

Argentina, the richest country of Latin America in terms of resource development and general levels of living, has suffered from political instability since the late years of the Perón era. The Administration of President Arturo Frondizi was buffeted, from its inception in 1958, from the left (represented by labor) and from the right (represented by the army). The left felt itself betrayed, in ideology and in pocketbook, by Frondizi's swing to the right after inauguration, in the face of his campaign commitments regarding economic and political nationalism and state control of national resources. His close relations with the United States, his emphasis on financial stabilization, and his conclusion of contracts with foreign petroleum companies alienated not only the Peronist wing of the left, but many within his own Radical Party. At the same time, Frondizi was constantly pressured by the military to check the left further, particularly Peronist and Communist labor groups. Moreover, the military, in February, 1962, forced him to break diplomatic relations with Cuba, just after the Argentine delegation had opposed strong anti-Castro measures at Punta del Este and, in the aftermath of the March elections, removed him from office.

In an attempt to escape his difficulties, Frondizi placed his faith in economic development, to the immediate neglect of social inequities and political disorganization. He seemed to believe that higher levels of living, attainable before the end of his term in 1964, would remove much of the dissatisfaction of labor, particularly the Peronists. In the meantime, he sought to assure himself of the support of the military by meeting their minimum demands. Despite this balancing of forces, and the lack of an acceptable alternative to him, Frondizi was forcibly removed from office by the military when the Peronists, whom Frondizi permitted to organize politically, emerged victorious in the March election. Although the July, 1963, elections paved the way for a return to constitutionality after eighteen months of a caretaker regime, the new government begins its life under inauspicious circumstances. Whether Argentina can escape a further bout with authoritarianism, and whether the country can return to the path of economic and social progress and political democracy, depends largely on the government's success in raising over-all living levels in the next several years. Much will depend on the ability of the farming sector to produce and sell profitably abroad, since Argentina's main source of foreign exchange still is provided by the sale of its agricultural products. These must supply the surpluses needed for expanding the industrial plant, from which the government has high expectations.

In short, Argentina has the material and human resources to approximate the social and political conditions of the more advanced countries of the West. Her problems are to use them efficiently, to assure an equitable distribution of the new wealth created, and to resolve her class conflicts in a spirit of compromise. The Argentine leaders are most willing to receive economic assistance for their development programs, but they are resistant to suggestions for social reforms under the terms of the Alliance for Progress. On balance, Argentina will probably avoid extremist solutions, because of widespread revulsion toward the Perón era, the basic wealth of the country, and the lack of severe disparities in wealth that plague most other Latin American countries.

Mexico, Costa Rica, and Uruguay unquestionably have the most stable political institutions, the most muted class conflicts, and perhaps the best-balanced economies in Latin America. They are not the richest countries in the area (Venezuela and Argentina rank above Uruguay; Costa Rica is no better than seventh; and half the countries enjoy a higher per capita GNP than Mexico), but all three have succeeded, in different ways, in finding workable methods to ease the conflicts within their societies. Costa Rica and Uruguay—small in territory and population, homogeneous in culture, and poor in natural resources, except for land—resolved their internal political and social quarrels without revolution, and virtually without outside interference. Mexico, on the other hand, carried out its reforms only after ten years of civil war and ten more of political conflict, and under constant threat from the United States. Mexico, too, faced far wider disparities in wealth and culture over a vast terrain, much of which was for a long time virtually inaccessible.

All three have largely removed the military from politics. All three have emphasized industry according to their capabilities, but unlike most of the remainder of Latin America, all three are presently concerned with increased and improved agricultural production. All three have extended, and are continuing to extend, social services, primarily to their urban population; but again unlike most of the remainder of Latin America, they are not neglecting their rural peasantry. All three have at least a strong semblance of political democracy, and have established firm traditions for the peaceful transfer of power to constitutionally elected administrations. Mexico, however, has virtually a one-party system, with wide representation of interests within the official party. Other parties present candidates, but are insufficiently organized and financed to win major power. The official party also falsifies returns, even when victory does not require it. Uruguay has a two-party system, and Costa Rica a multiparty system. In all the countries, however, the administrations may be characterized as centrist, committed to the reforms that have thus far been carried out, but cautious of proceeding rapidly to new measures. Mexican Presidents must speak in strongly "revolutionary" and leftist terms, but their actions do not have to match their words. Administrations in Uruguay and Costa Rica can speak more favorably of business interests and capitalism, but their actions do not vary much from those of a Mexican administration. They cannot, and do not, intend to undo the social reforms enacted—if anything, they continue to expand them. Differences between right and left in Uruguay, Costa Rica, and Mexico are differences of degree, not of kind.

This is not to deny the existence of any disequilibrium or unrest in these countries. Mexico faces the most severe problems, Costa Rica the least. Great poverty and suffering still exist among the lower classes in Mexico, especially among the rural peasantry. The rural workers of Uruguay have not had the same social benefits extended them that the workers of Montevideo have received. There is dissatisfaction, and there are political leaders who speak for these underprivileged masses. In Mexico, a new rich class has arisen from the revolution, many of whose members have little social consciousness. Taxes are not equitably distributed or efficiently collected. The land is overcrowded, and thousands of Mexicans yearly seek work in the United States. The list of problems could be extended for all three countries. The fact remains, however, that social unrest falls below the danger point of solution by revolt and violence. The reasons are obviously that reforms have already been undertaken and are continuing, albeit modestly; the economies are expanding; and there is basic confidence in the system—political, social, and economic—and that living conditions will improve materially and culturally. As long as this minimum confidence exists among the masses, there is little fear of insurrection or of Castro-Communist take-overs.

SUMMARY

Every Latin American country, even the most industrialized, diversified, and agriculturally modernized, is economically underdeveloped by comparison with U.S. or even Western European standards. Economic growth and development must continue at an accelerating rate. Social reform, too, is essential in Latin America, and must accompany the economic changes that are overtaking the area. In a few countries, basic changes in the social structure either have already occurred through violent revolution, or are in process of occurring through slower, evolutionary methods. In these countries, economic development must be stressed, since social reform can be deepened and broadened only by use of the profits accruing from greater productivity. In the majority of the countries of Latin America, however, though some change has taken place, it has been insufficient to establish a strong enough or deep enough current to assure basic modification of the traditionalist control over political, social, and economic life. Pressures for change are present, but so too are pressures to preserve the traditional order, even in those countries that have taken long and rapid steps toward industrialization and urbanization. In these areas, economic aid and social reform must go hand in hand; in that way, the benefits of economic growth may be equitably distributed among the lower-income groups to satisfy at least minimum demands and assure the political stability necessary for continued economic growth and peaceful social transformation. In those remaining countries in which few modern inroads have been made into the traditional order, rapid strides must be made in social reform, as well as in economic development, within the next few years. Economic growth cannot be ignored, but growth without better distribution of wealth will only accelerate increasingly bitter frustrations and hatreds.

Political democratization and stability will perhaps follow the economic and social changes, but they cannot be expected to precede these basic reforms. The lower classes will not continue to tolerate political processes that deny them access to decent living conditions, educational opportunities, and good health. If those masses should lose all hope that democratic political procedures can alleviate their wretchedness, the future of democracy in Latin America appears bleak. Castro has apparently persuaded at least a million Cubans that his authoritarian way offers them the only hope for escaping the chains of poverty. He is trying to convince the masses throughout the hemisphere. Whether he succeeds or not depends upon how rapidly those who proclaim democracy can move to meet the needs of the masses. The economic failures of the Castro regime in 1962–63 have dimmed the Cuban image for many, at least temporarily, in effect giving the democratic forces in the area extra time in which to produce acceptable results. However, laggard performance now by moderate reformers will only emphasize for the Latin American mass the efficacy of violent upheaval if a Sovietized Cuba begins to pay off economically by the end of the 1960's. Democracy, the United States, and moderates throughout the hemisphere are on trial. The outcome remains uncertain everywhere.

Appendix A

POPULATION GROWTH IN LATIN AMERICA, 1953–62

(*In Thousands*)

Country	July 1, 1953	July 1, 1959	July 1, 1962	Annual Rate of Increase
Argentina	18,400	20,614	21,800	1.9%
Bolivia	3,147	3,416	3,550	1.4
Brazil	55,772	64,216	74,500	3.0
Chile	6,437	7,465	8,000	2.5
Colombia	12,111	13,824	15,000	2.8
Costa Rica	884	1,126	1,250	4.1
Cuba	5,829	6,599	6,950	2.1
Dominican Republic	2,360	2,894	3,150	3.5
Ecuador	3,502	4,169	4,480	3.0
El Salvador	2,054	2,520	2,680	2.5
Guatemala	3,058	3,652	3,930	3.0
Haiti	3,327	3,464	3,570	1.2
Honduras	1,556	1,887	2,050	3.3
Mexico	28,057	33,304	35,750	2.9
Nicaragua	1,165	1,424	1,550	3.4
Panama	864	1,024	1,100	2.9
Paraguay	1,496	1,728	1,850	2.3
Peru	9,035	10,524	11,200	2.6
Uruguay	2,535	2,700	2,800	1.3
Venezuela	5,440	6,512	7,725	3.2
TOTAL	167,029	192,938	212,885	2.8%

Source: Figures are based on U.S. Census Bureau estimates, with adjustments from recent national census reports.

Appendix B

THE CHARTER OF PUNTA DEL ESTE

Establishing an Alliance for Progress Within the Framework of Operation Pan America

PREAMBLE

We, the American Republics, hereby proclaim our decision to unite in a common effort to bring our people accelerated economic progress and broader social justice within the framework of personal dignity and political liberty.

Almost two hundred years ago we began in this Hemisphere the long struggle for freedom which now inspires people in all parts of the world. Today, in ancient lands, men moved to hope by the revolutions of our young nations search for liberty. Now we must give a new meaning to that revolutionary heritage. For America stands at a turning point in history. The men and women of our Hemisphere are reaching for the better life which today's skills have placed within their grasp. They are determined for themselves and their children to have decent and ever more abundant lives, to gain access to knowledge and equal opportunity for all, to end those conditions which benefit the few at the expense of the needs and dignity of the many. It is our inescapable task to fulfill these just desires—to demonstrate to the poor and forsaken of our countries, and of all lands, that the creative powers of free men hold the key to their progress and to the progress of future generations. And our certainty of ultimate success rests not alone on our faith in ourselves and in our nations but on the indomitable spirit of free man which has been the heritage of American civilization.

Inspired by these principles, and by the principles of Operation Pan America and the Act of Bogotá, the American Republics hereby resolve to adopt the following program of action to establish and carry forward an Alliance for Progress.

TITLE I. OBJECTIVES OF THE ALLIANCE FOR PROGRESS

It is the purpose of the Alliance for Progress to enlist the full energies of the peoples and governments of the American republics in a great cooperative effort to accelerate the economic and social development of the participating countries of Latin America, so that they may achieve maximum levels of well-being, with equal opportunities for all, in democratic societies adapted to their own needs and desires.

The American republics hereby agree to work toward the achievement of the following fundamental goals in the present decade:

1. To achieve in the participating Latin American countries a substantial and sustained growth of per capita income at a rate designed to attain, at the earliest possible date, levels of income capable of assuring self-sustaining development, and sufficient to make Latin American income levels constantly larger in relation to the levels of the more industrialized nations. In this way the gap between the living standards of Latin America and those of the more developed countries can be narrowed. Similarly, presently existing differences in income levels among the Latin American countries will be reduced by accelerating the development of the relatively less developed countries and granting them maximum priority in the distribution of resources and in international cooperation in general. In evaluating the degree of relative development, account will be taken not only of average levels of real income and gross product per capita, but also of indices of infant mortality, illiteracy, and per capita daily caloric intake.

It is recognized that, in order to reach these objectives within a reasonable time, the rate of economic growth in any country of Latin America should be not less than 2.5 per cent per capita per year, and that each participating country should determine its own growth target in the light of its stage of social and economic evolution, resource endowment, and ability to mobilize national efforts for development.

2. To make the benefits of economic progress available to all citizens of all economic and social groups through a more equitable distribution of national income, raising more rapidly the income and standard of living of the needier sectors of the population, at

the same time that a higher proportion of the national product is devoted to investment.

3. To achieve balanced diversification in national economic structures, both regional and functional, making them increasingly free from dependence on the export of a limited number of primary products and the importation of capital goods while attaining stability in the prices of exports or in income derived from exports.

4. To accelerate the process of rational industrialization so as to increase the productivity of the economy as a whole, taking full advantage of the talents and energies of both the private and public sectors, utilizing the natural resources of the country and providing productive and remunerative employment for unemployed or part-time workers. Within this process of industrialization, special attention should be given to the establishment and development of capital-goods industries.

5. To raise greatly the level of agricultural productivity and output and to improve related storage, transportation, and marketing services.

6. To encourage, in accordance with the characteristics of each country, programs of comprehensive agrarian reform leading to the effective transformation, where required, of unjust structures and systems of land tenure and use, with a view to replacing latifundia and dwarf holdings by an equitable system of land tenure so that, with the help of timely and adequate credit, technical assistance and facilities for the marketing and distribution of products, the land will become for the man who works it the basis of his economic stability, the foundation of his increasing welfare, and the guarantee of his freedom and dignity.

7. To eliminate adult illiteracy and by 1970 to assure, as a minimum, access to six years of primary education for each school-age child in Latin America; to modernize and expand vocational, technical, secondary and higher educational and training facilities, to strengthen the capacity for basic and applied research; and to provide the competent personnel required in rapidly-growing societies.

8. To increase life expectancy at birth by a minimum of five years, and to increase the ability to learn and produce, by improving individual and public health. To attain this goal it will be necessary, among other measures, to provide adequate potable water supply and sewage disposal to not less than 70 per cent of the urban and 50 per cent of the rural population; to reduce the present mortality rate of children less than five years of age by at least

one-half; to control the more serious communicable diseases, according to their importance as a cause of sickness, disability, and death; to eradicate those illnesses, especially malaria, for which effective techniques are known; to improve nutrition; to train medical and health personnel to meet at least minimum requirements; to improve basic health services at national and local levels; and to intensify scientific research and apply its results more fully and effectively to the prevention and cure of illness.

9. To increase the construction of low-cost houses for low-income families in order to replace inadequate and deficient housing and to reduce housing shortages; and to provide necessary public services to both urban and rural centers of population.

10. To maintain stable price levels, avoiding inflation or deflation and the consequent social hardships and maldistribution of resources, always bearing in mind the necessity of maintaining an adequate rate of economic growth.

11. To strengthen existing agreements on economic integration, with a view to the ultimate fulfillment of aspirations for a Latin American common market that will expand and diversify trade among the Latin American countries and thus contribute to the economic growth of the region.

12. To develop cooperative programs designed to prevent the harmful effects of excessive fluctuations in the foreign exchange earnings derived from exports of primary products, which are of vital importance to economic and social development; and to adopt the measures necessary to facilitate the access of Latin American exports to international markets.

TITLE II. ECONOMIC AND SOCIAL DEVELOPMENT

Chapter I. Basic Requirements for Economic and Social Development

The American republics recognize that to achieve the foregoing goals it will be necessary:

1. That comprehensive and well-conceived national programs of economic and social development, aimed at the achievement of self-sustaining growth, be carried out in accordance with democratic principles.

2. That national programs of economic and social development be based on the principle of self-help—as established in the Act of Bogotá—and on the maximum use of domestic resources, taking into account the special conditions of each country.

3. That in the preparation and execution of plans for economic and social development, women should be placed on an equal footing with men.

4. That the Latin American countries obtain sufficient external financial assistance, a substantial portion of which should be extended on flexible conditions with respect to periods and terms of repayment and forms of utilization, in order to supplement domestic capital formation and reinforce their import capacity; and that, in support of well-conceived programs, which include the necessary structural reforms and measures for the mobilization of internal resources, a supply of capital from all external sources during the coming ten years of at least 20 billion dollars be made available to the Latin American countries, with priority to the relatively less developed countries. The greater part of this sum should be in public funds.

5. That institutions in both the public and private sectors, including labor organizations, cooperatives, and commercial, industrial, and financial institutions, be strengthened and improved for the increasing and effective use of domestic resources, and that the social reforms necessary to permit a fair distribution of the fruits of economic and social progress be carried out.

Chapter II. National Development Programs

1. Participating Latin American countries agree to introduce or strengthen systems for the preparation, execution, and periodic revision of national programs for economic and social development consistent with the principles, objectives, and requirements contained in this document. Participating Latin American countries should formulate, if possible within the next eighteen months, long-term development programs. Such programs should embrace, according to the characteristics of each country, the elements outlined in the Appendix.

2. National development programs should incorporate self-help efforts directed toward:

a. Improvement of human resources and widening of opportunities by raising general standards of education and health; improving and extending technical education and professional training with emphasis on science and technology; providing adequate remuneration for work performed, encouraging the talents of managers, entrepreneurs, and wage earners; providing more productive employment for underemployed manpower; establishing effective systems of labor relations, and procedures for consultation and collaboration among public authorities, employer associations, and labor organizations; promoting the establishment and expansion of local institutions for basic and applied research; and improving the standards of public administration.

b. Wider development and more efficient use of natural resources, especially those which are now idle or under-utilized, including measures for the processing of raw materials.

c. The strengthening of the agricultural base, progressively extending the benefits of the land to those who work it, and ensuring in countries with Indian populations the integration of these populations into the economic, social, and cultural processes of modern life. To carry out these aims, measures should be adopted, among others, to establish or improve, as the case may be, the following services: extension, credit, technical assistance, agricultural research and mechanization; health and education; storage and distribution; cooperatives and farmers' associations; and community development.

d. More effective, rational and equitable mobilization and use of financial resources through the reform of tax structures, including fair and adequate taxation of large incomes and real estate, and the strict application of measures to improve fiscal administration. Development programs should include the adaptation of budget expenditures to development needs, measures for the maintenance of price stability, the creation of essential credit facilities at reasonable rates of interest, and the encouragement of private savings.

e. Promotion through appropriate measures, including the signing of agreements for the purpose of reducing or eliminating double taxation, of conditions that will encourage the flow of foreign investments and help to increase the capital resources of participating countries in need of capital.

f. Improvement of systems of distribution and sales in order to make markets more competitive and prevent monopolistic practices.

Chapter III. Immediate and Short-Term Action Measures

1. Recognizing that a number of Latin American countries, despite their best efforts, may require emergency financial assistance, the United States will provide assistance from the funds which are or may be established for such purposes. The United

States stands ready to take prompt action on applications for such assistance. Applications relating to existing situations should be submitted within the next sixty days.

2. Participating Latin American countries should, in addition to creating or strengthening machinery for long-term development programming, immediately increase their efforts to accelerate their development by giving special emphasis to the following objectives:

a. The completion of projects already under way and the initiation of projects for which the basic studies have been made, in order to accelerate their financing and execution.

b. The implementation of new projects which are designed:

(1) To meet the most pressing economic and social needs and benefit directly the greatest number of people;

(2) To concentrate efforts within each country in the less developed or more depressed areas in which particularly serious social problems exist;

(3) To utilize idle capacity or resources, particularly under-employed manpower; and

(4) To survey and assess natural resources.

c. The facilitation of the preparation and execution of long-term programs through measures designed:

(1) To train teachers, technicians, and specialists;

(2) To provide accelerated training to workers and farmers;

(3) To improve basic statistics;

(4) To establish needed credit and marketing facilities; and

(5) To improve services and administration.

3. The United States will assist in carrying out these short-term measures with a view to achieving concrete results from the Alliance for Progress at the earliest possible moment. In connection with the measures set forth above, and in accordance with the statement of President Kennedy, the United States will provide assistance under the Alliance, including assistance for the financing of short-term measures, totalling more than one billion dollars in the year ending March, 1962.

Chapter IV. External Assistance in Support of National Development Programs

1. The economic and social development of Latin America will require a large amount of additional public and private financial

assistance on the part of capital-exporting countries, including the members of the Development Assistance Group and international lending agencies. The measures provided for in the Act of Bogotá and the new measures provided for in this Charter, are designed to create a framework within which such additional assistance can be provided and effectively utilized.

2. The United States will assist those participating countries whose development programs establish self-help measures and economic and social policies and programs consistent with the goals and principles of this Charter. To supplement the domestic efforts of such countries, the United States is prepared to allocate resources which, along with those anticipated from other external sources, will be of a scope and magnitude adequate to realize the goals envisaged in this Charter. Such assistance will be allocated to both social and economic development and, where appropriate, will take the form of grants or loans on flexible terms and conditions. The participating countries will request the support of other capital-exporting countries and appropriate institutions so that they may provide assistance for the attainment of these objectives.

3. The United States will help in the financing of technical assistance projects proposed by a participating country or by the General Secretariat of the Organization of American States for the purpose of:

a. Providing experts contracted in agreement with the governments to work under their direction and to assist them in the preparation of specific investment projects and the strengthening of national mechanisms for preparing projects, using specialized engineering firms where appropriate;

b. Carrying out, pursuant to existing agreements for cooperation among the General Secretariat of the Organization of American States, the Economic Commission for Latin America, and the Inter-American Development Bank, field investigations and studies, including those relating to development problems, the organization of national agencies for the preparation of development programs, agrarian reform and rural development, health, cooperatives, housing, education and professional training, and taxation and tax administration; and

c. Convening meetings of experts and officials on development and related problems.

The governments or abovementioned organizations should, when appropriate, seek the cooperation of the United Nations and its specialized agencies in the execution of these activities.

4. The participating Latin American countries recognize that each has in varying degree a capacity to assist fellow republics by providing technical and financial assistance. They recognize that this capacity will increase as their economies grow. They therefore affirm their intention to assist fellow republics increasingly as their individual circumstances permit.

Chapter V. Organization and Procedures

1. In order to provide technical assistance for the formulation of development programs, as may be requested by participating nations, the Organization of American States, the Economic Commission for Latin America, and the Inter-American Development Bank will continue and strengthen their agreements for coordination in this field, in order to have available a group of programming experts whose service can be used to facilitate the implementation of this Charter. The participating countries will also seek an intensification of technical assistance from the specialized agencies of the United Nations for the same purpose.

2. The Inter-American Economic and Social Council, on the joint nomination of the Secretary General of the Organization of American States, the President of the Inter-American Development Bank, and the Executive Secretary of the United Nations Economic Commission for Latin America, will appoint a panel of nine high-level experts, exclusively on the basis of their experience, technical ability, and competence in the various aspects of economic and social development. The experts may be of any nationality, though if of Latin American origin an appropriate geographical distribution will be sought. They will be attached to the Inter-American Economic and Social Council, but will nevertheless enjoy complete autonomy in the performance of their duties. They may not hold any other remunerative position. The appointment of these experts will be for a period of three years, and may be renewed.

3. Each government, if it so wishes, may present its program for economic and social development for consideration by an ad hoc committee, composed of no more than three members drawn from the panel of experts referred to in the preceding paragraph together with an equal number of experts not on the panel. The experts who compose the ad hoc committee will be appointed by the Secretary General of the Organization of American States at the request of the interested government and with its consent.

4. The committee will study the development program, exchange opinions with the interested government as to possible modifications and, with the consent of the government, report its conclusions to the Inter-American Development Bank and to other governments and institutions that may be prepared to extend external financial and technical assistance in connection with the execution of the program.

5. In considering a development program presented to it, the ad hoc committee will examine the consistency of the program with the principles of the Act of Bogotá and of this Charter, taking into account the elements in the Appendix.

6. The General Secretariat of the Organization of American States will provide the personnel needed by the experts referred to in paragraphs 2 and 3 of this Chapter in order to fulfill their tasks. Such personnel may be employed specifically for this purpose or may be made available from the permanent staffs of the Organization of American States, the Economic Commission for Latin America, and the Inter-American Development Bank, in accordance with the present liaison arrangements between the three organizations. The General Secretariat of the Organization of American States may seek arrangements with the United Nations Secretariat, its specialized agencies and the Inter-American Specialized Organizations, for the temporary assignment of necessary personnel.

7. A government whose development program has been the object of recommendations made by the ad hoc committee with respect to external financing requirements may submit the program to the Inter-American Development Bank so that the Bank may undertake the negotiations required to obtain such financing, including the organization of a consortium of credit institutions and governments disposed to contribute to the continuing and systematic financing, on appropriate terms, of the development program. However, the government will have full freedom to resort through any other channels to all sources of financing, for the purpose of obtaining, in full or in part, the required resources.

The ad hoc committee shall not interfere with the right of each government to formulate its own goals, priorities, and reforms in its national development programs.

The recommendations of the ad hoc committee will be of great importance in determining the distribution of public funds under the Alliance for Progress which contribute to the external financing of such programs. These recommendations shall give special consideration to Title I. 1.

The participating governments will also use their good offices to the end that these recommendations may be accepted as a factor of great importance in the decisions taken, for the same purpose, by inter-American credit institutions, other international credit agencies, and other friendly governments which may be potential sources of capital.

8. The Inter-American Economic and Social Council will review annually the progress achieved in the formulation, national implementation, and international financing of development programs; and will submit to the Council of the Organization of American States such recommendations as it deems pertinent.

Bibliography

The following compilation of newspapers, periodicals, books, and articles is selective. The newspapers listed include some—like *The New York Times*—that give rather full coverage, on a daily basis, to vital developments throughout Latin America, and others—like *The Wall Street Journal*—that provide only selective coverage, but supply analysis. The Latin American newspapers cited provide excellent information on political and economic events in their countries of publication and fair to good reportage on events elsewhere in the area. The periodicals listed range from fair to excellent as aids to understanding current Latin American affairs. The accompanying annotations explain the special interest of each of these periodicals.

The books and articles selected are, for the most part, recent publications. Change has been so rapid in the past five years that books on political and economic development rapidly become dated. A few old titles have been retained—for their insight into causes of recent problems, or for their treatment of certain of the area's vital constants. Realizing that this bibliography is too extensive for the general reader, we have marked the most important entries with asterisks. To afford further assistance, many of the entries are annotated.

One more comment concerning the organization of the books and articles section of this bibliography might be of value. The section is divided into three parts: General, U.S.–Latin American Relations, and Individual Countries. Each is divided into alphabetized listings of books and articles.

NEWSPAPERS

The Christian Science Monitor (Boston).
Corréio da Manhã (Rio de Janeiro).

O Estado de São Paulo (São Paulo).
Excelsior (Mexico City).
Miami Herald.
The New York Times.
La Prensa (Buenos Aires).
El Siglo (Bogotá).
El Tiempo (Bogotá).
Última Hora (Rio de Janeiro).
The Wall Street Journal.
The Washington Post and Times Herald.

PERIODICALS

American Universities Field Staff Reports (New York). Good to excellent reports by U.S. scholars on topics of current interest in the field of social, economic, and political problems in selected countries of Latin America.

Anhembi (São Paulo). Monthly review of current developments in the arts and sciences, with a good roundup of national and international news. Ceased publication November, 1962.

Atenea (Concepción, Chile). Quarterly devoted to art, science, and history, with occasional articles on political thought.

Brazilian Trade News (Rio de Janeiro and New York). Newssheet issued daily except Sunday; particularly valuable for its coverage of labor and economic affairs.

Combate (San José, Costa Rica). Bimonthly review of current politics and political thought, directed by outstanding leaders of the anti-Communist left, including Rómulo Betancourt, Víctor Raúl Haya de la Torre, José Figueres, Eduardo Santos, and Norman Thomas. Ceased publication, at least temporarily, early in 1963.

Cuadernos Americanos (México, D.F.). Bimonthly periodical on current politics, political thought, and international relations. The predominant tone is strongly anti-U.S. and nationalist, but not Communist. With a highly intellectual content, *C.A.* is one of the most respected periodicals of Latin America.

Current History (New York). Monthly publication devoting each issue to some particular problem or area. For several years, Latin America has been treated annually.

Estudios (Buenos Aires). Catholic monthly of centrist political views, containing articles and commentary on current politics.

Finis Terrae (Santiago, Chile). Quarterly publication concerned with current politics, history, and the arts.

Foro Internacional (México, D.F.). Quarterly review on international relations, including Latin American foreign policies, with a wide range of scholarly contributors.

Hispanic American Historical Review (Durham, N.C.). The leading historical review dealing with Latin America in the United States. Published quarterly by Duke University Press.

Hispanic American Report (Stanford, Cal.). Stanford University's monthly publication of current news on Spain, Portugal, and Latin America, including European overseas possessions in the area.

Inter-American Economic Affairs (Washington, D.C.). Quarterly review, containing documents, analyses, and descriptions of current economic problems.

Journal of Inter-American Studies (Gainesville, Fla.). Multilingual review, published by the University of Florida, covering a broad spectrum of Latin American affairs.

Noticias. Weekly Digest of Hemisphere Reports (New York). News reports—chiefly economic, but also political—gathered and edited from a wide variety of sources in the United States and Latin America.

Política (Caracas, Venezuela). Bimonthly review, liberal and leftist, but anti-Communist; similar to *Combate* although its lead articles have greater depth. Concerned primarily with current political and economic problems and, to a lesser extent, with history.

Revista Brasileira de Estudos Políticos (Belo Horizonte, Brazil). Semiannual review on politics, economics, and sociology, with emphasis on Brazilian developments and some interest in political theory and political behavior.

Revista Brasileira de Política Internacional (Rio de Janeiro). Quarterly review on Brazilian and Latin American foreign policies, with particular attention to U.S.–Latin-American relations.

Revista de Historia de América (México, D.F.). Semiannual, multilingual review, published by the Pan-American Institute of Geography and History. Leading journal of its type in Latin America; noted for its excellent bibliography.

Statistical Abstract of Latin America (Los Angeles). Yearly report by the staff of the Center of Latin American Studies at the University of Southern California at Los Angeles. Broad coverage of a wide variety of sociological, cultural, economic, and political matters that lend themselves to statistical tabulation.

Visión (Panama City). Biweekly general news magazine, providing good coverage of current politics in Latin America, with some attention to scientific, cultural, and economic developments. Virtually every issue contains a special section on Mexico, focusing primarily on economic aspects. A Portuguese-language edition, *Visão,* covers Brazil much more extensively than does *Visión.*

Note: For further references, see ZIMMERMAN, IRENE. *A Guide to Current Latin American Periodicals.* Gainesville, Fla.: Kallman Publishing Company, 1961. For brief reports on new books, see PARISEAU, EARL J. (ed.). *Handbook of Latin American Studies.* Gainesville, Fla.: University of Florida Press. Published annually.

BOOKS AND ARTICLES

GENERAL

ADAMS, MILDRED (ed.). *Latin America: Evolution or Explosion?* New York: Dodd, Mead, 1963. Papers from an international conference on the preconditions for economic and social development in Latin America and Latin American relations with the Common Market.

ADAMS, RICHARD N. *Cultural Surveys of Panama—Nicaragua—Guatemala—El Salvador—Honduras.* Washington, D.C.: Pan American Sanitary Bureau, 1957.

*———, *et al.* *Social Change in Latin America Today.* New York: Council on Foreign Relations; Harper & Brothers, 1960. A perceptive examination by six social anthropologists of changes in five countries, and of the significance of these changes for the United States.

*ALEXANDER, ROBERT J. *Communism in Latin America.* New Brunswick, N.J.: Rutgers University Press, 1957. The standard work on the subject. Some errors in fact, but excellent evaluation of Communist strengths and weaknesses (to 1957).

———. *Labor Relations in Argentina, Brazil, and Chile.* New York: McGraw-Hill Book Company, 1962.

*———. *Prophets of the Revolution.* New York: The Macmillan Company, 1962. Review of social reform and social revolution, with studies of selected countries.

———. *Today's Latin America.* Garden City, New York: Doubleday & Company, 1962.

ALLEN, ROBERT LORING. *Soviet Influence in Latin America: The Role of Economic Relations.* Washington, D.C.: Public Affairs Press, 1959. Points out the low level of Soviet trade with Latin America and obstacles to expansion—pre-Castro.

BENHAM, FREDERIC C., and HALLEY, H. A. *A Short Introduction to the Economy of Latin America.* London and New York: Oxford University Press, 1959. Brief but useful surveys of Argentina, Brazil, Chile, Mexico, Venezuela, and Colombia.

BLANKSTEN, GEORGE I., "The Politics of Latin America," in Gabriel A. Almond and James S. Coleman (eds.), *The Politics of the Developing Areas,* Princeton, N.J.: Princeton University Press, 1960.

CHRISTENSON, ASHER N. (ed.). *The Evolution of Latin American Government.* New York: Henry Holt & Company, 1951. A series of fifty-five readings, now somewhat dated, by distinguished scholars.

* Key works.

CLAGETT, HELEN L. *The Administration of Justice in Latin America.* New York: Oceana Publications, 1952.

COLEMAN, WILLIAM J., M.M. *Latin American Catholicism—A Self-Evaluation.* ("World Horizon Reports," No. 23.) New York: Maryknoll Publications, 1956. A frank appraisal of the spiritual and social weaknesses of Latin American Catholicism, by lay and clerical leaders of Catholic Action in Latin America.

Cosío VILLEGAS, DANIEL. *Change in Latin America: The Mexican and Cuban Revolutions.* Lincoln, Nebr.: University of Nebraska Press, 1961.

CRAWFORD, WILLIAM REX. *A Century of Latin American Thought.* Cambridge, Mass.: Harvard University Press, 1961. Updated version of a 1944 classic dealing with the social and political views of the great Latin American *pensadores* of the last century.

CREVENNA, THEODORE R. (ed.). *Materiales para el estudio de la clase media en América Latina.* Washington, D.C.: Pan American Union, 1951.

DAVIS, HAROLD E. (ed.). *Government and Politics in Latin America.* New York: The Ronald Press, 1958. A particularly good text.

———. *Latin American Social Thought Since Independence.* Washington, D.C.: The University Press of Washington, D.C., 1961.

GORDON, WENDELL C. *The Economy of Latin America.* New York: Columbia University Press, 1950.

*HANKE, LEWIS. *Modern Latin America: Continent in Ferment.* 2 vols. Princeton, N.J.: D. Van Nostrand Co., 1959. Excellent short introduction and selected readings for the nonspecialist by one of the leading Latin American scholars in the United States.

HAUSER, PHILIP M. (ed.). *Urbanization in Latin America.* New York: International Documents Service, Columbia University Press, 1961.

HERRING, HUBERT A. *History of Latin America.* Rev. ed. New York: Alfred A. Knopf, 1961. A readable and generally reliable history of the area.

*HIRSCHMAN, ALBERT O. *Journeys Toward Progress: Studies of Economic Policy-Making in Latin America.* New York: Twentieth Century Fund, 1963.

*——— (ed.). *Latin American Issues: Essays and Comments.* New York: Twentieth Century Fund, 1961. Highlights complexity of Latin American problems of economic development and the controversies raging in the area over means and methods.

INTERNATIONAL LABOR ORGANIZATION. *The Landless Farmer in Latin America.* Geneva, 1957.

*JAMES, PRESTON E. *Latin America.* 3rd ed. New York: The Odyssey Press, 1959. The basic work on economic geography.

*JOHNSON, JOHN J. *Political Change in Latin America.* Stanford, Cal.: Stanford University Press, 1958. Excellent survey of the political rise of urban groups in five countries, though it fails to clarify the meaning of middle class or sector in Latin America.

—————— (ed.). *The Role of the Military in Underdeveloped Countries.* Princeton, N.J.: Princeton University Press, 1962. Three chapters are devoted to the military in Latin America.

KALIJARVI, THORSTEN V. *Central America, Land of Lords and Lizards.* Princeton, N.J.: D. Van Nostrand Co., 1962. A brief survey by a former U.S. Ambassador to El Salvador.

KARNES, THOMAS L. *The Failure of Union: Central America, 1824–1960.* Chapel Hill, N.C.: University of North Carolina Press, 1961.

KIDDER, FREDERICK E. *Latin America and UNESCO: The First Five Years.* Gainesville, Fla.: University of Florida Press, 1960.

LAVELL, CARR B. *Population Growth and Development in South America.* Washington, D.C.: George Washington University, 1959.

LEONARD, OLEN E., and LOOMIS, CHARLES P. (eds.). *Readings in Latin American Social Organization and Institutions.* East Lansing, Mich.: Michigan State College Press, 1953.

*LIEUWEN, EDWIN. *Arms and Politics in Latin America.* Rev. ed. New York: Frederick A. Praeger, 1961. The first attempt to survey the role of the military in politics. This work also analyzes the U.S. military-aid program for Latin America and its political effects.

MACDONALD, AUSTIN F. *Latin American Politics and Government.* 2nd ed. New York: Thomas Y. Crowell Co., 1954. Outdated and sometimes inaccurate, this text is useful for its country-by-country approach to politics.

*MARTZ, JOHN D. *Central America. The Crisis and the Challenge.* Chapel Hill, N.C.: University of North Carolina Press, 1958. An accurate and useful survey of recent political history, but lacking depth in analysis of the social and economic factors that condition political life.

MECHAM, J. LLOYD. *Church and State in Latin America.* Chapel Hill, N.C.: University of North Carolina Press, 1934. The classic history of this problem, now outdated for much of Latin America, but indispensable for background.

MONTEFORTE TOLEDO, MARIO. *Partidos políticos iberoamericanos.* México, D.F.: National Autonomous University of Mexico, 1962.

MOSHER, ARTHUR T. *Technical Cooperation in Latin American Agriculture.* Chicago: University of Chicago Press, 1957.

PIKE, FREDERICK B. (ed.). *Freedom and Reform in Latin America.* Notre Dame, Ind.: University of Notre Dame Press, 1959.

* Key works.

PLAZA LASSO, GALO. Problems of Democracy in Latin America. Chapel Hill, N.C.: University of North Carolina Press, 1955. Valuable as the viewpoint of a moderate liberal and ex-President of Ecuador.

POBLETE TRONCOSO, MOISES, and BURNETT, BEN G. *The Rise of the Latin American Labor Movement.* New York: Bookman Associates, 1960. A brief survey of a vital topic.

Report of the Second Inter-American Conference for Democracy and Freedom. (Maracay, Venezuela, April 22–26, 1960.) New York: Inter-American Association for Democracy and Freedom, 1961.

RIO, ANGEL DEL (ed.). *Responsible Freedom in the Americas.* New York: Columbia University Press, 1955.

SILVERT, KALMAN H. The Conflict Society: Reaction and Revolution in Latin America. New Orleans, La.: The Hauser Press, 1961. Primarily a collection of reports from one of the most able scholars in the field; previously published by the American Universities Field Staff.

SMITH, T. LYNN. *Latin American Population Studies.* Gainesville, Fla.: University of Florida Press, 1961.

STARK, HARRY. *Social and Economic Frontiers in Latin America.* Dubuque, Iowa: William C. Brown Co., 1961.

STOKES, WILLIAM S. *Latin American Politics.* New York: Thomas Y. Crowell Co., 1959.

SZULC, TAD. *Twilight of the Tyrants.* New York: Holt, 1959. Interesting and balanced study of the rise and fall of five recent dictators of Latin America.

———. *The Winds of Revolution. Latin America Today—and Tomorrow.* New York: Frederick A. Praeger. Forthcoming.

TANNENBAUM, FRANK. Ten Keys to Latin America. New York: Alfred A. Knopf, 1962. Excellent summary of main aspects of Latin American life.

WHITAKER, ARTHUR P. *Nationalism in Latin America.* Gainesville, Fla.: University of Florida Press, 1962.

WILGUS, A. CURTIS. *The Caribbean: The Central American Area.* Gainesville, Fla.: University of Florida Press, 1961.

——— (ed.). *The Caribbean: Contemporary International Relations.* Gainesville, Fla.: University of Florida Press, 1957.

——— (ed.). *The Caribbean: Political Problems.* Gainesville, Fla.: University of Florida Press, 1956.

WOLFE, WAYNE. *Attitudes Toward the United States as Revealed in the Latin American Press.* Unpublished Ph.D. dissertation, Indiana University, 1961. Content analysis of twenty-one Latin American newspapers.

ADAMS, RICHARD N. "The Community in Latin America: A Changing Myth," *The Centennial Review,* Summer, 1962.

ALBA, VICTOR. "Communism and Nationalism in Latin America," *Problems of Communism,* September–October, 1958.

ALEXANDER, ROBERT J. "Central America: Three-cornered struggle," *Foreign Policy Bulletin,* December 15, 1960.

———. "The Latin American *Aprista* Parties," *Political Quarterly,* July–September, 1949.

ALVAREZ ROMERO, JOSÉ MARÍA. "Los partidos demócratas de izquierda en Ibero-américa," *Revista de Política Internacional,* July–October, 1961.

ANDERSON, CHARLES W. "Politics and Development Policy in Central America," *Midwest Journal of Political Science,* November, 1961.

BARANSON, JACK. "Industrialization and Regionalism in Central America," *Inter-American Affairs,* Autumn, 1962.

BETANCOURT, RÓMULO. "Communidad Interamericana sin Dictaduras," *Combate,* July–August, 1960.

BLANKSTEN, GEORGE I. "Political Groups in Latin America," *American Political Science Review,* March, 1959.

CHAPARRO, ALVARO, and ALLEE, RALPH H. "Higher Agricultural Education and Social Change in Latin America," *Rural Sociology,* March, 1960.

CUMBERLAND, CHARLES C. "Twentieth Century Revolutions in Latin America," *The Centennial Review,* Summer, 1962.

DELWART, LOUIS O. "Industrialization and Balanced Development in Semi-Industrialized Countries: Latin America's Postwar Experience," *Economic Development Digest,* May, 1961.

DREIER, JOHN. "The OAS and the Cuban Crisis," *SAIS Review,* Winter, 1961.

DRUCKER, PETER. "A Plan for Revolution in Latin America," *Harper's Magazine,* July, 1961.

FEDER, ERNEST. "Land Reform in Latin America," *Social Order,* January, 1961.

———. "Some Reflections on Latin America's 'Common Market,'" *American Journal of Economics and Sociology,* July, 1961.

FIGUERES, JOSÉ, and BERLE, ADOLF A. "Países Ricos y Países Pobres," *Combate,* July–August, 1960.

FISCHLOWITZ, ESTANISLAU. "Revoluçao social na América Latina em 1961," *Journal of Inter-American Studies,* July, 1962.

FITZGIBBON, RUSSELL H. "The Organization of American States; Time of Ordeal," *Orbis,* Summer, 1961.

———. "The Party Potpourri in Latin America," *The Western Political Quarterly,* March, 1957.

FRANKENHOFF, CHARLES A. "The Prebisch Thesis: A Theory of Industrialization for Latin America," *Journal of Inter-American Studies,* April, 1962.

HOSELITZ, BERT F. "Economic Growth in Latin America," *Proceedings of the International Conference on Economic History* (Stockholm), 1960.

KALVODA, JOSEF. "Communist Strategy in Latin America," *Yale Review,* Autumn, 1960.

KEUR, DOROTHY L., *et al.* "Social and Cultural Pluralisms in the Carribean," *Annals of the New York Academy of Sciences,* Vol. 83, No. 5 (1960).

"Latin America: The 'Fountain of Youth' Overflows," *Population Bulletin,* August, 1958.

LIPSET, SEYMOUR MARTIN. "Some Social Requisites of Democracy: Economic Development and Political Legitimacy," *The American Political Science Review,* March, 1959.

MCALISTER, LYLE N. "Civil-Military Relations in Latin America," *Journal of Inter-American Studies,* July, 1961.

MECHAM, J. LLOYD. "Democracy and Dictatorship in Latin America," *Southwestern Social Science Quarterly,* December, 1960.

MIKESELL, RAYMOND F. "Latin American Economic Development: Some Basic Issues," *Journal of International Affairs,* XIV, No. 2 (1960).

NEEDLER, MARTIN. "Putting Latin American Politics in Perspective," *Inter-American Economic Affairs,* Autumn, 1962.

PAGE, CHARLES A. "Communism and the Labor Movements of Latin America," *Virginia Quarterly Review,* Summer, 1955.

———. "Labor's Political Role in Latin America," *Virginia Quarterly Review,* Autumn, 1952.

PIKE, FREDERICK B. "The Catholic Church in Central America," *Review of Politics,* January, 1959.

PREBISCH, RAÚL. "The Role of Commercial Policies in Underdeveloped Countries," *American Economic Review,* May, 1959.

ROGGE, BENJAMIN A. "Economic Development in Latin America: The Prebisch Thesis," *Inter-American Economic Affairs,* Spring, 1956.

SMITH, T. LYNN. "Current Population Trends in Latin America," *American Journal of Sociology,* January, 1959.

SOUZA, JOAO GONÇALVES DE. "Aspects of Land Tenure Problems in Latin America," *Rural Sociology,* March, 1960.

TANNENBAUM, FRANK. "The Future of Democracy in Latin America," *Foreign Affairs,* April, 1955.

———. "Political Dilemma in Latin America," *Foreign Affairs,* April, 1960.

WOLF, ERIC R. "Types of Latin American Peasantry: A Preliminary Discussion," *American Anthropologist,* June, 1955.

Wyckoff, Theodore. "The Role of the Military in Latin American Politics," *Western Political Quarterly*, September, 1960.

U.S.–LATIN AMERICAN RELATIONS

Adams, Richard N., and Cumberland, Charles C. *United States University Cooperation in Latin America*. East Lansing, Mich.: Michigan State University Press, 1960.

*The American Assembly. *The United States and Latin America*. New York: Columbia University Press, 1959. A series of papers on social, political, and economic developments in Latin America, and their impact on U.S.–Latin American relations.

Arciniegas, German. *The State of Latin America*. New York: Alfred A. Knopf, 1952. Perceptive analysis of Latin America in the early postwar years by a Colombian intellectual.

*Bemis, Samuel F. *The Latin American Policy of the United States*. New York: Harcourt, Brace, & Company, 1943. This classic account of U.S.–Latin American policy up to World War II ably defends most U.S. actions in Latin America.

*Benton, William. *The Voice of Latin America*. New York: Harper & Bros., 1961. In this perceptive report of his findings on his tour of Latin America with Adlai Stevenson early in 1960, Senator Benton pleads for popular support for the Alliance for Progress.

Berle, Adolf A. *Latin America: Diplomacy and Reality*. New York: Harper & Row, 1962.

Bernstein, Harry. *Making an Inter-American Mind*. Gainesville, Fla.: University of Florida Press, 1961.

Dozer, Donald M. *Are We Good Neighbors?: Three Decades of Inter-American Relations, 1930–1960*. Gainesville, Fla.: University of Florida Press, 1960.

Dreier, John C. (ed.). *The Alliance for Progress. Problems and Perspectives*. Baltimore, Md.: The Johns Hopkins Press, 1962.

———. *The Organization of American States and the Hemisphere Crisis*. New York: Harper & Row, 1962.

Ellis, Howard S., and Wallich, Henry C. (eds.). *Economic Development for Latin America*. New York: St. Martin's Press, 1961.

Fabela, Isidro. *Buena y mala vecindad*. Mexico City: El América Nueva, 1958. A collection of pieces—some of which constitute a severe indictment of U.S. postwar policies toward Latin America—by a leading Mexican statesman, diplomat, and writer.

Gordon, Lincoln. *A New Deal for Latin America*. Cambridge, Mass.: Harvard University Press, 1963.

* Key works.

Latin American USOM's Seminar on Agrarian Reform. Report of ICA Seminar held in Santiago, Chile, on February 21–24, 1961. Washington, D.C.: International Cooperation Administration, 1961.

*LIEUWEN, EDWIN. *Arms and Politics in Latin America.* Rev. ed. New York: Frederick A. Praeger, 1961. Part II of this ground-breaking study analyzes and criticizes the U.S. policy of military aid to Latin America.

MADARIAGA, SALVADOR DE. *Latin America Between the Eagle and the Bear.* New York: Frederick A. Praeger, 1962.

MANGER, WILLIAM (ed.). *The Alliance for Progress: A Critical Appraisal.* Washington, D.C.: Public Affairs Press, 1963.

———. *Pan America in Crisis.* Washington, D.C.: Public Affairs Press, 1961. A valuable critique of the Organization of American States, by a former Assistant Secretary-General.

*MECHAM, J. LLOYD. *The United States and Inter-American Security, 1889–1960.* Austin, Tex.: The University of Texas Press, 1961. A thoroughly documented study of the Inter-American Security System, with an analysis of current problems.

PALMER, THOMAS W., JR. *Search for a Latin American Policy.* Gainesville, Fla.: University of Florida Press, 1957.

*PERKINS, DEXTER. *Hands Off: A History of the Monroe Doctrine.* Boston: Little, Brown & Co., 1941. The standard one-volume work on the subject.

———. *The United States and Latin America.* Baton Rouge, La.: Louisiana State University Press, 1961. A broad survey of the history and problems of inter-American relations in three lectures by a distinguished scholar.

*QUINTANILLA, LUIS. *A Latin American Speaks.* New York: The Macmillan Company, 1943. Friendly criticism of U.S. policy toward Latin America from a leading Mexican diplomat.

———. *Pan-Americanism and Democracy.* Boston: Boston University Press, 1952.

RADLER, D. H. *El Gringo: The Yankee Image in Latin America.* Philadelphia: Chilton Company, 1962.

RIPPY, J. FRED. *Globe and Hemisphere: Latin America's Place in the Post-War Foreign Relations of the United States.* Chicago: Henry Regnery Co., 1958.

STUART, GRAHAM. *Latin America and the United States.* 5th ed. New York: Appleton-Century-Crofts, 1955. The standard one-volume text on the subject.

*SUBCOMMITTEE ON AMERICAN REPUBLICS AFFAIRS OF THE COMMITTEE OF FOREIGN RELATIONS, UNITED STATES SENATE. *United States–Latin American Relations.* Washington, D.C.: Government Printing Office, 1960.

1. Post World War II Political Developments in Latin America
2. Commodity Problems in Latin America
3. The Organization of American States
4. United States Business and Labor in Latin America
5. United States and Latin American Policies Affecting Their Economic Relations
6. Problems of Latin American Economic Development
7. Soviet Bloc Latin American Activities and Their Implications for United States Foreign Policy.

On the whole the economic studies are superior to the political ones; the work on the Soviet bloc, however, is an excellent supplement to Robert J. Alexander's book.

*VILLOLDO, PEDRO A. *Latin American Resentment*. New York: Vantage Press, 1959.

WHITAKER, ARTHUR P. *The United States and South America: The Northern Republics*. Cambridge, Mass.: Harvard University Press, 1948.

*————. *The Western Hemisphere Idea: Its Rise and Decline*. Ithaca, N.Y.: Cornell University Press, 1954. A leading Latin Americanist's critical analysis of the idea that "the peoples of America are bound together in a special relationship which sets them apart from the rest of the world."

*WOOD, BRYCE M. *The Making of the Good Neighbor Policy*. New York: Columbia University Press, 1961. A thoroughly documented study of U.S.–Latin American Relations from 1926 to 1943.

BALL, M. MARGARET. "Issue for the Americas: Non-Intervention v. Human Rights and the Preservation of Democratic Institutions," *International Organization*, Winter, 1961.

BERLE, ADOLF A., JR. "Our Role in Latin America," *The Reporter*, November 23, 1961.

CORNELIUS, WILLIAM G. "The 'Latin American Bloc' in the United Nations," *Journal of Inter-American Studies*, July, 1961.

DAVIS, HAROLD E. "A New Look at Latin American Relations," *World Affairs*, Summer, 1959.

DILLON, DOUGLAS. "The New Social Development Program," *Inter-American Economic Affairs*, Autumn, 1960.

FEINSTEIN, OTTO. "A Changing Latin America and U.S. Foreign Policy," *New University Thought*, Spring, 1960.

FURNESS, EDGAR S., JR. "The United States, the Inter-American System, and the United Nations," *Political Science Quarterly*, September, 1950.

GAOS, JOSÉ. "Los Estados Unidos y la revolución de América Latina," *Cuadernos Americanos*, July–August, 1962.

* Key works.

GORDON, WENDELL. "The Contribution of Foreign Investments," *Inter-American Economic Affairs*, Spring, 1961.

HICKEY, JOHN. "The Role of Congress in Foreign Policy: The Cuban Disaster," *Inter-American Economic Affairs*, Spring, 1961.

HIRSCHMAN, ALBERT O. "Second Thoughts on the Alliance for Progress," *The Reporter*, May 25, 1961.

"Importance of the U.S. Naval Base, Guantanamo, Cuba," *Inter-American Economic Affairs*, Autumn, 1960.

MANSFIELD, MIKE. "New Horizons for the Americas," *Inter-American Economic Affairs*, Autumn, 1960.

MATTHEWS, HERBERT L. "The United States and Latin America," *International Affairs*, June, 1961.

OWEN, C. F. "U.S. and Soviet Relations with Underdeveloped Countries: Latin America, a Case Study," *Inter-American Economic Affairs*, Winter, 1960.

PREBISCH, RAÚL. "Joint Responsibilities for Latin American Progress," *Foreign Affairs*, July, 1961.

RIPPY, J. FRED. "U.S. Postwar Aid to Latin America," *Inter-American Economic Affairs*, Spring, 1961.

————. "Vague Plans and Huge Expenditures for the Solution of Hemispheric Problems," *Inter-American Economic Affairs*, Autumn, 1960.

————, and TISCHENDORF, ALFRED. "The San José Conference of American Foreign Ministers," *Inter-American Economic Affairs*, Winter, 1960.

WOODS, RICHARD H. "The Servicio and Other Joint Methods of Administering U.S. Technical Assistance," *Economic Development and Cultural Change*, January, 1962.

INDIVIDUAL COUNTRIES

Argentina

*ALEXANDER, ROBERT J. *The Perón Era*. New York: Columbia University Press, 1951.

*BLANKSTEN, GEORGE I. *Perón's Argentina*. Chicago: University of Chicago Press, 1953.

FILLOL, TOMÁS ROBERTO. *Social Factors in Economic Development; The Argentine Case*. Cambridge, Mass.: M.I.T. Press, 1961.

KENNEDY, JOHN J. *Catholicism, Nationalism, and Democracy in Argentina*. Notre Dame, Ind.: University of Notre Dame Press, 1958.

PENDLE, GEORGE. *Argentina*. London: Royal Institute of International Affairs, 1955.

*RENNIE, ISABEL F. *The Argentine Republic*. New York: The Macmillan Company, 1945. Best single volume on Argentine history up to the rise of Perón.

WHITAKER, ARTHUR P. *Argentine Upheaval: Perón's Fall and the New Regime.* New York: Frederick A. Praeger, 1956.

*————. *The United States and Argentina.* Cambridge, Mass.: Harvard University Press, 1954. Attempts to assess long-term factors in Argentine internal and international developments.

BAKLANOFF, ERIC N. "Argentina, Chile and Mexico: Contrasts in Economic Policy and Performance," *Journal of Inter-American Studies,* October, 1961.

ELENA, ITALO V., and PALERMO, EPIFANIO. "Las 'villas miserias' y el desarrollo industrial en la Republica Argentina," *Cuadernos Americanos,* July–August, 1962.

GERMANI, GINO; GRACIARENA, JORGE; and MURMIS, MIGUEL. "La asimilación de los inmigrantes en la Argentina y el fenómeno del regreso en la inmigración reciente," *Revista Interamericana de Ciencias Sociales* (Washington, D.C.), I, No. 1 (1961).

PEFFER, LOUISE E. "The Argentine Cattle Industry Under Perón," *Food Research Institute Studies,* May, 1960.

————. "State Intervention in the Argentine Meat Packing Industry, 1946–58," *Food Research Institute Studies,* February, 1961.

POTASH, ROBERT A. "Argentine Political Parties: 1957–58," *Journal of Inter-American Studies,* October, 1959.

————. "The Changing Role of the Military in Argentina," *Journal of Inter-American Studies,* October, 1961.

Bolivia

*ALEXANDER, ROBERT J. *The Bolivian National Revolution.* New Brunswick, N.J.: Rutgers University Press, 1958. An enthusiastic endorsement of the revolution by a U.S. scholar.

LEONARD, OLEN E. *Bolivia: Land, People and Institutions.* Washington, D.C.: Scarecrow Press, 1952. Sociological account.

*OSBOURNE, HAROLD. *Bolivia: A Land Divided.* 2nd ed. London: Royal Institute of International Affairs, 1955. A balanced view of the revolution.

OSTRÍ GUTIÉRREZ, ALBERTO. *The Tragedy of Bolivia. A People Crucified.* New York: The Devin-Adair Co., 1958. An exile's bitterly critical account of the revolution of 1952.

ARNADE, CHARLES W. "Bolivia's Social Revolution, 1952–59," *Journal of Inter-American Studies,* July, 1959.

HEATH, DWIGHT B. "Land Reform in Bolivia," *Inter-American Economic Affairs,* Spring, 1959.

————. "Land Tenure and Social Organization: An Ethnohistorical Study from the Bolivian Oriente," *Inter-American Economic Affairs,* Spring, 1960.

* Key works.

PATCH, RICHARD W. "Bolivia—diez años de la revolución nacional," *Cuadernos,* September, 1962.

STOKES, WILLIAM S. "The Revolución Nacional and the MNR in Bolivia," *Inter-American Economic Affairs,* Spring, 1959.

Brazil

FREE, LLOYD A. *Some International Implications of the Political Psychology of Brazilians.* Princeton, N.J.: Institute for International Social Research, 1961.

FREYRE, GILBERTO. *Brazil, An Interpretation.* New York: Alfred A. Knopf, 1945. Freyre sees in the cultural and racial heterogeneity of Brazil an explanation for the country's progress.

————. *New World in the Tropics: The Culture of Modern Brazil.* New York: Alfred A. Knopf, 1959.

MORSE, RICHARD. *From Community to Metropolis. A Biography of São Paulo, Brazil.* Gainesville, Fla.: University of Florida Press, 1958.

PETERSON, PHYLLIS J. *Brazilian Political Parties: Formation, Organization, and Leadership, 1945–1959.* Unpublished Ph.D. dissertation, University of Michigan, 1962.

SCHURZ, WILLIAM L. *Brazil, the Infinite Country.* New York: E. P. Dutton & Co., 1961.

SMITH, T. LYNN, and MARCHANT, ALEXANDER. *Brazil. Portrait of Half a Continent.* New York: Dryden Press, 1951.

————. *Brazil. People and Institutions.* 3rd ed. Baton Rouge, La.: Louisiana State University Press, 1963.

SPIEGEL, HENRY W. *The Brazilian Economy: chronic inflation and sporadic industrialization.* Philadelphia: Blakiston, 1949.

TAVARES DE SA, HERNANE. *The Brazilians: People of Tomorrow.* New York: The John Day Company, 1947.

WAGLEY, CHARLES. *Amazon Town: A Study of Man in the Tropics.* New York: The Macmillan Company, 1953.

————. An Introduction to Brazil. New York: Columbia University Press. Forthcoming.

BASTOS DE AVILA, FERNANDO. "Immigration, Development, and Industrial Expansion in Brazil," *Migration,* July–September, 1961.

BRESSER PEREIRA, L. C. "The Rise of Middle Class and Middle Management in Brazil," *Journal of Inter-American Studies,* July, 1962.

DELL, EDMUND. "Brazil's Partly United States," *Political Quarterly,* July 9, 1962.

DONALD, CARR L. "Brazilian Local Self-Government: Myth or Reality?," *Western Political Quarterly,* December, 1960.

FREYRE, GILBERTO. "Misconceptions of Brazil," *Foreign Affairs,* April, 1962.

HUTCHINSON, HENRY W. "The Transformation of Brazilian Plantation Society," *Journal of Inter-American Studies,* April, 1961.

QUADROS, JÂNIO. "Brazil's New Foreign Policy," *Foreign Affairs,* October, 1961.

RODRIGUES, JOSÉ HONÓRIO. "Aspirações e Interesses de Brasil," *Journal of Inter-American Studies,* April, 1961.

VON GERSDORFF, RALPH. "Agricultural Credit Problems in Brazil," *Inter-American Economic Affairs,* Summer, 1961.

WYCKOFF, THEODORE. "Brazilian Political Parties," *South Atlantic Quarterly,* Summer, 1957.

Chile

BAKLANOFF, ERIC N. *Chile: Balance of International Payments, Economic Development, and Foreign Economic Policy.* Unpublished Ph.D. dissertation, Ohio State University, 1959.

BUTLAND, GILBERT J. *Chile: An Outline of Its Geography, Economics, and Politics.* 3rd ed. London: Royal Institute of International Affairs, 1953.

COHEN, ALVIN. *Economic Change in Chile, 1929–59.* Gainesville, Fla.: University of Florida Press, 1960.

EDWARDS VIVES, ALBERTO, and FREI MONTALVA, EDUARDO. *Historia de los Partidos Políticos Chilenos.* Santiago: Editorial del Pacifico, 1949.

ELLSWORTH, P. T. *Chile, an Economy in Transition.* New York: The Macmillan Company, 1945.

GIL, FEDERICO. *Genesis and Modernization of Chilean Political Parties.* Gainesville, Fla.: University of Florida Press, 1961.

PENDLE, GEORGE. *The Land and People of Chile.* New York: The Macmillan Company, 1960.

*PIKE, FREDERICK B. *Chile and the United States, 1880–1962: The Emergence of Chile's Social Crisis and the Challenge to United States Diplomacy.* Notre Dame, Ind.: University of Notre Dame Press, 1963.

ABBOTT, ROGER S. "The Role of Contemporary Political Parties in Chile," *American Political Science Review,* June, 1951.

BAKLANOFF, ERIC N. "Argentina, Chile and Mexico: Contrasts in Economic Policy and Performance," *Journal of Inter-American Studies,* October, 1961.

———. "Model for Economic Stagnation: Chile's Experience with

* Key works.

Multiple Exchange Rates," *Inter-American Economic Affairs,* Summer, 1959.

————. "Taxation of United States-Owned Copper Companies in Chile: Economic Myopias vs. Long-Run Self-Interest," *National Tax Journal,* March, 1961.

BONILLA, FRANK. "The Student Federation of Chile: 50 Years of Political Action," *Journal of Inter-American Studies,* July, 1960.

FEDER, ERNEST. "Feudalism and Agricultural Development: The Role of Controlled Credit in Chile's Agriculture," *Land Economics,* February, 1960.

JOBET, JULIO CÉSAR. "Acción e Historia del Socialismo Chileno," *Combate,* September–October, 1960.

PIKE, FREDERICK B., and BRAY, DONALD W. "A Vista of Catastrophe: The Future of United States–Chilean Relations," *The Review of Politics,* July, 1960.

WHITE, C. LANGDON, and CHILCOTE, RONALD H. "Chile's New Iron and Steel Industry," *Economic Geography,* July, 1961.

Colombia

*FLUHARTY, VERNON. *Dance of the Millions: Military Rule and the Social Revolution in Colombia, 1930–56.* Pittsburgh, Penn.: University of Pittsburgh Press, 1957. An attempt to explain the Bogotá riots of 1948 and the advent of dictator Gustavo Rojas Pinilla.

GALBRAITH, W. O. *Colombia: A General Survey.* London: Royal Institute of International Affairs, 1953.

GUZMÁN, GERMÁN; FALS BORDA, ORLANDO; and UMAÑA LUNA, EDUARDO. *La violencia en Colombia.* Bogotá: Editorial Iqueima, 1962.

*MARTZ, JOHN D. *Colombia: A Contemporary Political Survey.* Chapel Hill, N.C.: University of North Carolina Press, 1962. A survey of Colombian politics basically substantiated by the March, 1962, elections.

WHITEFORD, ANDREW H. *Two Cities of Latin America: A Comparative Description of Social Classes.* Beloit, Wis.: Beloit College, 1960. A sociological study of Querétaro and Popayán.

WILGUS, A. CURTIS (ed.). *The Caribbean: Contemporary Colombia.* Gainesville, Fla.: University of Florida Press, 1962.

BEYER, ROBERT C. "Land Distribution and Tenure in Colombia," *Journal of Inter-American Studies,* July, 1961.

HELGUERA, I. LEON. "The Changing Role of the Military in Colombia," *Journal of Inter-American Studies,* July, 1961.

JOHNSON, KENNETH F. "Colombia: External Assistance and Political Change," *The Western Political Quarterly,* September, 1962.

Costa Rica

ARCE, ANTONIO M. *Sociologia y desarrollo rural.* Turrialba, Costa Rica, 1961.

BIESANZ, JOHN and MAVIS. *Costa Rican Life.* New York: Columbia University Press, 1944.

JONES, CHESTER L. *Costa Rica and Civilization in the Caribbean.* 2nd ed. San José, Costa Rica: Editorial Borrasé Hermanos, 1941. Outdated, but still of some value.

KANTOR, HARRY. *The Costa Rican Election of 1953: A Case Study.* Gainesville, Fla.: University of Florida Press, 1958.

LOOMIS, CHARLES P., *et al.* (editors and directors). *Turrialba—Social Systems and the Introduction of Change.* Glencoe, Ill.: The Free Press of Glencoe, Ill., 1953.

MAY, STACY. *Costa Rica: A Study in Economic Development.* New York: Twentieth Century Fund, 1952.

BUSEY, JAMES L. "Foundations of Political Contrast: Costa Rica and Nicaragua," *Western Political Quarterly,* September, 1958.
———. "The Presidents of Costa Rica," *The Americas,* July, 1961.

KANTOR, HARRY. "Tambien hay democracias en el Caribe," *Combate,* March–April, 1960.

KARNES, THOMAS L. "The Origins of Costa Rican Federalism," *The Americas,* January, 1959.

PACHECO, LEÓN. "Evolución del pensamiento democrático de Costa Rica," *Combate,* March–April, 1961.

RYS, JOHN F. "The Costa Rican Revolution of 1955 as a Case Study in Intra-Regional Collective Security," *West Virginia University Bulletin,* December, 1960.

Cuba

*DRAPER, THEODORE. *Castro's Revolution: Myths and Realities.* New York: Frederick A. Praeger, 1962. The most objective and analytical work yet to appear on Castro's Cuba.

FRANK, WALDO. *Cuba: Prophetic Island.* New York: Marzane and Munsell, 1962.

GUEVARA, ERNESTO "CHE." *Che Guevara on Guerrilla Warfare.* New York: Frederick A. Praeger, 1961.

HUBERMAN, LEO, and SWEEZY, PAUL. *Cuba: The Anatomy of a Revolution.* New York: Monthly Review Press, 1960.

JAMES, DANIEL. *Cuba, the First Soviet Satellite in the Americas.* New York: Avon Book Division of the Hearst Corporation, 1961. Moderate and rather objective in its single aim to explain the Communist take-over in Cuba, this work has the built-in thesis that Castro was a Communist before he came to power.

* Key works.

*MacGaffey, Wyatt, and Barnett, Clifford H. *Cuba, Its People, Its Society, Its Culture*. New Haven: Human Relations Area Files Press, 1962. Best account of pre-Castro Cuba.

Matthews, Herbert. *The Cuban Story*. New York: George Braziller, 1961. A now disillusioned former admirer of Castro, the author still believes that there is some good in Castro and lays much blame upon U.S. policy for driving him toward the Soviet bloc.

*Meyer, Karl E. and Szulc, Tad. *The Cuban Invasion: The Chronicle of a Disaster*. New York: Frederick A. Praeger; Ballantine Books, 1962. An examination and critique of U.S. policy with respect to the April, 1961, invasion.

Miller, Warren. *90 Miles From Home*. Boston: Little, Brown & Co., 1961.

*Mills, C. Wright. *Listen, Yankee: The Revolution in Cuba*. New York: Ballantine Books, 1960. Valuable as the official Castro line.

Nelson, Lowry. *Rural Cuba*. Minneapolis, Minn.: University of Minnesota Press, 1950.

Pflaum, Irving Peter. *Tragic Island: How Communism Came to Cuba*. Englewood Cliffs, N.J.: Prentice-Hall, 1961. Holds the thesis that the United States lost its opportunity with Castro by failing to offer aid during Castro's visit of April, 1959.

Phillips, R. Hart. *Cuba: Island of Paradox*. New York: McDowell, Obolensky, Inc., 1959.

Rivera, Nicolás. *Castro's Cuba: An American Dilemma*. Washington, D.C.: Robert B. Luce, 1962. A rather balanced view of a Cuban exile who served under both Batista and Castro and broke with both.

Roca, Blas. *The Cuban Revolution*. New York: New Century Publishers, 1961. A Communist interpretation of the Cuban revolution.

Sartre, Jean-Paul. *Sartre on Cuba*. New York: Ballantine Books, 1961.

Smith, Earl E. T. *The Fourth Floor: An Account of the Castro Communist Revolution*. New York: Random House, 1962.

Smith, Robert F. *The United States and Cuba: Business and Diplomacy 1917–60*. New York: Bookman Associates, 1961.

Weyl, Nathaniel. *Red Star Over Cuba: The Russian Assault on the Western Hemisphere*. Rev. ed. New York: The Devin-Adair Co., 1961.

Berle, Adolf A., Jr. "The Cuban Crisis: Failure of American Foreign Policy," *Foreign Affairs*, October, 1960.

Gil, Federico. "Antecedents of the Cuban Revolution," *The Centennial Review*, Summer, 1962.

HALPERIN, ERNST. "Why Castro Can't Be Neutral," *The New Republic,* November 27, 1961.

VILLAREJO, DONALD. "American Investment in Cuba," *New University Thought,* Spring, 1960.

Ecuador

*BLANKSTEN, GEORGE I. *Ecuador: Constitutions and Caudillos.* Berkeley, Cal.: University of California Press, 1951.

LINKE, LILO. *Ecuador. Country of Contrasts.* 3rd ed. London: Royal Institute of International Affairs, 1960.

SAUNDERS, JOHN V. D. *The Population of Ecuador: A Demographic Analysis.* Gainesville, Fla.: University of Florida Press, 1961.

PAREJA DIEZCANSECO, ALFREDO. "Democracia o Demagogía en el Ecuador," *Combate,* March–April, 1961.

SAUNDERS, JOHN V. D. "Man-Land Relations in Ecuador," *Rural Sociology,* March, 1961.

El Salvador

OSBOURNE, LILLY DE JONGH. *Four Keys to El Salvador.* New York: Funk and Wagnalls, 1956.

SELVA, MAURICIO DE LA. "El Salvador: tres décadas de lucha," *Cuadernos americanos,* January–February, 1962.

WALLICH, HENRY, and ADLER, JOHN H. *Public Finance in a Developing Country. El Salvador—A Case Study.* Cambridge, Mass.: Harvard University Press, 1951.

Guatemala

ARRIOLA, JORGE LUIS (ed.). *Integración Social en Guatemala.* Guatemala: Ministerio de Educación Pública, 1956.

BISHOP, EDWIN W. *The Guatemalan Labor Movement, 1944–59.* Unpublished Ph.D. dissertation, University of Wisconsin, 1959.

JAMES, DANIEL. *Red Design for the Americas: Guatemalan Prelude.* New York: The John Day Company, 1954.

KELSEY, VERA, and OSBOURNE, LILLY DE JONGH. *Four Keys to Guatemala.* Rev. ed. New York: Thomas Y. Crowell Co., 1961.

LABARGE, RICHARD A. *Impact of the United Fruit Company on the Economic Development of Guatemala 1946–54.* New Orleans, La.: Tulane University Press, 1960.

MONTEFORTE TOLEDO, MARIO. *Guatemala, monografía sociológica.* México, D.F.: Universidad Nacional Autónoma de México, 1961.

ROSENTHAL, MARIO. *Guatemala: The Story of an Emergent Latin American Democracy.* New York: Twayne Publishers, 1962.

* Key works.

*SCHNEIDER, RONALD. *Communism in Guatemala, 1944–54.* New York: Frederick A. Praeger, 1959. The definitive study on the subject.

*SILVERT, K. H. *A Study in Government: Guatemala.* New Orleans, La.: Tulane University Press, 1954.

U.S. DEPARTMENT OF STATE. *A Case History of Communist Penetration: Guatemala.* (Department of State Publication No. 6465.) Washington, D.C.: Government Printing Office, 1957.

*WHETTEN, NATHAN L. *Guatemala: The Land and the People.* New Haven, Conn.: Yale University Press, 1961.

GRANT, DONALD. "Guatemala and U.S. Foreign Policy," *Journal of International Affairs,* IX, No. 1, 1955.

JAMES, DANIEL. "Church and State in Guatemala," *Commonweal,* September 30, 1955.

TAYLOR, PHILIP B. "The Guatemalan Affair: A Critique of United States Foreign Policy," *American Political Science Review,* September, 1956.

Haiti

COOK, MERCER. *An Introduction to Haiti.* Washington, D.C.: Department of Cultural Affairs, Pan American Union, 1951.

DE YOUNG, MAURICE. *Man and Land in the Haitian Economy.* Gainesville, Fla.: University of Florida Press, 1958.

LEYBURN, JAMES G. *The Haitian People.* New Haven, Conn.: Yale University Press, 1941.

PATTEE, RICHARD. *Haití, pueblo afroantillo.* Madrid: Ediciones Cultura Hispánica, 1956.

RODMAN, SELDEN. *Haiti: The Black Republic.* New York: The Devin-Adair Co., 1954.

Honduras

CHECCHI, VINCENT. *Honduras: A Problem in Economic Development.* New York: The Twentieth Century Fund, 1959.

STOKES, WILLIAM S. *Honduras, An Area Study in Government.* Madison, Wis.: University of Wisconsin Press, 1950.

ROSS, DAVID F. "Economic Theory and Economic Development: reflections derived from a study of Honduras," *Inter-American Economic Affairs,* Winter, 1959.

Mexico

*BRANDENBERG, FRANK R. *Mexico: An Experiment in One-Party Democracy.* Unpublished Ph.D. dissertation, University of Pennsylvania, 1955. A comprehensive study of Mexico's official Institutional Revolutionary Party (PRI).

*CASTANEDA, JORGE. *Mexico and the United Nations.* New York: Manhattan Publishing Co., 1958. Valuable as a semi-official account of the government's foreign policy positions.

*CLINE, HOWARD. *Mexico, 1940–60: Revolution to Evolution.* London: Royal Institute of International Affairs, 1962.

*————. *The United States and Mexico.* Cambridge, Mass.: Harvard University Press, 1953. The best single volume on Mexican developments since 1910.

GARCÍA VALENCIA, ANTONIO. *Las relaciones humanas en la administración publica mexicana.* Mexico City: Editorial Porrúa, 1958. The author sees *"servilismo"* and the lack of a merit system as the primary weaknesses in public service and an expansion of social-welfare services as a solution.

GEISERT, HAROLD L. *Population Problems in Mexico and Central America.* Washington, D.C.: George Washington University Press, 1959.

GLADE, WILLIAM PATTON, JR. *The Role of Government Enterprise in the Economic Development of Underdeveloped Regions: Mexico, A Case Study.* Unpublished Ph.D. dissertation, University of Texas, 1955.

JAMES, DANIEL. *Mexico and the Americans.* New York: Frederick A. Praeger, 1963.

PARKES, HENRY B. *A History of Mexico.* Boston: Houghton Mifflin Co., 1950. Standard "liberal" interpretation of Mexican history.

POWELL, J. R. *The Mexican Petroleum Industry, 1938–50.* Berkeley, Cal.: University of California Press, 1956.

*SCOTT, ROBERT E. *Mexican Government in Transition.* Urbana, Ill.: University of Illinois Press, 1959. A comprehensive study of the Mexican political system.

*SENIOR, CLARENCE. *Land Reform and Democracy.* Gainesville, Fla.: University of Florida Press, 1959. An analysis of the Laguna collective-farm system and its relationship to political democracy.

*TANNENBAUM, FRANK. *Mexico: The Struggle for Peace and Bread.* New York: Alfred A. Knopf, 1950. A classic study of the Mexican revolution and its accomplishments and failures by one of its most ardent admirers among U.S. scholars.

WALKER, DONALD A. *The Nacional Financiera of Mexico.* Cambridge, Mass.: Harvard University Press, 1961. The first major study in English of the role of this semiautonomous agency that directs Mexican government investments.

WHETTEN, NATHAN. *Rural Mexico.* Chicago: University of Chicago Press, 1948. A comprehensive study; now somewhat dated.

* Key works.

WHITEFORD, ANDREW H. *Two Cities of Latin America: A Comparative Description of Social Classes.* Beloit, Wis.: Beloit College, 1960. A sociological study of Querétaro and Popayán.

ANDRADE M., CARLOS. "La tenencia de la tierra y la evolución política de México," *Política* (Caracas), February–March, 1961.

*AUBREY, HENRY G. "Structure and Balance in Rapid Economic Growth: The Example of Mexico," *Political Science Quarterly,* December, 1954. One of the earliest studies to point out the fact of Mexican concern for agricultural development and the benefits derived from this concern.

BAKLANOFF, ERIC N. "Argentina, Chile and Mexico: Contrasts in Economic Policy and Performance," *Journal of Inter-American Studies,* October, 1961.

BRANDENBERG, FRANK R. "Organized Business in Mexico," *Inter-American Economic Affairs,* Winter, 1958.

CLINE, HOWARD F. "Mexico, Fidelismo and the United States," *Orbis,* Summer, 1961.

FENN, PEGGY. "Non-Intervention and Self-Determination as Cornerstones of Mexican Foreign Policy: Their Application to the Cuban Issue," *Topic,* Fall, 1962.

FLORES, EDMUNDO. "The Significance of Land-Use Changes in the Economic Development of Mexico," *Land Economics,* May, 1959.

GRAHAM, DAVID L. "The Rise of the Mexican Right," *Yale Review,* Autumn, 1962.

NEEDLER, MARTIN C. "The Political Development of Mexico," *American Political Science Review,* June, 1961.

ROSENZWEIG HERNÁNDEZ, FERNANDO. "El proceso político y el desarrollo económico de México," *El Trimestre Económico,* October–December, 1962.

SCRUGGS, OTEY M. "Evolution of the Mexican Farm Labor Agreement of 1942," *Agricultural History,* July, 1960.

SHELTON, DAVID H. "Mexico's Economic Growth: Success of Diversified Development," *Southwestern Social Science Quarterly,* December, 1960.

VILLORO, LUIS. "La cultura mexicana de 1910 a 1960," *Historia Mexicana* (México, D.F.), October–December, 1960.

WYLIE, KATHRYN H. "Mexico's Agrarian Reform," *Foreign Agriculture,* February, 1961.

Nicaragua

INTERNATIONAL BANK FOR RECONSTRUCTION AND DEVELOPMENT. *The Economic Development of Nicaragua.* Baltimore, Md.: The Johns Hopkins Press, 1953.

ALISKY, M. "Our Man in Managua," *The Reporter,* December 22, 1960.

BUSEY, JAMES L. "Foundations of Political Contrast: Costa Rica and Nicaragua," *Western Political Quarterly,* September, 1958.

Panama

BIESANZ, JOHN and MAVIS. *The People of Panama.* New York: Columbia University Press, 1955.

EALY, LAWRENCE O. *The Republic of Panama in World Affairs, 1903–50.* Philadelphia: University of Pennsylvania Press, 1951.

GOLDRICH, DANIEL. "Toward an Estimate of the Probability of Social Revolutions in Latin America: Some Orienting Concepts and a Case Study," *The Centennial Review,* Summer, 1962.

PEREIRA BURGOS, CESAR ANTONIO. "Socialismo y sindicalismo en Panamá," *Política* (Caracas), January, 1961.

ROSA, DIÓGENES DE LA. "Panamá, Problema Americano," *Política* (Caracas), March, 1960.

Paraguay

PENDLE, GEORGE. *Paraguay: A Riverside Nation.* 2nd ed. London: Royal Institute of International Affairs, 1956.

RAINE, PHILIP. Paraguay. New Brunswick, N.J.: Scarecrow Press. 1956.

WARREN, HARRIS G. *Paraguay. An Informal History.* Norman, Okla.: University of Oklahoma Press, 1949.

ZOOK, DAVID H., JR. *The Conduct of the Chaco War.* New York: Bookman Associates, 1960.

Peru

FORD, THOMAS R. *Man and Land in Peru.* Gainesville, Fla.: University of Florida Press, 1955.

KANTOR, HARRY. *The Ideology and Program of the Peruvian Aprista Movement.* Berkeley, Cal.: University of California Press, 1953.

WHITE, C. LANGDON, and CHENKIN, GARY. "Peru Moves onto the Iron and Steel Map of the Western Hemisphere," *Journal of Inter-American Studies,* July, 1959.

Uruguay

FITZGIBBON, RUSSELL H. *Uruguay: Portrait of a Democracy.* New Brunswick, N.J.: Rutgers University Press, 1954. A labor of love that fails to see some of Uruguay's weaknesses.

* Key works.

*PENDLE, GEORGE. *Uruguay.* 2nd ed. London and New York: Oxford University Press, 1957.

*TAYLOR, PHILIP B. *Government and Politics of Uruguay.* New Orleans, La.: Tulane University Press [1962].

URUGUAYAN INSTITUTE OF INTERNATIONAL LAW. *Uruguay and the United Nations.* New York: Manhattan Publishing Company, 1958.

CASTRO, JULIO. "La reforma agraria en el Uruguay," *Política* (Caracas), June–July, 1961.

Venezuela

*BETANCOURT, RÓMULO. *Venezuela: Política y petroleo.* México, D.F.: Fondo de Cultura Económica, 1956. The political views of President Betancourt during his years in exile.

LIEUWEN, EDWIN. *Petroleum in Venezuela: A History.* Berkeley, Cal.: University of California Press, 1954.

———. *Venezuela.* London: Royal Institute of International Affairs, 1962.

RANGEL, DOMINGO A. *La Industrialización de Venezuela.* Caracas, Venezuela: Ediciones Pensamiento Vivo, 1958. An associate of President Betancourt when he wrote this work, Rangel has since broken with Acción Democrática to become one of the leaders of the leftist coalition.

SERXNER, STANLEY J. *Acción Democrática of Venezuela: Its Origin and Development.* Gainesville, Fla.: University of Florida Press, 1959.

BEATLY, DON W. "Venezuela: A New Era," *International Affairs,* May, 1959.

COOK, HUGH L. "The New Agrarian Reform Law and Economic Development in Venezuela," *Land Economics,* February, 1961.

DELWART, LOUIS O. "Land for Venezuelans," *Americas,* August, 1961.

KANTOR, HARRY. "The Development of Acción Democrática de Venezuela," *Journal of Inter-American Studies,* April, 1959.

LOTT, LEO B. "The Nationalization of Justice in Venezuela," *Inter-American Economic Affairs,* Summer, 1959.

WASHINGTON, S. WALTER. "Student Politics in Latin America: The Venezuelan Example," *Foreign Affairs,* April, 1959.

Index

302